Life is Funny!

Sometimes It's Not.

Frank Penley

ISBN 978-1-64569-811-1 (paperback)
ISBN 978-1-64569-812-8 (digital)

Christian Faith Publishing, Inc.
832 Park Avenue
Meadville, PA 16335
www.christianfaithpublishing.com

Printed in the United States of America

Introduction

Everybody's life experience is different. No two of us are exactly alike. I am in the fifty-eighth year of my adventures and have decided to write some of them down. Even with the differences we experience in life, I have found that there are some things we all have in common. This journey we call life will throw some of the same things at us, but in different ways. Everyone will experience love, hate, joy, pain, life, death, romance, bitterness, brokenness, and healing at different times throughout life.

I am just now beginning to understand that I have had to live until I'm this old to finally begin understanding how to do it. What a wonderful thing it would be to be able to take my life lessons and what I know now and go back to sixteen years of age and start again. Just imagine how different our lives would be if we could do that. Impossible, right?

That brings me to the point in writing this book of life stories (lessons, if you will). It is my hope that some of these stories will offer help to the readers when they are faced with the same type of experiences recorded on these pages. It is also hoped that it will bring enjoyment and laughter to your hearts as well. Some of this stuff is funny!

I am not writing this because I think life is focused on me. It is not that at all, I promise you. I am nothing special. I have honestly and accurately recorded these stories without exaggeration and as best as my memory can produce. I hope that you will see in this work that the stories are not so much about me. The stories are about life and the things we all go through while living it.

I am not proud of some of the things I bring into account here, but I believe the lessons learned in the process will benefit readers. I was an atheist early in my adult life and have been a Christian for some time now. As much as I wish each one who reads this will come to Christ, that is not the reason for the writing. I write this book because I believe that the only true fulfillment in a person's life comes from dealing with the truth about God.

I am not trying to convert you with these words. I am offering my true life experiences as examples of the true God and how he works in anyone's life who will let him. It's not about church. It's not about me being right and you being wrong. It's about life and the God who authors it who wants to journey with each of us through it. I hope you will keep an open mind as you read and I wish the best for each one of you!

I have a selfish reason for writing this book also. I want my children and grandchildren to have a copy of it so they can remember all of the prayers God answered for our family. I want them to remember God is faithful and Jesus is our help in every time of need. Isaiah 46:9 is the verse the Lord gave me for this book! "Remember the things I have done in the past. For I alone am God! I am God, and there is none like me" (NLT).

Last of all, some things in life are just plain funny! I wanted to write some of the funny things in my life that will bring laughter to your hearts. Life is funny sometimes (sometimes it's not)!

Alone

It's funny what we remember from our childhood. Our family didn't go on many vacations, but when we did, it was always to the ocean. My dad loved the beach, and any memory I have of vacations was always going to or from or at the ocean.

One of my earliest memories was on such an occasion. We had been at the beach for a week and were in the car beginning the long trip home. It was my dad, mom, my blind brother, Adrian, my older sister, Gail, and me. It was a hot summer day, and our car was a two-door Chevy of some kind with no air-conditioning.

We were driving along on this long Florida highway that seemed as if we were the only ones on the road. We had been driving long enough for us kids to start getting on our tired parents' nerves, and a break was soon to happen. Remember the gas stations where they had gas attendants that would clean your windows and check your oil and pump your gas for you? We came up on such a place and stopped for gas and bathroom breaks.

This gas station was one that had one handle on each side of the pump and two pumps on two different islands. There was room for eight cars at the same time in four different lanes (a huge station back in the day). There was a small glass-front store to the left side of the building for buying snacks, drinks, or beach balls and such. To the right of the building was two large open bays where mechanics were working on cars. The bathrooms were around the right side of the building and toward the back. It was the typical old-style gas station with a larger capacity for customers.

When we pulled up to the pump, my dad told us kids to go to the bathroom so we would not have to stop again anytime soon. They asked the attendant to fill up the car and went inside the store to get snacks and drinks as we headed around the corner and visited the restroom. All was well, and by the time we all got back in the car, we were about to pull out and back on the road. My dad remembered something he wanted to get, so he ran back in the store to get it. I was probably just barely four and decided I had better run back to the bathroom one more time because I didn't want to be the one to have to ask my dad to stop again, and I kind of needed to go again.

My mom and sister and brother were all arguing about something, so I jumped out the door on mom's side and ran around the corner to go. I had to wait on someone, and then it was my turn to go. I went in and took care of my business and knew I was making everybody wait, so I was a little nervous heading back to the car.

This is where the story is significant, at least as far as life is concerned. I have very few memories of my early childhood. This one moment is as clear to me now at fifty-eight as if it was happening again in front of my own eyes. As I walked around the corner of the gas station, there was my car pulling out and driving away at a high speed. I just froze right there in my tracks. My family was going down the highway away from me, and *I was alone!* Being alone is a feeling that I do not know how to properly describe. It is a pain unlike any other and should not be wished on anyone. No wonder God says he is the God of the orphan and the widow!

I have no idea how long I stood there, but it seems, in my mind, like a short eternity. I remember thinking, *My mom left me!* I have never cried easily, but right there at the sight of my family driving away, I started crying uncontrollably. Not loud, but very deep and inside my heart. I was just barely four and abandoned by my family. I am crying now as I remember it.

There were five men working at the station, and it was not really busy. One of the mechanics noticed me first and came out and started to try and help me, I guess. I remember him coming up to me, and I was about knee-high to him, and he touched my arm and I freaked. Next thing I know, there were these five guys all around me, trying to get me to calm down, and they were all big and ugly, and I did not know them or anybody else.

After a while, I started calming down, and they would try to take me back in the store to make me comfortable, I'm sure. I would bust out crying again when they took me away from being able to see the road where my mom (family) left me. The older man finally brought me out a chair and a hat like his and an ice-cream. He told me not to worry, that I could eat that ice-cream and wait, and my family would be back any minute to get me. He fixed the hat and put it on me, and I ate the ice-cream, never taking my eyes off that spot in the highway where I last saw our car pull away.

The next three hours was sort of the same and went something like this: I would be staring at the road, and then one tear would come followed by another, and before I knew it, I would be crying and hyperventilating. Sometimes one of the men would speak to me, and then I would just go ballistic.

After a long time, the older man would just bring me out an ice-cream or candy bar or drink. If I was eating candy or ice-cream, I was quiet. I sat there for three hours, and finally, I remember seeing my car turning back into the gas station. As I watched it pull in, I just started crying again, but this time because my mom was there and it was okay again.

"Pray for Me!"

One of my earliest memories, if not my earliest, is of being in church with our family. My family, for most of my pre-adult life, was not religious at all. Quite the opposite. In many ways, we were anti-Christian in lifestyle and practice.

Before my brother died, we went to church faithfully. I have just a few memories of going and, only because for me, going to church was a terrible experience. I was a very active child and, had I been born today, I would probably have been heavily medicated. I could not stand or sit still for any length of time.

In those days, the only cure for not sitting quietly in class or church was the woodshed. If you do not know the meaning of the wood-shed, then that is the place that bad little boys were taken, and then their parents would commence to beat the hell out of you (literally)! In any case, for me—not so much my brother or sister—going to church is what you would do two times on Sunday and one time on Wednesdays before you got a spanking.

I was three going on four and had not yet figured out that just because you want to play does not mean you can play. I did not understand then how us children behaved in church was a direct reflection to the other church members of how good or bad they were as parents. As I began to understand this, I used to wonder who was the most upset at my behavior—my parents, other church parents, the preacher, or God. I am sure now that God never was as mad at me as the rest of the aforementioned became on a regular basis.

Our church was an old-fashioned, independent, fundamental Baptist church. Women did not wear pants (in public), and almost everything fun was sin. You had a suit on in church with 100-degree weather and old funeral home fans with which to fan yourself. We did not have air-conditioning in the church house, and on hot summer days, you could relate when the preacher preached on hell because it felt like you were in it, sitting on a crowded pew. Our church had big open windows with no screens. In the summertime, there was no wind, no shade. All I had was sweat and resolve to make it through a church service without a spanking, which I never did make it all the way through.

One Sunday, I remember on the way to church thinking today is going to be the day that I would not get into trouble. I determined I was going to make it through Sunday school and church without one single beating (two or more was not uncommon). I went to my class and sat in my seat with my hands under my legs and looked straight down. When I was tempted to do something, I would shut my eyes and pray for God to help me! I am proud to write to you that with the pain of a mother in labor, I made it through Sunday school class without the teacher saying the dreaded words, "I am going to speak with your parents, young man."

I proudly walked out into the crowded sanctuary and found my parents sitting in the middle of a pew on the left side of the church near the window. As I slid in toward where my parents were sitting, my dad picked me up and put me on the pew in front of him and mom. Dad said, "I want you where I can keep my eyes on you."

I didn't say anything, but I was thinking, *You just wait, I'm going to make it all the way through, no matter how long and hard, without getting in trouble.*

I was somewhat exhausted by all the effort I had put into not getting in trouble in Sunday school. But I was determined and had made it this far. When the preacher came to the pulpit to pray to start the service, I decided that I would pull the same deal as at Sunday school. I felt that if I did not get in trouble for not standing with everyone else to sing or what not, I could sit on my hands again, look straight down, and not move for the entire service.

I sat down on my hands and picked a spot on the old wood floor and stared at it. I tried not to get caught up in any of the activity of the worship so as not be tempted. I would pray for help when I was tempted to look up or move. I made it through the singing and the special song and was just getting to the long hard part—the message. Our preacher could preach for hours no matter how hot it was. In fact, I think that man was energized by heat and misery.

Anyway, I was getting a little antsy but holding up when the preacher started his introduction. About that same time, a little butterfly flew in the window and straight toward me. It flew into my peripheral vision, and I was thinking, *Get away, devil!* About the time the preacher was through his introduction and began praying, I started praying for help. As he was praying, that butterfly flew down between my eyes and my legs. I tried to grab him with one hand while my dad's eyes were closed for the prayer.

The next few seconds are kind of hard to tell as my hard work to that point was in serious trouble. I grabbed for the butterfly, and it shot straight up. I grabbed for it with both hands, and it was just above my reach. In the next second, three things happened at the exact same time. First, the preacher said amen and looked up. Second, my dad opened his eyes that were pointing right at me. Third, I leaped up on the pew and jumped up as high as I could for one last grab for the butterfly. The whole church froze in silence as I came down on my feet, standing on the pew where my butt had been at the start of the prayer.

The butterfly flew away as the preacher asked, "Don, can you not control your son in church?"

My dad threw me over his shoulder and started out to the back doors of the church toward the dreaded woodshed. As we were going out, I looked up at the whole church staring at me and shouted as loud as I could, "Ya'll pray for me!"

Tim

There are in some lives what is called a life-defining moment! That is truly the case in my life. This one is not a funny or happy moment but one that has shaped my life all the same. With the exception of a few events in my life, like I just shared, I have very little memory of anything before Tim.

My parents were just getting by and had three kids. Adrian, my brother who was blinded at birth by the doctor, was the oldest. My sister, Gail, was the middle, and I was the baby. Both of my parents came from very hard backgrounds. My dad joined the navy at fifteen during the Korean War to get away from home. My mother ran away from her abusive father and was homeless until marrying my dad and having Adrian at age fourteen. Neither of my parents had a functional family growing up.

I was just about three when my mom and dad found out Mom was pregnant with who was to be my brother, Tim. They had just become Christians from my Uncle Cork sharing with them about his conversion to Christ. Mom and Dad joined and began attending church but knew very little of the Bible. A family secret is that they both were looking into ways to terminate the pregnancy because of fear of not being able to afford another child. They did not, and sure enough, nine months later, Tim was born.

I was the baby before Tim and do not remember this but was told that I was a jealous brother. I often did mean things to Tim because of his taking over my spot in the family. None of this is from my memory. I was told this by my parents.

My childhood memories begin with Tim at nine months old. He and I were in the basement with my dad who was working on a project of some kind. I had just turned four, and my carpenter dad had started a nail in a board and was letting me play with trying to drive the nail into the wood. My brother, Tim, was crawling around like nine-month-olds do. At some point, Tim was crawling up my back as I was leaning over the wood, hitting the nail. I drew the hammer back and hit Tim in the forehead with the claws.

Tim started screaming and ended up having to have stitches from the claw marks. When my parents came home from the doctor's office, my dad beat me with a leather strap. He said I hit Tim on purpose and beat me to blood over it. I honestly do not remember hitting Tim and hope I didn't do it on purpose, but I may have. I remember waking up the next morning and having to pull the sheets loose from me because the dried blood made them stick to my back and legs.

The next morning, Tim's head was three times the normal size. My parents rushed him to the doctor and then rushed him to the big hospital in Atlanta. Tim was diagnosed with a type of leukemia in his brain. In the sixties, they did not know what they know now. The doctor told my parents that Tim's leukemia was dormant and could have stayed that way until his adult years. They believed that when I hit him with the hammer, the injury caused the cancer to wake up, if you will. In any case, that was the beginning of the next nine months of Tim's suffering.

Tim was put into the hospital for fifty-two days. My mom stayed with him the entire time. She never came home. At the end of the fifty-two days, the insurance ran out, and they sent Tim home to die. The leukemia was in Tim's brain. Tim, being a baby, would scratch his face, trying to get to the pain. My parents had to strap his hands to his sides to keep him from scratching his face.

The doctors gave my parents morphine for pain and told them to give it to him every four hours. They did not worry about him becoming addicted, because he was terminal. Toward the last two months, Tim would pass out for two hours after the morphine and then cry for two hours from pain until the next shot.

One day, as my dad was rocking Tim, his eyes exploded, covering my dad's shirt. Tim lived for nine months in great pain and suffering. When he died, his feet and hands were already turning black from dead tissue. The doctors told my parents because of his youth, his will to live was what caused him to last so long.

My parents were part of a Baptist Church where my dad had been made a deacon, and he even preached some as a layman preacher. After Tim became sick, no one from our church ever came by to visit or check on our family. After Tim's eyes burst, a group from a local church of God came by to ask my parents if they could lay hands on Tim and ask God to heal him. My dad had to be talked into it and tried to tell them that Tim was hard to look at in his present condition. They assured Dad it was all good, and when Dad took them into where Mom and Tim where, they covered their mouths and left the house without any words or prayer. In nine months of suffering, not a single person from our church contacted us, and the church of God tried to help but was overwhelmed by the sight. Tim died one afternoon with my dad holding him.

After we buried Tim, our home changed. My dad and mom tried to stay in church for a few months but finally stopped going. My dad began to drink, and my mom began to run around on my dad. They became bitter with each other and began horrible fighting.

One day, my dad visited his pastor to try to get some kind of grip on his life. He told me this on one of many late night talks. He went into his preacher's office and asked for help (only time I ever heard of him asking anyone for help). The pastor told him, "Don, I have enough problems of my own, I cannot help you with yours!" That was the last time in years my dad went anywhere near a church.

My mom and dad both blamed me for Tim's death. Throughout my early years into my late teen years, they would both remind me often of how I had killed Tim and screwed up our family. My mom became a very wild woman, sleeping around with everyone she could. My dad crawled into a bottle and hid.

From after Tim's death until I became old enough to stop taking it, my dad would make me sit with him while he drank. He would drag me everywhere like a security blanket. After midnight, he would begin talking about my hitting Tim. He would, for the next four to five hours, rehearse the entire experience again to me, reminding me that it was my fault. He would constantly tell me how I had ruined everything and would always ruin everything. He told me I would never be able to do anything right. He would force me to sit and listen to him until about 4:00 or 5:00 in the morning when he would pass out drunk. He did that to me 1,000 times or more until I was big enough to stop it.

I do not know if I hit Tim on purpose. I always thought I did not, but deep down, I am not sure. I bore the blame of Tim's death from my mom and dad all my childhood and most of my teenage years. I have been told forever by them all of our problems were and are my fault. For a time in my early adult life, I accepted that burden. My identity was, for some time, that of being the one who killed Tim and messed up everyone and everything in our family. I took that abuse until I became grown up enough to start kicking back instead of being my parents' punching bag.

I have learned a lot in my life about bitterness. I know that it can destroy you. I still deal with that day in the basement long ago. I

15

remember Tim's suffering and the damage it brought to our family. I do not know how to undo it. I do know this: I have given this to God and trust Jesus to make it all okay one day. I plan on seeing Tim and both of my parents again, and when I do, everything will be made right!

Peeping Tom

In the early days, our family's life centered around my blind brother's school. In Macon, Georgia, there was a special school just for blind people. It offered a way for them to get educated while learning survival skills. We moved close to that school so my brother could get his special needs met, and we would be together as a family.

I was about third grade, and my sister was about fourteen or fifteen. We lived in a lower middle-class neighborhood. It was one of those neighborhoods that if you were playing in one of the other yards with your friends and did something wrong, their mother would come out and whip you and send you home. On your way home, the mom would call your mom, and as soon as you walked in your house, your mom would whip you again. You could count yourself lucky if, when your dad got home, you did not get a third one.

We had close friends and a common ground type of community, and everybody watched out for each other. One of the houses was broken into, and some things were stolen. That never happened back in that day and was big business in our neighborhood. One of the mothers caught someone peeping at her through her window, and soon, every house in the area was watching for the Peeping Tom thief. It was assumed that it had to be the same person.

We (as did most people back then) slept with our windows open at night. One night, a few hours after bedtime, I woke up with someone crawling through my window. I started screaming, and the person jumped back out just as my dad came in the room, gun in hand. He saw the person but not well enough to get a shot off at him or recognize who he was. It was soon determined to be a young man in his early twenties from a couple of people who had caught glimpses of him. At any rate, life went on in our neighborhood with everybody a little jumpy as there were a few more sightings during the next few weeks.

My sister became very worried about this guy. She was all the time looking out her window or sleeping with her windows shut. It had become a big deal to her, and she was clearly shaken up by it. My dad, at the time, was an insurance salesman and was often meeting with clients to sell them policies. One evening, there was this young married couple in our living room meeting with Dad. They had our coffee table covered with papers that Dad was going over with them. My sister had just got home from practice and going to get in the shower. I was bored and looking for something to do as it was just after sunset, and all my friends were at home. Sitting in my room, I got the idea that I would scare my sister.

As I said, my sister had just got into the shower, and I went out into the backyard and dragged the doghouse over under the bathroom window. The window was just by the shower. I imagine that if someone wanted to peek in on someone, that window would give a perfect peek. Anyhow, I had to climb up on the doghouse to get high enough to the window to do something scary.

As I climbed up on top of the doghouse, I could hear my sister but was not tall enough to see anything in the window. As it was, I could just reach the bottom of the screen with my hand. So I reached up and scratched the screen and bent back down in case Gail looked out. As I said, I could not tell what, if anything, was happening in the bathroom, but this was a classic opportunity for the perfect joke on Gail. So I reached up and scratched on the window as loud as I could and bent down, waiting. I did this about six or seven times waiting to hear Gail flip out. My plan was to scare her, then I could run around the house and walk in the front door like I did not know what was happening.

It did not go as planned. What happened was that the very first time I reached up and started scratching the window, Gail saw it and was trying to scream but couldn't. Unbeknownst to me, Gail ran out of the bathroom, soaking wet and butt naked and into the living room, jumped over the coffee table, and into my dad's lap. He, his papers, and his potential clients all became wet from Gail, and there Gail sat in Dad's lap, naked and afraid. My dad jumped up and ran to his room for his pistol as I was still scratching the screen and bending down, laughing.

My dad burst out the back door with gun in hand, and there I was, laughing my head off with my back to him. I must tell you that after that moment, I was not laughing!

Who Are You Going to Live with?

In the third grade, my biggest worries were what G.I. Joe to get next or who to play with. My mom and dad were fighting all the time, and home was kind of rough, but I was young and tried not to let it mess with me too much. My dad was making a lot of money at the time, and he and Mom were partying hard also.

We lived in a wealthy neighborhood and became "that family" as the fights often spilled over into the ears of our neighbors. My dad was a very successful insurance salesman but hated the job. He was in the top ten in the country with his company but only worked four days a week. He would go to work on Monday, and by Thursday afternoon, he was drinking. He would drink straight until Sunday night, then pass out, and start over again the next day.

One day, my parents' fighting came to a head. My dad came home drinking, and my mom left the dinner table, walked out of the house, and left with another man in plain sight. My dad just sat on the couch, drinking until she walked back in. When she did, they started fighting, and Dad began hitting Mom, and Mom broke a bottle over Dad's head, cutting him deeply. Mom was bloody and Dad was bloody. My dad took a bunch of pills and cut his wrist and fell over on the floor, foaming at the mouth.

My sister called the ambulance while my blind brother was putting pressure on Dad's wrist. He was throwing up and choking and he stopping breathing. I was trying to keep his mouth clear and giving him mouth-to-mouth. We were trying to keep him alive. When the ambulance arrived, they transported both my parents to the hospital.

The next week, when I walked in from school, Mom and Dad were sitting at the table, each at one end facing the other. They told me to sit down, and I did. My dad looked at me and said, "Your mom and I are getting a divorce. Who do you want to live with?"

I sat in the middle of the table between my parents and was just asked which one I wanted to live with. I was in the third grade!

The reason for sharing this story is because of what happened in me with that question. I did not feel ready to have to make that type of decision, but I did. I looked at both of them and said, "You two have messed your lives up so much, I am not going to let you mess up mine anymore." I told them from that time on, I would be on my own. I said I would move in with Mom because she would need my help, but from that day forward, I would make my own decisions.

I grew up that moment. I began to think as an adult from that time on. I decided what I would do or not do. It was a "not so funny time" in my life. It was one that changed the way I did things from then on. I was relieved that my parents were getting away from each other before they killed one another. I think back to that moment and remember when I decided to become my own man.

Creature from the Black Lagoon

Back in the days of twelve channels on your TV was a thing on Friday nights called *Friday Night Frights!* Every Friday night, we kids would gather around the TV and watch the scary movies and hug our pillows and such. On one certain Friday night, there was a thunderstorm and hard rain outside with lightning every few minutes. It was the perfect night for scaring and being scared.

My sister, Gail, and stepsister, Kelly, were huddled up on the couch, and my dad and stepmom had already gone to bed. I was stretched out on the floor, and the second movie of the night was just starting. It was *The Creature from the Black Lagoon!* I was about eleven or twelve, and Gail and Kelly were fourteen and fifteen respectively.

The movie plot started getting intense, and we were acting like we were not scared, but we were. Gail and Kelly started laughing at the movie, trying to act brave. We got to the scene in the movie where the creature's hand came up out of the Black Lagoon and grabbed the rail of the boat with suspenseful music playing. Gail and Kelly freaked out and threw the blanket they were sharing over their heads. When the creature's head came out of the water, they both screamed and went to bed. It was too much for them, and they were scared past their comfort zones.

As it was back in those days, our family was a large one living in a small house. Gail and Kelly shared a bedroom with an old big bed with the wooden slats holding the mattress and box springs up between two metal frames that fit into the bedposts. Anyway, they ran and jumped in their bed and were hiding under the covers, hoping the creature would not get them. I was left in the living room alone and watching the movie. As I was lying on the floor with the lightning flashing and rain coming down, I got this wonderful idea for a joke on my sisters.

We lived in an area surrounded by woods. Our yard was a couple of acres, and we raised some animals and had a large garden for food. Well, we also had a pigpen where we raised pigs for sale and slaughter. I put on some cut-off shorts and went outside to the pigpen. It was about eleven at night, and I was trying to be quite sneaky. I went into the pigpen and caught a little pig about twenty pounds. It was not a baby, but small enough to be able to handle alone.

I walked back to the house and into the back door. My dad's room was on one end of the house, and Gail and Kelly's room was on the other end and down the hall, last door on the right. I was sneaking down the hall, soaking wet with a muddy wet little pig in my arms. I turned the doorknob on the bedroom door, real quiet like, and they were in bed, lights out, and asleep...or almost asleep. I stepped in the room and growled the most monster-like growl I could come up with and threw the pig. It flew across the room in the air, landing in the middle of the bed with Gail and Kelly. I then jumped out of the room and slammed the door.

The lightning flashed, and Kelly, Gail, and the pig were all fighting each other to get away. The mattress and bedsprings dropped between the frames onto the floor. Gail, Kelly, and a little frightened pig were screaming and running all around this dark room, thinking that the creature from the Black Lagoon was jumping on them. Little piggy was not thinking anything; it was just screaming and running all around the room, bouncing off the walls in a panic-driven state.

Kelly wet the bed and just sat there, staring and crying. Gail, who was a fighter, jumped up and attacked her dresser, knocking it over onto their floor. Gail then landed beside the dresser, and the pig ran to a corner, squealing, trying to root a place to hide out off the floor. I was not expecting the trick to work out quite this well or quite this loud. The whole house was shaking, and I was trying to run before my dad came out of his room. My problem was I was laughing too hard to run.

The next thing I remember is seeing my dad running down the hall, butt naked with a pistol in his hand. He jumped over me and opened the girl's door, turning on the light. There was Kelly in bed, crying, with a giant wet spot all around her and her mattress on the floor. Gail was on the floor, holding her leg from having kicked the dresser over, which was beside her with all their stuff all over the floor. Over in the corner was a very frightened little "creature from the black lagoon," still squealing, and trying to dig through the floor to hide. I cannot say that it was worth the punishment I took for that little joke on my sisters, but I can say that in my lifetime, that was one of my best memories of fun times, except the last part.

Possums and Persimmons

Our backyard was large and surrounded by a large tract of woods. Much of my time as a kid was spent in those woods and around the lake, which was in the middle of the woods, hunting, fishing, camping, and everything in between. One tree directly behind our house on the edge of the woods was a persimmon tree. If you don't know what a persimmon is, it is a fruit that is extremely tart and bitter until the first frost. After the first frost, the persimmons turn sweet and enjoyable. They are about the size of an average fig, and this tree was loaded up with persimmons every year.

We did not live on a farm, but we did have a large garden and raised animals for food and to sell. We also hunted for food and raised and sold hunting dogs. I was always hunting and catching any kind of animal I could. One of the favorite foods for our local population of possums was persimmons after the first frost. Possums were one of the animals that we could catch and sell for a decent profit. We would catch them and pen them up for a couple of weeks and feed them corn to clean them out and then sell them.

Catching a live and often angry possum is tricky, and you have to be careful. They are fighters, and if they get you, they can tear you up. It was always exciting to catch them because you never really knew who would win when you got them cornered. We used traps and would run them down if we caught them in the yard before they made it to the woods.

But the best time to catch possums was just after first frost for about three weeks or so. The persimmon tree would be loaded with them. You had to wait till after dark, and then you could go down to the persimmon tree and shine a flashlight up in the branches and look for their eyes. You could tell how big the possums were by how far the space was between their eyes. It was not unusual to see four or five or more in the tree at any given time until the fruit was eaten up.

To catch the possums, we would take a ladder, a blanket, and flashlights down to the persimmon tree after dark. It would take three of us and some luck. The plan went like this: We would set the ladder up so I could climb it without too much noise to get to the lowest branches (fifteen feet or so). Then I would climb up the tree. Dad and Gail or whoever helped Dad would shine lights throughout the tree at the possums and pick out the ones big enough to catch. When they got the light on one they wanted, I would climb up to the possum and kick it out of the tree, and they would catch it in the blanket, wrapping it up, and then carry it to the pen. That was how it was supposed to happen and did most of the time. Believe it or not, we caught most of the ones we went after. This brings me to one of the funny times I look back on with fond memories.

My dad was drinking heavily during this time of his life and was the kind of man that did not take no from any of the family. He ruled the roost. This one night, he had been drinking quite a bit and decided it was time to catch a possum. So he got Gail and me and the stuff, and we headed quietly down toward the persimmon tree.

It was a dark night and cold. When we got to the tree and set the ladder up, we could see eyes about halfway up the tree. So my dad and Gail got the blanket ready, and up the tree I went. When I got up to the limb the possum was on, it was the biggest possum I had ever seen in my life. We knew this was a big one, because his eyes had a hammer handle space between them. But he was not just big; this possum was mean! When I got to the limb and was where

26

I could climb out and kick him down, he just looked at me and growled. It was like he was saying, "Come on, big boy, let's see what you got." It was dark, and I was twenty-five-plus feet up a tree with this possum who was as big as my dog, and he was not happy.

I shouted out to my dad, "I don't want to mess with this one!"

My dad was a man's man, and he shouted back up at me to quit being afraid and "man up and kick that possum out of the tree."

This possum was mean and mad, and I was being yelled at by my drunk father to attack it. The only reason I went toward the possum was that I was more afraid of my dad than I was of it. I climbed out toward the possum who was hissing and lunging at me. I would kick at it, and it would bite at my foot or try to grab it. It was a real battle for a while when the possum lunged at my leg, giving me the chance to get a lucky kick in, knocking it almost off the limb. I yelled for them on the ground, "Get ready, here it comes!" And I began shaking the limb as hard as possible to shake him off.

I was standing on the middle of this limb, holding onto the limb above me, shaking it like a springboard. It just so happened that as I pushed down hard on the limb, the possum holding on by two claws got flung up in the air and out into the night. The rest of the story was told to me by Gail as it was too dark to see the ground. I was also dealing with fright from this possum and was really relieved he was gone.

My dad and my sister were holding the blanket to catch it, but it was flung out of the tree with more spring than they guessed. It came down and landed on my dad's face. It should have broken his neck; it was so big! It was one of the funniest things I have ever heard.

That possum and my dad were both screaming, and Mr. Possum latched onto my dad's face, and my dad was wailing and flinging his arms in the air. I almost fell out of the tree. I was laughing so hard. My dad and that possum where fighting and carrying on like they were both fighting for their lives (the possum was anyway).

After what seemed a few minutes (seconds) of fighting, the possum jumped off my dad's face and headed for cover. As it happened, the old possum got away to live another day. I made it out of the tree without injury, and my sister was scared but unhurt and crying. My dad got the worst of it. His glasses were broken and his face was torn up pretty bad. He was bleeding all over, and his nose was broken; but other than that, he was fine. I never reminded him this to his face afterward, but I tried to tell him that old possum was one we should probably not mess with while he was eating! He did not get that big and old by being stupid or soft.

Bull Riding

I n the fourth grade, our class went to a Mennonite farm for a field trip. We were supposed to see how the farms worked before the days of electricity. There were three classes going, and we pulled into the farm and lined up to see the various workings of the dairy farm. The farm was very big with a large number of milking cows. We walked all over, seeing all the animals and fields and pens and such.

This farm had a prize bull that was the largest bull I had ever seen. It had short legs for a bull, but this thing was huge. Our class walked through the barn where this bull had his own living space, half the size of the barn all to himself. There was a fence inside the bull's room that had room for people to walk through and view the bull and walk out into the barnyard at the end of the barn wall. The classes came in and walked along the fence and back out the door at the other end.

Inside the bull's room, the farmer had two of his sons washing it. The bull was standing there calmly while the boys had these brushes on poles, dipping them in buckets of soapy water and scrubbing the bull like it was a car. My buddy, Granville, and I were at the back of the line, and the teacher guide said for everyone to follow him out into the barnyard.

Granville and I climbed through the fence and walked over to the farmer's sons. We asked if we could help clean the bull, and they said, "Sure." We started scrubbing the bull with it just standing and looking at us carefree and calm. I asked the guys if the bull was ever mean. They said that it was like a giant pet. I started petting him on the side of his face, and he didn't move.

One of the farmers' sons (they were in their late teens, early twenties) asked me if I had ever ridden a bull. I told him I had not but that I wanted to. He picked me up and put me on its back. This thing was so large that I could not get my legs around its back. I scooted up to its neck where I just could get a leg hold on him. He just stood there with me sitting on his shoulder/neck area.

I asked the guys to get him to move so I could ride him. There was a board laying on the ground, and Granville slapped the bull on the butt with the board. When he did, the bull took off, out toward the corral in the barnyard!

He was not bucking, just running at a slow run, but it was all I could do to hold onto his neck and shoulders. The bull ran out of the barn into the corral area outside. The bull was running beside the fence where my class was walking. I rode right by my teacher, just a few feet and a fence between us, on the back of this huge running bull. I heard the teacher say, "My heavens! He is mine!" as we passed.

The bull was running toward the end of the fence where the farmer had a wood post wrapped in carpet stretched out between two posts with a chain. It was a thing he had made for the bull to walk under, and it would brush the flies and bugs off its back in the hot summer days.

The bull ran straight to the post and under it, brushing me off his back like a bug. I landed on my back with a thud into a pool of mud, urine, and bull doo-doo. I was laughing so hard that I couldn't get my breath, and Granville came running up, screaming that it was his turn.

The farmers' sons came up next, and then the farmer and my teacher and everyone was freaking out. I was not hurt in any way. I was still laughing from the fun of riding that bull who was now standing in the middle of the corral just watching. I was completely soaked in the type of mud that puddles up at the feeding spot of a corral. I had my hair caked in bull stinky, and all my clothes were wet from the puddle I landed in.

After everybody (mainly my teacher) had calmed down, the farmer had his boys take me over to the side of the barn and hose me off. It took a while, and finally my hair, ears, and clothes were less green and more their natural color. I had to sit by the bus until the field trip was finished, and for the rest of the year, I sat in the principal's office during class field trips. But if anyone ever asks if I have ever ridden a bull, I can say, "Yes, in the fourth grade!"

Molly

I n my early years, I was extremely shy and very energetic. I was not rebellious or defiant. I was the kid who would figure out a way to get into the return air vents to explore the tunnels. I was a very large kid and was that kid that other kids picked on. I didn't mind being picked on nor did it bother me what others thought about me. I just wanted to play. I lived for recess.

In the third grade, there was this girl that, for some reason, did not like me. Molly was her name, and she was the perfect kid in everybody's book but mine. She was the kid that you would put in the Sunday school poster for third-grade kids who would someday solve world hunger.

Molly was always dressed in the nicest, newest, and most expensive clothes. Every other kid wanted Molly to like them so they could be popular. Molly was a true class leader, and all the teachers and office people loved her to death. She could do no wrong. I did not dislike Molly. I just didn't chase after her or try to fuss for her attention.

Molly, however, did not like me at all. She was always getting me in trouble by telling on me. I was talking to my buddy during quiet time, and Molly would burst out crying and run to the desk of our teacher, telling her I was talking. One day at lunch, I shot a spitball at my friend, and Molly jumped up crying and ran to the principal's office, telling him what I did. Every time I would do something, Molly was there to make sure I paid for my actions.

She was also very mean in secret. She would say mean things about me to other kids, and they would laugh. She was the biggest bully I faced, and no one would ever believe me if I tried to tell on her. I got to the point I was having bad dreams, and instead of a monster or wild animal trying to get me, it was Molly. I cannot say it strong enough how much grief that sweet little girl caused me for months.

That brings me to this funny memory. We were in class one spring day after lunch and were supposed to be sitting quietly at our desks. Molly had been on my case again, and I was just about to the point of going nuts. Our teacher had left the room to speak to someone down the hall. Molly was sitting across the aisle from me and one chair ahead. She was wearing this nice cashmere sweater and matching skirt. I was trying to sit still (not easy) and not get in trouble when I looked on the floor and, under my chair, was a palmetto bug (giant roach). I reached down and scraped it up in my hand.

I said out loud, "Molly," and she turned and looked at me as I threw the bug at her. This giant roach hit her right in her chest, getting caught in the cashmere material of her sweater, kicking and struggling, trying to fly away but to no avail. Molly jumped up and started slapping herself and screaming at the top of her lungs. The class was shocked, and teachers were running into our classroom to see what was going on. At some point, the roach got free from Molly's sweater, but not before she had wet herself and the floor where she was standing. Molly was standing in a puddle of pee on the floor, and the class was shocked, and I was the only one laughing. So everyone knew who was guilty.

Molly went home early, and I got to spend the rest of the day thinking about my paddling in the principal's office. In most cases, I would have felt bad about that situation, but in Molly's case, that was my first understanding of the phrase "poetic justice." Funny thing, Molly never picked on me after that day.

Drugs in Our Schools!

Our culture has changed a lot from when I was in high school. Back in 1978, our high schools were different than today. I was in an English class during our lunch period. The way it worked was that we would do our class, then go to lunch eat and return to that class where we had a twenty-minute wait period before the bell. This class was taught by a teacher who was openly gay. Not a big deal now, but back then, it was not a normal situation. This teacher had flowers growing on a table by his desk and watered them during this free period.

One day, he asked the class for a volunteer for someone to water his plants for him. He said he wanted it to be a guy that did it. His reason: "I want you to be able to get in touch with your feminine side." I was half-kidding and raised my hand to do it. The teacher was excited that I would volunteer and gave me the job. He was openly expressing his hopes for me to be more feminine at our class's amusement.

Let me say two things here so you do not get the wrong impression. I did not have any ill-will toward the teacher nor did I really want to water his plants. I was just wanting to play a prank on him for embarrassing me in front of the class. I planted seven marijuana seeds in his plants to see if they would grow. Sure enough, over a little bit of time, I had seven pot plants growing in my English teacher's flowers in class.

The plants grew to the place where they were a little taller than the flowers, and the teacher even noticed them. He mentioned to the class that he had these weeds growing in his plants. He said he normally would pull them up, but they were pretty, and he decided to keep them. I did not tell anyone what I had done, so no one really knew what they were until one day.

We had left lunch and were heading upstairs back to class when police and drug agents with dogs ran past us to guess where? Sitting on the floor in the hall next to the door to our class was our English teacher hyperventilating. Inside the classroom, the drug agents were bagging up the plants and taking pictures. In the late seventies, pot was treated like a major drug, and this deal became headline news. "Drugs in Our Schools" was the headline with pictures of the flowers on the front page of the paper.

Whenever anything like this happened at our school, my counselor would come to me and ask me if I had anything to do with what happened. I would always tell her the truth. If I did it, I would not lie about it. Well, on this given time, she never asked me about it. They were going to hang whoever was guilty. I never told anyone about my guilt.

I visited the school several years after the pot incident, and my counselor was now the principal. I had become a Christian by this time and was there on business. As we were finishing our business and rehashing old times, she said that she was dying to ask me something. Without hesitation, I told her, "Yes, it was me (the only one I told at that point)." I was wondering why she had not asked me when the incident happened. She said she thought it was me but didn't want it to go any further than it had. She knew it would be blown way out of proportion and did not want to see me have that on my record.

Welcome to the Neighborhood

One of the funny things about life is that it can change on you without notice. We lived in a nice neighborhood and enjoyed the comforts of my father's large salary and all the benefits that came with it. Then, overnight, we were moving into government housing after a bitter divorce and everything changing.

My blind brother and I stayed with my mom, and my sisters went with my dad. We moved into government housing in the bad side of Macon, Georgia. It was a very violent area with a lot of racial tension. After living there long enough, I realized it was not so much racial tension as it was just poor people with a lot of problems, looking for someone to hate. Hating other people is easier when they have different skin or culture or whatever. In any case, it was a very different neighborhood than our wealthy private school with nice everything that we had just moved away from.

I was just in my early teens and had never been in a fight other than kid-type fights on the playground at school. We had just finished unloading our stuff into our new home and were sitting in the living room. My mom had left for some reason. I heard a voice from outside calling, "Hey! You in the house!"

I opened the door, and standing in front of our porch were three ugly white guys staring at me. These guys looked rough, and the big one in the middle was obviously the leader. He had a chain in his hand and outweighed me by fifty pounds easily. To his right was a skinny small kid holding a ball bat, looking at the leader. The guy on the left was considerably older and was a tall lanky fellow, holding a pipe with this silly grin just staring at me. They were the welcoming committee for the neighborhood. The leader was telling me to come out and fight.

I was scared to death. I was thinking, *These guys are going to kill me.* I slammed the door and ran back to my room and hid under my bed. My older brother, who is legally blind, came into my room and told me that I needed to go outside and fight them. I told Adrian that he was only saying that because he was blind and could not see how mean those guys looked. What my brother said to me next changed my life and is the main reason I am sharing this story with you.

Adrian was my older brother and was blinded at birth by the doctor who delivered him. Adrian said to me, "Frank, we are going to have to live here for some time, and if you run from these guys, you will be running from now on. Go outside and face them, and even if you get beat up, it is better to attack your fears than to run from them." He said that he had learned that life lesson by being blind. He said he had no choice but to face life (fears) blind and not run from his condition. He decided to fight through his fears rather than live hiding from them.

I was really scared of these guys, but I knew in my heart, my brother had just spoken truth to me. I knew I had to go outside and face these guys.

The house was old WWII army housing. The front of it had four steps up to a four-foot by four-foot landing or porch, which then led into the house. I opened the door, and standing directly in front of the steps were these guys trash talking and waving their weapons. At this point, I was not a fighter and was not sure if my brother was all that smart. I noticed that the two guys kept watching the big guy

37

in the middle, so he had to be the leader. I knew I had to deal with him first and needed to do it before I lost my nerve.

I was four steps higher than those guys and about four steps away from where they stood. I screamed as loud as I could and ran and jumped off my porch onto the big guy's chest and shoulders. He fell backward onto the ground, and I was on my knees, on top of his chest, screaming like a wild man, punching him in the face as hard and as often as I possibly could. I kept waiting for the other two to start hitting me, but they were just standing there, watching me beat their buddy in the head. They dropped their weapons and ran away.

I stepped off the guy who had quit moving and stood beside him, looking at him breathing heavy and crying. He was bleeding from his nose and mouth and was swelling up a bit. He sat up and stared back at me. I told him I didn't want to fight them and that he had made me. He got up and walked away and down the street toward what I found out later to be his house. I walked back into my house to my brother and told him what happened.

Just a little while later, I heard a knock at my door, and it was those same three guys. I went outside and sat on the porch with them. We introduced ourselves to each other and ended up becoming close friends. From that time forward, they thought I was a bad dude, but truthfully, I was just a scared dude in a very new world who decided not to hide from my fears and my circumstances. I will never forget my brother's wisdom.

Your Last Look at Freedom

My best friend and I were known to hang out at the skating rink. Tony was a third-degree black belt and a ladies' man. We were dating these girls who were best friends at the time. So it was a best friends dating best friends type thing. We spent our Tuesdays at the skating rink and knew most of the people there. There was this one girl who got it into her head that she was going to make Tony her man. She had no shy bone in her body and was outspoken about her intentions.

We were hanging out, and Tony's girl was not there yet, so we were just waiting on the girls to show up. Well, this girl began to come on to Tony in an obvious way. Tony was not at all interested and did not want to have his girl hear that he had been flirty with another girl. So he told her several times to go away and leave him alone.

When the girls showed up, we had been skating and ended up standing beside the floor, talking, and this girl came up to Tony and threw herself on him, hugging him. Tony pushed the girl way and told her to leave him alone. When Tony pushed the girl away, being on skates, she lost her balance and fell forward. It was no big deal, and everybody was laughing at the girl more because of her throwing herself at Tony and him pushing her away.

The girl flipped out and started screaming that Tony had punched her and she was going to tell her dad and have Tony thrown in jail. The push was no big deal, and the girl fell from her own skates more than from the push. She was not hurt, and Tony had not struck her anywhere but her rejected heart. We just thought it was funny as the girl began throwing a tantrum because Tony turned her away.

Sure enough, the next week, Tony was arrested for hitting this girl and had to get a lawyer and go to court. I was ignorant to how the world worked in these situations. I'd come to find out the girl had a wealthy dad who had a lot of influence in the county. The girl was a spoiled brat that got anything she wanted (but Tony). The dad had taken out a warrant for Tony for punching his daughter. Tony was seventeen and had to go to adult court. I was there when all this stuff happened and knew Tony never touched the girl. It was a complete lie. In any case, we ended up in a Georgia state superior court having to answer charges.

The day of the trial, I was so sure that Tony was innocent that I was kidding him while walking to the courtroom. I told Tony to look at the bird on the phone line outside the window. I asked him if he knew what that bird was. Tony said he didn't, and I said, "Look at it long and hard as that bird is your last look at freedom." Tony was all nervous, and I was laughing at him. After all, I was his best friend!

When we got into the courtroom, I was the only witness that showed up. I didn't think anything of it at first. The courtroom was packed with cases, and Tony's last name started with a W, so I knew we would be there for a while. When the judge entered the courtroom and the court began, Tony's case was called first. I was a little taken back by that but still didn't fully see what was going on. Immediately, the girl and her father and their lawyer started by telling her story. She basically told the court that Tony was chasing her, and she was trying to get him to leave her alone and he wouldn't. She said that Tony came up to her and hugged her and tried to kiss her and she pushed him back. She then claimed Tony slapped her in the face, knocking her down and sending her to the doctor with injuries.

Tony gave his side, and I was called up as the only witness. When I was finished, the judge sat there a minute and then said, "Guilty." He gave Tony thirty days in jail, a $1,000 fine, and one-year active probation.

I was shocked. I stood up and said, "Hold it, Judge! You can't do that! He was not guilty!"

The judge told me to be seated or I would be in contempt of court. I told him that his court was in contempt of itself and that he was full of doo-doo. I then turned and left the court.

The judge told the bailiff to get me, and I took off running down the hall. Next thing I know, these four sheriffs were dragging me back in front of His Honor in handcuffs. The judge asked me if I had anything to say to the court, like an apology, and I told him that I did not have anything to apologize for because what I said was the truth. The next thing I know, he charged me with contempt of court and a felony charge for resisting arrest, and then I was in jail.

I know that I was wrong to say what I said in open court with it in session. I also know that at that time in my life, I was full of bitterness and had a bad attitude. The funny thing was that Tony's lawyer signed Tony out and made an appeal, and he went home. I, however, was in jail, thinking about that bird on the wire.

FYI, the charges were dropped against Tony for several reasons. One, it was not supposed to be in state court. Two, the judge was the girl's uncle and had business with her dad. Third, witnesses proved true. I, on the other hand, was in county jail eight days before being released. It was a time that helped me come to grips with needing to change my outlook on life and attitude. I'm thankful for the lesson!

Grandmothers' Prayers

I am not proud of the person I was before I became a Christian. I had—from my brother Tim's death to the time I was twenty—become a very bitter and faithless person. I claimed to be an atheist and had a bad addiction to drugs and alcohol. I was very anti-Christian and would not talk with anybody about Christ. I hated Christ and the church and did not trust Christians. I was not a heavy dealer in drugs but sold some from time to time. I sold drugs to Christians who would not admit they knew me unless they needed some dope.

I was not really a person who carried emotional ties with anyone. I was not afraid of any man, and the only person I feared was my little ninety-pound grandmother. Nanny (as I called her) had whipped me with switches growing up and she was one person who always loved me. I feared her out of respect and cared about her.

My dad told me one day that Nanny had not been well and that she went to the doctor. He and Uncle Cork had just found out she had cancer. Her cancer was advanced, and they felt that she had three months at most to live. Then my dad told me that he and my uncle Cork had decided along with the doctor not to tell her. I did not feel good about Nanny having three months to live and no one telling her. To me, it was a matter of respect. So I decided to tell her myself.

I was always high during this time in my life and could not function without being high. I drove to the hospital where Nanny was and went into her room to tell her about her fate. The past few years, I had not seen her much because I was not living right, and I was ashamed to be around her. My Nanny was a Christian; not like all the other ones I knew and did not like. She was a different kind of Christian. She never said anything to me about it, but she always had her Bible close and would read it and cry and pray. She had a direct line to God, it seemed.

I walked into her room, hoping she could not tell how high I was, and said my hellos. I was just about to start telling her, and she looked right at me and spoke. "Harry (*what she called me*), sit down and shut up. God told me last night that I am going to die soon." She then said this: "I told him I was not going to do it. I will not die and go to heaven with my grandson going to hell!" She then told me, "Now you get out of my room and don't come back until you are saved!"

I left her room, thinking, *Man, whatever drugs she was on were better than mine.* I knew she knew and didn't think anything much more about it. What I didn't know was that my grandmother began to pray for me to come to Christ. I didn't have contact with her again for nine months, but things began to happen in my life that made me begin to think about God and if he could be real. Everybody said he was not, and I did not believe in him, and thought only people with no sense believed in Jesus.

Shortly after the visit to my grandmother's room, a friend of mine was killed in a drug deal that went bad. Story was he killed himself, but word on the street was he was killed. We threw a big party for him after his funeral, and I could not get the thought of him being dead out of my mind. What happens when you die?

One of my good friends and I were in a store getting beer shortly after that, and this little old lady came up to Larry and tried to give him a religious pamphlet. I am ashamed of it now, but I told the lady to go away and take her religion with her. Larry and I were talking to each other about our funerals. Neither one of us thought we would live much longer and had both written out how we wanted to be buried. The old lady tried to give the pamphlet to Larry again, and I raised my voice to her and told her to go away. She said God had told her to give it to Larry, and I told her to go away.

Larry told me that he wanted to read it because he was wondering if any of the Christian stuff was real. I told him that it was all a big con and to forget about it. The next day, Larry was thrown off a building and killed. We buried him just like he wanted, according to his requests that he had written. I often wonder if Larry would have been saved if I had not stopped that old lady from giving him the Gospel pamphlet.

Soon after that funeral, I began thinking about taking my life. I was not depressed or crazy. I was just not seeing any reason to keep on in this life with no purpose or meaning to anything. In this mindset, I decided to see if there was anything to Jesus and church. I decided I would try going to church and see. The next Sunday morning, I went into the first church I thought of. Our little town was the kind where a person could get a reputation and be looked down upon. My hair was very long, and I wore t-shirts and blue jeans all the time.

Sunday morning, First Baptist Church, I went in with my long hair and Led Zeppelin t-shirt checking church out. I had not been in a church in seventeen years. To my surprise, I saw some people that I partied with, so I went and sat down beside them. You would have thought I had leprosy. They jumped up and moved away, hoping nobody saw me sit beside them. I kid you not, this happened several times over the next few weeks. I would go into a church, wanting to know if Jesus was real, see someone I partied with or sold drugs to, and they would run and hide from me. I realized I was not welcome as their friend unless it was in my world. The church folk did not want anyone to know they knew me.

I finally decided I was going to try one last time to see if Jesus was real. There had been one more church that I wanted to try before I gave up on God. I decided I would not do anything but go in and sit alone and see if God somehow would show me that he was real. I pulled into this parking lot that was full. I waited until the service had started, and then I got out and walked into the foyer. There were two swinging sets of doors going into the main church, and I looked through the window and found a spot I could go to and sit by myself.

I did not know how to pray, but for the first time that I can remember, I tried a prayer. I said to God, "If you are real, will you please show me if you want me to follow you?" I then added, "I am going into this service and am going to do anything you tell me to do!" I meant it. I was not sure that there was a God to talk to, but if he was there, I had just asked him to show himself to me.

I opened the door and walked halfway down toward the front of the church to an empty seat on the left side. I was about eight rows from the pulpit, closer to the front than the back. It was the only empty place where I wouldn't offend someone by sitting too close to them. The choir was singing, and I sat down and sat on my hands and looked straight to the floor, just like I used to do when I was three years old so as not to get into trouble. I had my eyes closed and was just waiting to hear God say something.

I felt someone poke me on my shoulder from behind. I looked back, and this little bald dude was standing in the aisle (while the choir was trying to sing), looking at me. He spoke in a normal voice. "I am a deacon here," he said, then he stared at me.

I answered, "I am proud of you," and looked toward the front.

He poked me again and said, "We don't want any trouble, and you can't sit here. You are not dressed right, and we are on TV. You can go and sit in the back, or better yet, there are the back doors. Don't let them hit you on the way out."

I didn't want trouble nor did I want anything but to know if God was real. I could have broken that little man in half, but at that point in my life, I was not concerned about him or anyone else. I walked out the back doors into their foyer again. I thought about the prayer I had said just a few minutes before. It seemed that if God was real, he had just answered. If God existed, he did not want my kind. I was convinced that I was okay to die. God either was not real or he did not want me. Either way, I had my answer.

I decided I would take my own life. It was the first time in a long time I felt peace about something. I did not let anyone know what I was planning and was going to do it in such a way that no one else would be bothered by it. I spent a few weeks getting things ready and taking care of my car and finances. I picked the night I was going to do it, and the time finally came.

I lived close to a grocery store that had an alley behind it that was blocked by a hill, so it was not in clear view of anyone unless they intended to go back there. It had places where cars could park and not be suspect. The dumpster was emptied early in the morning. My plan was to park there in the middle of the night, crawl into the dumpster under the garbage, shoot myself, and be buried in a land-fill the next morning. It would be several days or even a week or so before anyone tried to find me, and by then, I would be long gone.

I pulled into the spot at about 1:30 and decided I would listen to my favorite tape then do it. I had a letter in the passenger seat explaining things and giving my car to my little sister. I sat in the dark car, smoking dope and waiting. The alley was very dark, and I was just about finished with my tape, getting ready to get in the dumpster, when there was a knock on my window. It scared me to death!

I rolled down my window, and a friend of mine was standing there. He and I used to be friends but about a year before he became a Christian and I broke off our friendship. He was never out after 11:00, and there was no reason for him to be next to my car after 2:00 in the morning. His car had a flat tire that night, and he had tried to change it for several hours, but everything kept going wrong. Finally, he gave up and decided to walk home and try again tomorrow. It just so happened that alley was a shortcut toward his house, and he was as surprised to see me as I was to see him.

He started to try to talk to me about accepting Christ again and had no idea of my plans. I told him to leave me alone, and he said something to me that shook me up. He looked at me and said, "Frank, you are determined to die and go to hell aren't you?" And he walked away.

I did not know it then, but I know it now that God's Holy Spirit entered that car and convicted my heart. I became afraid and didn't know what to do, but I wanted to know some way to find peace. I had a little Bible in my drawer at home and drove to it. I got into my room and opened the little bus Bible someone had given me years before that I had never read. I sat down and opened it. I did not know any verses or anything about it or where to look.

The Bible fell open to John 15:15. It said, "I no longer call you a slave, for a slave does not know what His master is doing. I have called you a friend, for I have made all things known to you (paraphrased)." In that moment, God opened my heart to the fact that He wanted a friendship with me! I knew it but did not know what to do with it. I remember it well as I write this, just like it happened yesterday.

I got on my knees and prayed. I said, "God, if you are real, why would you want to be my friend?" I said to him, "The problem is I am a sinner and I mess up everything I touch." I told him I was addicted to drugs and alcohol and other sins and I was not sure I could stop. I finally said, "God, if you want to be my friend, I will be your friend and Christ's if you would forgive my sins and help me!" I then promised him that I would do any and everything he ever asked me too! That night or morning, God entered my life, and I have had Jesus in my heart ever since.

It was God's mercy, but I slept a few hours and woke up the next morning a different person. God took my main addictions away without withdrawals. I was different inside. Things that controlled me were gone, and my heart was different. I didn't know what to do or how to tell anyone. I decided I needed to tell my grandmother. It had been nine months since I had been to her room. I drove to the hospital to see her.

When I got to ICU where she was, they said I could not see her because she was in a coma and could not hear me. I told them I really needed to see her, and reluctantly, they let me into her room.

When I took her hand and told her I was there, Nanny opened her eyes and asked me, "Are you saved, boy?" I told her I was, and she said, "Harry, boy, don't you lie to me." She had her Bible beside her on the nightstand and asked me to open it and read John 14 and 15 to her. I opened it and began reading it to her. She listened a little then reached over and patted my hand. She said, "Yep, you got it." She smiled and slipped back into her coma. Nanny passed just a few hours later that evening.

At Nanny's funeral a few days later, I was standing back behind the crowd at the graveside service. My t-shirt had a pot plant on it and read, "Nature's way of say hi!" As I was standing there, this lady came up to me and asked me if I was Harry. I told her that was what Nanny called me. She asked me, "Are you saved yet?" I was a little taken aback as just a few days before, those were fighting words, but now they were wonderful words.

I told her I was and asked her why she asked. She informed me that she had been Nanny's night nurse for the past months and that she would go by her room night after night and hear her calling out to God for me to get saved. She said that she and others had joined her in her prayers for me and needed to know. I told her that I had just put my faith in Christ the day she passed.

Here is to each of you who are praying for loved ones. I know that the reason I am going to heaven and God saved me is because of my grandmother's prayers. I believe God sent that friend by my car that night just before I ended my life because of that church's cold heart to a sinner that day. I opened my heart to him in that foyer, and they turned me away. My grandmother did not give up, and I ask you not to either. God answered Nanny's prayer in my life, and if God will save me, he will save anyone. Do not give up on your loved one.

Call

I was amazed that the Christian faith was true. I was even more amazed at how easy it was to come to God through Christ. I had heard the church spiel on Jesus dying on the cross and so on, but I had never understood that Jesus died on the cross so Frank Penley (and anyone else) can be forgiven freely. I remember lying in bed at night and thinking about all the people I knew who did not know how easy it was to come to Christ. I decided that praying was just simply talking to God, so I would talk to him about everything.

One night, I was praying and I was asking God why no one was telling all my friends about how easy it was to be saved. Anybody could be saved; all they had to do was ask. I was naming people who meant a lot to me, those I thought would go to hell if somebody did not tell them. God spoke to my heart (not audibly, but very real) and said, "I want you to tell them."

I promised the Lord I would do anything he asked me. I knew he was asking, and I didn't know how to talk to people about him, but I thought it was a very serious thing to do. It was important to say the right stuff, so I remember praying and saying to God I would do my best to let people know how to be saved. During this prayer, it was dawning on me that God was calling me into my life's purpose.

A funny thing happened after I realized God was calling me to serve him with my life. He put it very strongly on my heart that while serving him with my life that I would not seek money or wealth. I have often wondered why God was so strong with me about this, but I have followed him, not letting money be my influence the best I have known how.

I still would hang out with my friends and I was adamant that they become Christians. I would go to parties and tell everyone they needed to get saved. I would go into parties and turn the lights on and the music off. I would tell everybody, "You guys have to get saved. It's easy, and Jesus loves you too."

One night, I went to the parking lot where all of us kids would park and hang out. It would have several hundred kids some weekends. On this night, I was getting really brokenhearted for my friends who just were not understanding their need for Jesus. I was parked where most of the main guys parked, and it was crowded. I got up on the hood of my Nova and shouted for everybody to come around. I needed to tell them something. I started pointing at everybody and naming all the stuff they were doing wrong (I was worse than any of them) and telling them they needed to get saved. I told them, "Come on now, guys, get down on your knees, and let's pray and ask Jesus to save you." They were very patient with me as we were close friends. They gathered around, and I got off the car, and they told me that they knew how to get saved but were not ready to give up their party life yet. They said that as soon as my religion wore off, they would be the first ones to get me high again.

My religion has not worn off, but I had to learn that a lot of people are not lost in sin because they don't know the truth; many simply don't want the truth. I also learned that people don't come to Christ by force. My grandmother's example is the way. Prayer is what opens the doors to people's hearts.

Brother Joe

I cannot remember anyone talking to me about faith until after I became a Christian. I had very little if any Bible knowledge, and now suddenly people started telling me all these things I must do now to be saved. This was after I already was saved. Where were they when I did not know Christ? Now one person tells me I'm not saved yet unless I get baptized, someone else tells me I'm not saved unless I speak in tongues, others say I must go to church on Saturday if I'm saved.

I remember these two guys at my work (Kroger). They were meat-cutters, and I worked on stock crew. I started reading or trying to read my Bible on break, and they noticed. They came to me one day and said that I needed to be baptized or I was not going to heaven. They told me I could go to their church and get baptized.

The next day that I had off, I met them at their church, and they and their pastor took me in, and I got baptized. It was a Friday, and they didn't pray or do anything, and nothing happened other than I changed clothes, got baptized, changed back into my clothes and left. Not anything other than I just let them get me wet. I did not understand any of it and felt like I had been tricked more than I had done something God wanted.

I had all these people telling me different things that their church taught that was so different from the next guy's thing. "God wanted me to do." I was so confused, I felt like just giving up on all of it altogether. I have often wondered how many people have come to Christ and then been confused and discouraged by other religious people telling them all these different demands that God wants from them. I wanted to do anything God wanted me to do, but I couldn't tell what God wanted from what people wanted. I was going crazy inside.

I met this truck driver, Joe Hunter. He was a humble man and was a preacher to truck drivers. I had started missing the church I was going to and one day ran into Joe who asked where I had been. I told him that I was really getting confused and had doubts that any of it was real. He was leaving that night on an overnight run to Miami and then back to Atlanta the next day. I had those two days off from work, and he asked me to ride with him so we could talk about it. I decided to go.

We left that night and headed toward Miami. When we got to Miami the next morning, Joe's Trucking company changed his load. They did not know he had a rider with him, and he did not want to tell them, so he had to take the load. Long story short, Brother Joe and I went from Miami to New Orleans, to Texas, Mississippi, and several other places. We stayed two weeks on the road. I lost my job and, not to mention, made a few people mad, but God put me in a place where I could talk with a Christian man who was real.

In the time we spent together, Brother Joe helped me to understand that Jesus was alive, and when I accepted him, we started a relationship. The important thing about relationships is time spent together. Joe told me that I needed to read my Bible for myself and that if I did that and prayed, God would show me what he wanted me to do. I should not listen to all these voices from well-meaning (some not so well-meaning) people about what God wanted me to do. I needed God to show me what he wanted me to do. I should spend time reading God's word and praying and learning how to hear from him and speak to him.

I thank God for that man. God used him to help me understand one of the most basic but important things a believer needs to know. Being a Christian is a relationship with God through His Son, Jesus. You can talk to Jesus and to God with an open heart once you repent and put your faith in Christ. In other words, your faith is not a relationship with a church. Your relationship is now with Jesus and God the Father, and God takes you just as you are and begins his work in you as you begin to walk with him. I follow Jesus and I obey his word. My church activity is because of my Christianity, not what makes me a Christian. Far too many "Churchians" are walking around confusing people. Thank God for Christians like Brother Joe!

The Bible

I have never in my life had anyone love me enough to give themselves to take God's punishment for my mess-ups and sins. Jesus
forgave me, he washed away all my sins, and he made me his friend.
I knew I could talk to him openly about my stuff, but I did not
know a lot about him. After my cross-country trip with Brother
Joe, I decided I was going to start reading the Bible on my own. I
did not know much about the Bible, but I knew Jesus was in there
somewhere. I was determined to find him!

I lived with my divorced dad, and our house was a party place for
so long. I came and went through my bedroom window, and so did
my friends. It was not unusual to wake up with one or two of my
friends crashed on my floor after coming in the window during the
night. For that reason, I started locking my room door and window
and hiding under my bed with a flashlight to read my Bible. I did
not know John 3:16, much less the difference between the Old
Testament and the New Testament. All I knew is that everything I
needed to know about Jesus was in this book. I was going to find
every bit of it.

I used drugs for the last three years and was not a good reader. I
could not retain to memory anything I read. I was burnt out and
my mind was undisciplined. I did not know that there were Bible
translations written in English that were easy to understand (go
figure). I thought that it had to be old English if it was a Bible. So
here I was, under my bed with a flashlight, reading a King James

Bible with a damaged brain and no knowledge of proper Bible interpretation. But I had one thing, I knew Jesus was Real, I knew he heard me when I prayed, and I knew he wanted me to know him.

There is so much about the Christian faith and Christian walk that I still don't understand. I don't know why it took so long to hear God speak to me through His word, but it took over six months. I read my Bible three to four hours most every day and did not understand a thing. I would read and pray, asking Jesus to open the Bible to me so I could know Him better. I read and could not remember what the first part of the verse said by the time I got to the end of it. I often became discouraged, but I knew Jesus was in there and he was in me. I refused to not learn the Bible. I read and re-read the Bible from Genesis, all the way to James in the New Testament before God ever spoke to my heart through the Word.

I remember this moment as if it just happened. I was under my bed, reading, and my heart was so discouraged. I was not getting anything, and I had put months into this. I was desperate. I don't cry easily, but that night, I started crying. I was telling Jesus that I was not going to get this without His help as I had said 100 times before. I had tears dripping on my Bible pages as I begged God for understanding.

I started reading James chapter 1. Verse 5 says, "If anyone lacks wisdom, ask God who gives it to all men liberally without holding back. If you ask, don't do it half-hearted or you won't get it (paraphrased)." I understood it! Not only did I understand it, I remembered it. I could tell you what it meant. I read it out loud to Jesus, and I said, "Lord you did not say if any man but ex-drug addicts lack wisdom, let them ask of God."

I began right that moment begging God for wisdom in his Word so I could know Jesus! I cried and prayed and begged God to open his Word to me. After long months of failing over and over, night after night, and not giving up, God answered my prayer. He spoke to my heart through his Word. I began to understand verses and then passages and chapters. I still ask God daily to give me wisdom and understanding in his Word. I still read it almost every day, and I am still learning more about my Jesus and my God that I do not know. I am so thankful for his answers to prayer and his desire to teach us more about himself.

After almost forty years of reading the Bible, I know this book is God's Word and complete truth to man! So many people, Christian and non-Christian, criticize and claim it's falseness and contradictions without spending proper time reading and studying it.

I want to finish this chapter by saying a little about hearing God speak to you. So many people claim so many things about what God says to them. Some are plain nuts! But I want to say that God speaks to people in many ways. I have never heard him speak to me audibly. I cannot put into words how God speaks to me other than one instant I know he did. I would never let anyone tell me how God can or cannot speak to his children. I will not tell you how he will speak to you. I will tell you that I notice how he spoke to his people in scripture, and that's one way of seeing how he spoke in the past. I do want to tell you some things about how God wants to speak to you and some things you must not do!

God wants to speak to you through the Bible, and the Bible is God's Word! You should read it daily, alone in a quiet place, asking for God to speak to you. You should always take everything that you think God says and match it to the Bible. God will never ask you to do anything that contradicts his Word! Also, whenever you hear from God, ask him to help you realize his voice. The most important thing you should do is to seek his voice in your life. Do not go through this life without it! Please learn to speak with and hear from God! if you have never heard God speak to you, go somewhere private, bow your head, and ask him to. Then wait, and you will see!

Toccoa Falls

I soon realized I needed Bible training to be able to teach the Bible properly. I started going to a little Bible school at night and began studying scripture on a college level. I was not a good student in high school and not at all comfortable with going back to school. I said to God I would do anything he asked me, and soon it became evident God was asking me to go to school. I needed to be more serious about my training than part time. I found and enrolled full-time in a Bible college in North Georgia, Toccoa Falls College. I promised God I would trust in him to provide the money. I worked all summer and got enough money to start and moved into the dorms that fall.

I assumed everyone in Bible college would be a passionate Christian. I found out that is not the case. Toccoa Falls is a good college, and the people who lead that college are serving God in a very needed ministry. The fact is a lot of kids attend Bible colleges for many different reasons. In any college of faith, there are every type of student from the sold out to the lost and everything in between. I was young in the Lord and had been converted from a very sinful lifestyle. I did not understand or have much patience (I'm sad to say this) for kids that did not live for Christ. I was more like a Pharisee than a believer in those days.

There was this one guy who was on our college's baseball team. He was a cocky guy and known for doing things against the rules. He would also bully other guys when he was around girls and enjoyed being a jerk. One day in gym class, we were doing intramural basketball. Our team was all the guys that were not athletically inclined. We gave each one of us one job and did it every time we were on offense. One guy on our team—little bitty guy with thick glasses and shy—was under our basket. We would just get the ball to him, and he would lay it up in the basket. It's all he knew how to do.

We all worked as a team, and each person did the same thing with each possession, and our team ended up beating the athletes' team. This cocky baseball player punched this little bitty shy guy in the face and hurt him badly and broke his glasses. It was just a gym class basketball game, no big deal. I went over to the guy and slapped him and asked him to punch somebody who was not afraid of him. Coach (his baseball coach) broke it up, and we helped the little guy up, and nothing was done to the baseball player for hurting that guy. He hit that kid way too hard and hurt him pretty badly. I let myself get really mad at the jerk and began looking for a way to get him for hurting that kid.

God began dealing with me about this guy and about my heart toward him that was not a Christian's heart. I began to pray about my heart and forgave the guy and started praying for him. One month or so passed, and I would run into him from time to time. I became burdened for him. One night, God really put it on my heart to go to this guy's room to talk with him. I went down to his room, and he was not there. I sat down and waited, and curfew came, and he still was not back. I sat there until about one in the morning.

He finally came stumbling down the hall. He had been out drinking. He opened his door and asked me what I was doing there. He wanted to know if I was going to turn him in for drinking. I told him no and that I came to apologize for slapping him that day at the gym. I also told him I had been praying for him and that God had told me to come and talk with him. I said to him I was sitting there because God told me to talk with him and I didn't want to not do what God said.

That night, this guy ended up breaking down and telling me that his family was wealthy and that his dad and mom had given him pretty much everything he wanted. He was a very good ball player and came to Toccoa on scholarship to play ball. He found out just before he came to school that year that his dad and mom told him they were divorcing. He was really messed up inside and mad at the world. He also told me that he was not truly a Christian. He had been fake and had never given His heart to Christ. In his room that night, he accepted Christ.

This guy wanted to be baptized that night. We got some guys up and walked down to the falls. We had to climb over the gate that was locked and dodge security, but we made it to the falls. It was winter, and the falls were iced over. The little guy that the baseball player had punched that day in the gym and myself walked out onto the ice and had to jump up and down to get it to break so we could baptize him. We all prayed and then we baptized him and made it back to the dorms without getting caught by security. God really did a real change in this guy's life, and he became a good guy.

Funny story about that night baptizing at the falls. The next day in chapel, the dean of students announced that they knew that students had broken into the falls and went swimming the night before. They claimed that they knew who we were and that we had until noon to turn ourselves in or our punishment would be greater. After chapel, the guys that were there at the baptism came up to me and asked what we were going to do. I told them, "Nothing." if they knew who we were, they would have come to us. We all decided to not tell anyone anything other than the guy was saved and was baptized. Think about it; getting in trouble at a Bible college for baptizing after-hours! I can live with that on my record.

Dr. "K" Ludwigson

P eople are put in our path by God, even if we do not see it at
the time, but time often reveals this as true. I was a struggling
student and failing every class I was taking. It was my third semester
in college, and I had not yet passed one class that mattered toward
my degree. I was starting my third semester of college, and Toccoa
Falls made the Bible school I started at seem like a K–4 school. I
had struggled at the first one and now I was drowning.

I signed up for an English Lit. class with Dr. "K" Ludwigson (K was
for kick-butt). She was a woman of small stature but very com-
manding in her class. She had like three PhDs and was working
on another one. Her class was four term papers of various subjects,
each with different styles of writing required. Each paper was one
quarter of our grade.

My first paper (ever) was a twelve-page paper with X number of
footnotes required. I sat down the evening before the paper was due
and started typing (pecking). I finished the paper with just enough
time to make it to class. I ran to class, turned in my paper, so proud
I had completed my first college paper. I had high hopes for a good
grade. I spent all night on this bad boy and was still in my clothes
from the day before and was very ragged looking. I laid it on Dr.
K's desk.

The next Monday, we got our papers back, and I was blown away.
The subject of our class that day was, "The lack of Respect for the

English Language in Our Present Generation." My twelve-plus-page paper had more red words from her pen on the first two pages than typed words on them. I will never forget the comment she put in quotations and capital letters at the top of the title page. "*In the beginning was the word; however, it was written nothing like this!*" She had another comment on the second page that summed it up well. "Mr. Penley, my only regret with this paper is that I can only fail you one time for it!"

I was shattered. I went to her after class, hoping to get positive reinforcement or something from her but only got chewed up and spit out. She said that my first-grade point deduction was that I had used two different types of typing paper (I didn't know I had). She failed me in the first two pages and did not look at the rest of it.

I was thinking I had to do something different to overcome a zero for a quarter of my final grade. If my next three papers were perfect, I would make at best a C, which I had to have in this class to count it toward my major. I was taking a full load of eighteen hours of classes, working scholarship and odd jobs to pay my bill, and it was not looking like I was going to pass a single class again. I received a note in my box from the dean asking me to come by his office. I did, and he advised me to pray about serving God in some other way than college. He was very sincere in not telling me to leave but asking me to pray about my calling and make sure I was doing the right thing. I was spending a huge amount of hard-earned money to fail classes.

I paid someone to correct my second paper and made a C. I was just barely thinking I could possibly make it until my third paper. I was behind in my payments, failing everything but gym, and there was not much hope of having any credit for my third semester toward a Bible degree. I was at the point I needed to hear from God.

LIFE IS FUNNY! SOMETIMES IT'S NOT.

I had a roommate named Will who was a walking brain. He and I stayed up, praying for God to tell me if I should quit or keep trying. I turned my third paper in and got a forty-nine. Dr. "K" gave the papers out at the first of class, and when I saw the grade, I just snapped. I started crying openly, walked up to her desk, and threw my paper in her trash can, interrupting her lecture, and walked out of class. I was done. I had every intention of packing my stuff and quitting.

Dr. "K" came after me in the hall and started yelling at me to stop. "May I ask you what on earth you are doing?"

I told her I was through. I was quitting!

She asked me if God had called me to serve him or not? I told her he had, and she said, "Then turn yourself around and go back to your seat and sit down! You may fail, but do not quit! God cannot use a quitter!"

I turned around and went back to my seat. A few classes later, Dr. K gave us a short story to do an allegorical interpretation on for extra credit. I got one called, "A Tree, a Rock, and a Cloud." The story was about this teenager who had a paper route in the inner city. He would go everyday into this bar early in the morning and get coffee before delivering his papers. The bartender was very mean and critical of the boy, because he liked cats. There was a drunk who rebuked the bartender and praised the boy for loving. The boy got up and walked out of the bar and the sun rose.

That was my story. It was not enough extra credit to help me, but at this point in my college career, I was just focusing on not quitting and praying for God to somehow give me relief. I did my allegorical interpretation (comments on the spiritual meaning behind the story) as follows.

The boy represented mankind, the bartender was the devil, the drunk was a misguided picture of Christ, and love was the point of the story. Cats were the unlovable objects. The boy chose to love cats, and the drunk commended him for doing so. When the boy walked out into the sunrise, it represented victory. The tree was the cross, the rock was the tomb, and the clouds were heaven. I turned in my paper and did not think much about it.

A few classes later, Dr. K gave the papers back but did not give me mine. After class, I asked her if she got mine, and she said she had. She asked me if I had time to talk, and I did. She said that my interpretation was deeply moving. She then asked me if she could rewrite it for me. I agreed and said that she could do one better. If she rewrote it, she could have the work and claim it as her own. I asked her, "Dr. K, if you want the work, you can have it if you pass me with a C."

She thought about it for a little time, then she agreed with one condition. If I would read the class grammar book, without skimming, in its entirety, she would pass me with a C. She did, I did, and I passed my first college class toward my major with a C.

Dr. "K" Ludwigson was God's answer to my prayer during a very difficult time in my early Christian walk. She forcefully and gracefully led me to not give up and to keep on, no matter what the circumstances were telling me. I have no idea if she ever used that work for anything, but I know God used her for answering my prayers and led me to keep going and trusting God! Please do the same thing. If God has asked you to serve him, do not quit; just trust and wait. God will send a Dr. K into your life!

Bad Dream

The church I attended in my early days was a good church full of loving people with a passion for Christ. I enjoyed and am thankful for those dear folks. Our church was one that emphasized miracles, visions, and prophetic words and so on. I came to a place in my life where I was unbalanced in my walk with Christ and my interaction with him. I was always seeking God to show me a sign or a miracle or a dream but was spending very little time reading my Bible. I also wanted God's will in my life. God gave me an experience that adjusted my faith and my way of communicating with him.

It was one night while still at Toccoa Falls that God gave me a dream that was supernatural. In my dream, this guy I have never met or seen was speaking in chapel about a children's home in central Florida. After chapel, the man was in the student center taking applications for potential workers for the home. I went to the table and applied to work at the children's home, and the guy hired me on the spot. He promised me a salary and assistance toward finishing my college degree in a Bible college near their home. It was the most realistic dream I had ever had and the only one of this type. It was supernatural in the sense of the person I had never met, and I had never heard of this children's home.

The next day in chapel, to my excitement and amazement, the guy in my dream was speaking. It was the guy in my dream as close as if I had a photo of him. He was representing a children's home in central Florida. He announced he would be in the crow's nest (student center) after chapel, taking applications for anyone who felt the call to work with troubled kids. I told my roommate that I was going to apply and that the guy was going to hire me on the spot. I knew it was God. He gave me a dream that could not happen unless God did it.

After chapel, I went to the crow's nest, and this man was seated at a table exactly where he had been in my dream. It was like a recording being replayed as it happened. It was a supernatural thing! I went to the table and met the man and told him I had a dream the night before. I told him that he was going to hire me and pay for my continued college education while I worked at the home.

He hired me on the spot and offered me everything exactly like in the dream the night before. I had a few weeks left in that semester, and we agreed to me coming the week following the end of my classes. I was so excited. Not so much about the job as much as it was because of the realness of the dream and the miracle of the accuracy of the details. I told my pastor from home, and he and my church were so excited, because God had given me a dream.

My dad was out of church for years and was far from being a spiritual man. He was, however, my father, and when I told him about the dream, he asked me if I had prayed about it. I asked him, "What is there to pray about?" God had given me a supernatural dream. It was his call to go. My father just told me that I should pray about it, and I just thought, *What does he know?*

Soon my car was packed, and I was on my way to this new level of serving God. I was living the dream God had given me. I got to the children's home midafternoon and pulled up to the visitor's center and walked inside. The director of the home was not there and did not know I was coming. I was told that he would be back the following morning and could meet with him then. They did not have a place for me to sleep, but they had a camper that did not have water or electricity that I could stay in that night. I was not at all worried as I knew God had given me the dream.

The next morning, I met with the director in his office. He informed me that he did not intend to hire me and that they were not going to pay for any college while I was there. I was floored! I told him of my dream and of the man who hired me and arranged for my coming with the promised salary and college. The director knew about the man hiring me, but he said he had never approved it and that the guy had been fired in the time between my hiring and my coming. He told me that I could stay in the camper for a day or two if I wanted and dismissed me from his office. I could not put in words my confusion and disappointment.

I went back to this trailer with no electricity or water and sat down alone. I thought through the situation and came to this conclusion. I did not make up the supernatural nature of the dream. God had to have done that. I obeyed the dream, and everything I did was just as the dream had shown me it would be. I told my church, and they all were excited with me that God was sending me. I left my college and my girlfriend and my church and moved to the place God had called me. My conclusion was that God did give me that dream. I was supposed to come to this home, and God was in control.

I spent the rest of that day, praying and asking God why this was happening. I slept that night in the trailer, no AC or water. I could have gone home, but my dad who was ungodly was the only one who was against me coming here. I was too proud to go back home and I also wanted God to show me my next move. The next day, the director told me that I could stay and cut grass and work around the place as needed for living in the trailer and three meals in the cafeteria. I would not have electricity but could hook up a hose and have showers. I had to use the bathroom in the dining hall.

I accepted the offer to stay and work for room and board. I also prayed. I asked God to show me why he did this and what he was wanting me to learn. I promised not to eat a bite of food until God showed me why and what to do next. I decided that I would spend every minute I had reading scripture and that I would make a list of the things I believed, based solely on the scripture—not dreams, not visions, not people or the church. My statement of faith would come only from what God showed me in the Bible.

I spent twenty-eight days doing odd jobs for the home and reading the Bible. All I had was water as I prayed and waited for God to tell me why this dream had turned out this way. The people at this home were not friendly, and I spent my time alone unless duties put me with the staff. On the afternoon of the twenty-eighth day without food, God gave me his word. Ecclesiastes 5:1–6 was the passage. God spoke to me about my way of serving him and my heart and attitude toward him. Here's what he gave me:

1. Be careful when you enter God's presence.
2. Listen instead of talking too much.
3. Don't be careless with your prayers and promises to God.
4. Let your words be few.
5. Do not let your mouth cause your flesh to sin.
6. Do not be quick to make a vow to God.
7. If you make a vow, keep it!
8. Do not trust in dreams.

God's Word said I would lose the work of my hands with a careless walk with him. I was seeking supernatural things from God and was passionate about God, but I was all about me and mine and not him and his. I was too reckless and selfish and self-centered in my walk with God. I was more about show than seeking God's face. I was immature, and God gave me just what I wanted so I could get what I needed to serve him.

I prayed and promised God from that day forward I would not speak in tongues anymore and that I would serve him with more fear and awareness of who he is and less of who I am. I promised that I would seek his will and word for me through the Bible. If I heard from him in any other way, I would not obey unless it lined up with the Bible. My Christian walk would be following God's will in my life and serving Jesus by walking every day in his Word!

I lost everything through that time—my car, my girl, my school, and hopefully some of my pride. I went to the director and told him that I would stay and fulfill my vow to God. I told him that even though they did not keep their word to me, I would stay and work until he was satisfied I had finished my vow to God in coming there.

I stayed several more months until one day, I was free to go with the director's blessing. I can only speak for myself on this matter. My Christian life was unbalanced and too fleshly. I was seeking miracles from God and supernatural works, hoping for recognition by others. I was not stable. One day, I would be ready to charge hell with a squirt gun, and the next, I was needing to get saved again. God used the very things I was caught up in to get me to humble myself and center my faith on him and his Word.

I am not saying that God never does supernatural things. I am saying when God does supernatural things, he is the one who is glorified, not man. I hope that my walk is more about Jesus and his will and death, burial, and resurrection than about myself and my will. Be careful with your attitude and words to God and seek his attitude and Word for your life or you may have bad dreams.

"Do What God Says"

After I went back home, I began working to pay off my debt and get my life on track to finish school. I was attending the same church. I shared with my pastor the 28 day fast and the things I wrote down during it that I knew I believed. The pastor and I concluded that I was not in agreement with his church. He suggested I would do better in a Baptist Church based on my biblical beliefs. I visited around for one to attend but was not comfortable in any I visited. Most of them did not agree with long hair and blue jeans. So I still visited around but mainly worked all the time to get money for school.

Early summer, I had several people bring up Tennessee Temple University to me. It was random people separate from each other and in just casual conversation. I noticed that every time I turned around, it seemed like somebody else would tell me to check out Temple. So I called them up and asked if I could come visit. A few weeks later, I walked on the campus and was shocked by the fact it was in the middle of a rundown slummy area of Chattanooga, Tennessee.

It was summer school, and the few students there were the adult married students. I walked around the campus and was impressed with the size of the college and the huge church. I walked around, asking people if they liked it, and they kept handing me tracts on how to be saved. I thought then that they were just being friendly but found out later that because of my hair and t-shirt and jeans that they were thinking I needed to be saved. In any case, the summer students were mature and friendly.

I watched a group all going into a building and down to a classroom, so I followed them. I walked into a class of about forty, and the professor was standing down at the front of the lecture hall. I asked if I could visit his class, and he welcomed me as long as I did not disturb the teaching. I agreed.

Dr. Porter was his name, and he was teaching on a passage of scripture that day dealing with speaking in tongues. I was amazed, because I was trying to figure that out from scripture myself. About three-fourths the way through the class, I was getting schooled as he was speaking against a lot of the things that I believed. He was using the same scripture I did for my beliefs but concluding entirely different views than I did.

I finally stood up and interrupted the class and stated that I spoke in tongues and even used the same scripture he was teaching from to prove it was scriptural. Dr. Porter kindly asked me to sit down and remain quiet and speak with him after class. I did, and after class, he took two hours sitting with me, answering every question I had, giving me biblical reasons for everything he believed. He was one of the kindest men I had ever disagreed with. I left our conversation, wishing I knew my Bible and what I believed like that man did.

The pastor of Tennessee Temple was a man named Dr. Lee Roberson. He started the college and built the church and school to international proportions. He was like a Moses of his day to most everyone at Temple. Going to his office was like visiting Peter or Mary or Moses. I did not know who he was, but he had an office that had a glass front view where he could see and be seen with ease. I walked by his office and thought, *That man looks important, so I will go ask him some questions.*

Dr. Roberson had an office in front of his office that anyone would have to go through to get to him. His secretary was a very good screener. It so happened that she had just walked out of her office with the door left open. I walked in and through her office and opened Dr. Roberson's door without knocking and stuck my head in and said, "You look important, may I ask you a few questions?" I had no idea how unconventional I was being nor how many people got rebuked after I left for letting me get to Dr. Roberson that easily and without screening.

I walked in and told Dr. Roberson that I was needing to finish my Bible school and was thinking about coming to this one. I asked him what he did around this place and began to realize who I was speaking to. I asked him how I could find out if I should come there or not.

He stopped his focus and looked at me and gave me some of the best advice I have ever been given. He told me I should not decide where I chose to go. His quote to me was, "Young man, you need to first learn how to pray, then you need to pray and let God tell you where to go. Then when you have done that, *do what God says!*"

After he said that, he had me up by the hand, walked me to the door, put one hand in the air while still holding my other one and prayed one sentence: "God, show this young man your way!" He told me to do what God said when I knew, patted me on the back, pushed me out the door, shut it, and locked it.

I walked out of his front office, out of the building, and looking through the window, he was back at his desk, writing. I thought, *This place is crazy.* I could not get away from the fact that at that time, I did not agree with a lot of their beliefs, but they knew from scripture why they believed and could show you in the Bible. I knew that I needed that ability and wanted to do what the Bible said, not what I wanted it to say. That day with Dr. Porter and Dr. Roberson made a huge impact on my heart. Best advice in the world: "Pray and ask God his will, then do what God says!"

God Says Go!

That summer, I did what that crazy old man told me to do. I asked God to help me learn how to pray and didn't pray as much about going to that school as I did to be able to "know and do" his will in my life. The thing that I realized I needed was a consistency in my walk. I needed discipline and guidance in my daily walk with Christ. I worked all the time, but when I was not working, I was looking for somewhere to help me get to the place I could be what God was calling me to be. I finally concluded that as crazy as those people were at Temple, I needed some of what they had. That Dr. Porter was what I needed to be more like, and that Dr. Roberson knew how to talk with God and know what God was saying to him.

I knew inside that God wanted our lives with him to be that way. He speaks with us, and we speak with him, and both of us understand each other. I also knew that spending time with God and communication with him took time being still and meditation. My life was too busy and undisciplined to do it. Looking back at it, I was just too invested in myself to want to spend the type of time with Christ to hear his voice. I knew in my heart I needed to go to "them men's" school.

I called and found out I was almost too late to sign up for that fall semester. I rushed an application to them and began making my plans for school. I had about three weeks and also had enough work to help me pay everything off that I needed to pay before I left. I was good to go. I painted houses and did construction for work and hoped I could pick up work at Temple.

I did not really know how Bible school worked as far as signing up and scheduling classes and such, with Temple anyway. I packed my clothes in a backpack and tied a ladder into my dad's car. I took a five-gallon bucket and three or four brushes with other odds and ends for painting in the bucket and headed for school. I got to Temple the morning of registration, and my dad dropped me off and patted me on the back and wished me well and drove away. I had to look like some hillbilly as I put my ladder and bucket and backpack out of the way of the front entrance sidewalk and got in line to register.

I have never let people's opinions bother me, but as I stood in line, I noticed that everybody there had very short hair, was wearing a suit, and had a folder of information with them. I had just untied a thirty-foot ladder off a car, set it in the bushes outside the window, and walked inside to get in line. My hair was halfway down my back, I was wearing blue jeans, sandals, and a Boston t-shirt. I smiled at everyone who was in line and staring at me and just kind of realized I was not sure what I was getting myself into.

The line was long, and it was over an hour before I got to the window to begin registration. The man at the window was Dr. Lockery who I became very good friends with later. He just looked at me in shock. "May I help you?" he asked, and I told him I was here to start school. He asked me for my folder with my registration information and my acceptance letter. I told him I had no idea what he was talking about. I informed him I had sent my application in a few weeks ago and was here to start.

Dr. Lockery wrote down my name and asked me to step aside until he called me. I sat down beside the window and waited. I sat politely from 9:00 to 3:30, waiting on him to call me. The line finally was gone, so I walked up to the window again and asked Dr. Lockery what he was waiting on.

Dr. Lockery informed me that he had checked and found out that my application had been denied. "How can you deny someone Bible college?" I asked.

He said that you had to be accepted into Temple and that I was not.

I asked him how long he had known and why he waited to tell me.

He looked at me and said, "Young man, you need to leave before I call security!"

I walked over to the seat I had been in all day and sat down. I thought about my conversation with Dr. Roberson. He said for me to go home, learn how to pray, ask God, then do what God says! He never said, "Then hope you get accepted if God says yes;" and he had. So I walked up to the window and said to Dr. Lockery that he was mistaken and I needed my registration. I told him that Dr. Roberson told me to pray and ask God what to do. Then I was supposed to, "Do what God said," and God had said, "Go to Temple." I looked him in the eyes and said I was going to do what God said and was not leaving until he put me in school.

Dr. Lockery threatened to call security, and I said for him to call them because I was not leaving. Besides, my dad was 200 miles away, and I had nowhere else to go. He threatened to call the police, and I said I was not trying to cause trouble. I was trying to do what God said for me to do! Dr. Lockery called Dr. Roberson and told him he had a guy refusing to leave who had been denied entrance. Dr. Roberson told him to send me to his office.

I walked into Doc's (name I came to know him by) office and sat down. He asked me what was the problem, and I told him they were not letting me do what God said! I explained that I did everything he told me to do earlier that summer. I spent time praying and asking God what to do. I told him that God said come to Temple.

Dr. Roberson said that God did not tell me to come with hair as long as mine.

I said that God told me to come, and I was willing to do whatever I had to get into school.

Dr. Roberson picked up his phone and called Dr. Lockery and told him to put me in school. I cut my hair four times that day before they said it was acceptable. I only had $150 bucks on me, and they wanted $3,500 to start the semester. I put $120 on the counter, and Dr. Lockery put me in school. I told Dr. Lockery I could not believe people turned guys down for Bible school and that I prayed and God said for me to come. I did what God said, and God made a way! Funny thing is my last year at Temple. I was elected student body president.

Temple

Temple was hard for me. My dad had been disabled in a work-related accident. I was supposed to get tuition paid for because of it. I applied for the payment and was denied and told to reapply. After several attempts to collect it, I began to realize that God wanted me to trust Him for my college tuition. I prayed about it and promised God I would depend on him for my bill. I worked all I could and took eighteen to twenty credit hours (sometimes more) each semester. We did not get our food card from the cafeteria unless our bill was up to date. So most of my semesters, I could not eat in the dining hall because I hardly ever caught up until the end. I learned to trust God for food and tuition. My classes were on a much more difficult level at Temple, but God was helping me.

I could go on forever telling of all the times every semester where I would come down to the last day and be needing huge amounts of money to take my finals. I had my roommates and their churches and everyone I knew praying, and every single time, God would bring in just enough to break even and start the next semester. I could not only not get a food card, I also could not take my midterms until my bill was paid for the semester. Every semester (I believe), without fail, I had to take both my midterms and finals the last week of the semester. I spent hours at night, praying for God to provide. He always did and he did it in such a way that the next time, my need was even bigger and my faith was tested/stretched more and more.

One would think that when a person decides to follow God with their life and to seek and do his will, things would come easily. I hear a lot of preacher's saying it's that way, even promising wealth and health if you do. I have just not found that to be true. Following God and doing his will puts us at odds with the powers of this world. To be a follower of Christ is to be an enemy of this world and the powers of Satan. When some of the times I was almost crazy with stress, trying to work, do school, pay bills, and preach on Sundays, I would think, *This is too hard*. God was training me and teaching me how to trust him.

Serving Jesus is a battle, and the victory is every person who comes to Jesus for salvation. It is also a great privilege to be able to serve Christ, and with the battles and hardships come the great blessings of doing his will and seeing his hand in people's lives!

I also was able to meet and become friends with so many good people. Larry Meade was my roommate and one of my closest friends. I remember many times we held each other up, serving in our ministries and school. Bill and Alice Simmons—dear friends that God taught me so much from each of them. Dr. Porter, Dr. Afman, Dr. Nat Phillips, Dr. Young (Greek teacher from hell), and Doc (Dr. Roberson)—God used these people to help me and many others develop the abilities to carry out service to Christ. These people and more unnamed were not wealthy or well-known famous people. But in heaven, they will be standing behind Jesus and are well-known by him!

Lonely in a Crowd

One of the unexpected truths about Bible College is how hostile of an environment it could be and how uncaring we as Christians are with each other at times. I thought that going to Bible college would be like walking around in a constant state of revival. Man, that was so far from true. Christians are some of the meanest people on earth to each other at times. It's unbelievable how selfish and uncaring and hard-hearted Christians can be to each other.

I was always running full speed, always almost late for something. I was always needing to finish some project that took more time to finish than I had to complete it. We all were that way—four thousand-plus people on this Christian campus, running around, stepping all over each other, trying to become something for God—doing this while we were forgetting the main thing God was asking of us: love!

I was walking to class one day and I noticed this girl (pretty) named Annie standing at the corner of a building, hiding her face in a window and just standing there. I rushed past her as that was what we did all the time to each other. God spoke to me and said, "Stop and go back and check on her."

I'm like, "Lord, if I do that, I will be late for my class!" It was like the Lord spoke to me and asked what would he rather me do? Obey his voice or ignore it so I could go to class to learn how to serve him?

I turned around and went back and met Annie. I told her I noticed her hiding in the corner and asked if she was okay. She was crying and was embarrassed, but she said that someone close to her was having serious issues and she was hurting for them. I asked her if we could stop and pray about it. You would be surprised at how many people look at you funny if you stop and pray together in public in a Bible school.

Annie and I joined hands, bowed our heads, and asked God together for his intervention in Annie's loved one's life. We also asked for his help in our lives. When we got through, people were passing and staring like we were nuts. It dawned on me that it was them that was nuts. We were all nuts, running around like chickens with our heads cut off, trying to impress God but too busy or embarrassed to stop and pray in public when a need was evident. I had been and was just as hard-hearted and busy and nuts as these people staring! I decided then and there that from that time forward, I was going to let God use me to care about people, even in Bible college.

I went through that year (both semesters) watching for people struggling and praying with them. One day, I heard that a girl I knew, a sweetheart, was in the hospital. I asked around and found out she tried to commit suicide the night before in her dorm room. I went to the hospital and asked her what was going on. She had been dealing with panic attacks and battles with fear. She said that over the past few weeks, she just kept feeling so lonely. The night before, she was overcome with fear and loneliness and lost hope.

I prayed with her, and she took some time off school and turned out okay. I was so convicted as a person who knew this girl and her feeling so alone in a crowded place. Crowded by Christians at that! Can you imagine what it must be like to be surrounded by so many people, and yet feel all alone? Some of you reading this know how that feels.

My dad was not a Godly man at this time in his life, but I called him for advice that night. I asked what he thought about people walking all around each other in a Christian college and not seeing the ones who were hurting. He said to me that people must decide if they will care, Christian or not. Each person must decide for themselves if they are willing to take the time needed and make the sacrifices required to care for others. That was some of the best "Christian" advice coming from a drunk man than I have had come from "church men!"

I promised God I would do all I could to make myself care. I would sacrifice whatever if he would show me the people who were hurting. It has been one of the hardest things to do consistently to care for others. I'm still trying!

God tested my promise that same semester. I was careful not to waste my time or purposely try to stop and pray or talk with people. I did not stop to help when I could do so at other times or when there were better ways of handling situations. I did stop when God spoke to me to do so or when I noticed someone in a serious frame of mind. It did not take long before my eyes were opened to a huge need on our campus.

People, problems, and issues were all around us, and if you had eyes to see, some were in a bad way. I stopped and prayed with every person I noticed who was going through something. Most of the time, it was a, "Hey dude, (or "dudess"), my name is Frank. I can tell something is bothering you, can I pray with you about it?"

Ninety percent of the time, that was all that was needed, and the rest of the time, it would be enough to get them through until more effort could be put toward the issue.

The semester was almost over, and I was all out of late passes to every one of my classes. I was running to a class that if I was late again, I would fail. If you had three tardies, it was an absence, and

I was down to no more tardies in this one class. I had just enough time to get there when, sitting on this bench in front of the building, was a girl crying. She was openly crying, and people (just like me that day) were passing her, ignoring her pain. I ran past because I could not fail my class. God spoke to me as I did and reminded me of the promise I gave him.

I stopped and turned around and sat down beside the girl. I asked her what was wrong. She explained that she had just opened a letter from home with bad news. The late bell was ringing in the background as she said her parents were getting a divorce and she was broken over it. We held hands and prayed and gave the problem to Jesus, and I asked him to give her strength and peace. We finished, and I went to my class, tardy.

I walked in the class and sat down and looked up to a class full of students without a professor. No sooner had I sat down than in he came. He looked at the class and said that in the first time in twenty years, he got to school and had left his briefcase on his dresser at home. He had to go back home and get it. He then started class. I passed all my classes that semester.

That Is the Girl I Am Going to Marry

The greatest gift God gave me at Temple is my wife. She was no easy catch and well-worth the chase. I am and will remain in awe that God would give me such a lady as Sharon Rose Van Kleeck.

I was visiting the dorm room of a friend one day when I looked on his dresser and saw a picture of the most beautiful girl I have ever seen. She took my breath away. I asked the guy, "Who is this in the picture?"

He said, "As a matter of fact, that is the girl I am going to marry."

I thought to myself, *Good luck with that one, buddy.* I was a firm believer in all is fair in love and war.

I knew about where this guy sat during church services, so the next Wednesday night service, I walked by where he should be, and sure enough, there he sat. Sitting beside him was the girl in the picture. She was prettier in real life than in her picture. I walked over to them and said hello to the guy, and I asked him to introduce me to his girl. He told me, "Get out of here, man!"

But I stepped past him and stuck my hand out and said, "My name is Frank, and I would like to meet you."

She looked away, and Charlie said, "Man, get out of here!"

I stepped into the direction of where she turned her head and said that my name was still Frank and I would like to meet her. I held out my hand for a handshake, and she just sat there and ignored me. Not to be rude, I told her and Charlie to have a good night and walked away. It was not exactly a good start, but she did not tell me no, so I felt it was at least a start.

I looked for her around campus during the next few weeks but did not see her. I didn't want to be to bold, but I was going to give us every shot possible as a couple, even though she did not know me yet. I did not go home for summer break. I just stayed at college until I finished. I had picked up work scholarship by this time, which meant I worked for the school forty hours for room and classes. I still had to buy books and everything else, but I had the big stuff covered.

Sharon had stayed for summer classes also. I drove the college garbage truck for Temple during the summer. It was a very hot and stinky job, but somebody had to do it.

One evening, I had just parked the truck and finished for the day and had a test the next day. I decided to go by Happy Corner (student activity center) and get coffee for the evening and go back to my dorm room to study. I was sweaty and smelled like the garbage truck and in much need of a shower.

I walked out of the student center, and over to my left, sitting on the wall beside the grass, was Sharon. I had not seen her since she had not spoken to me in church that night, but I decided to give it a shot. I walked by and said, "Sharon, isn't it?"

She said yes, and I sat down and explained I had just gotten off work and stopped for coffee. I sat beside her downwind and asked why she was staying at school for the summer. I also asked her where Charlie was at.

She said she stayed for work scholarship and that she had broken up with Charlie. I was feeling better about our chances by the minute. We ended up talking until I walked her to her dorm for the night.

The next day, I went by the same spot, looking for her after work. She was not there or anywhere else I looked. It was several days later, I was walking by the post office, and there she was, sitting on a bench with this other guy I did not know. They were just talking, and I decided to see if there was a chance of cutting in. I walked by and said hello to Sharon.

She said hello.

I asked her, "Who is this guy with you, your brother?"

Sharon said that he was not her brother, so I asked her if he was her brother's friend.

The guy was glaring daggers at me. Sharon (not having a clue) said, "No, he does not know my brother."

I said to her, "You did not tell me the other night that you had another boyfriend."

She said, "He is not my boyfriend, he is just a friend."

I looked at them both and asked her if I was her friend, and she said, "Well, yes, I guess."

So I sat down beside the guy on the same bench with them and said, "Hello, friend."

He got up and stormed off. Sharon and I sat and talked for a time. I was encouraged by the fact that as we talked, it was very evident that she had a walk with Christ that was real. She prayed for guidance and seemed sincere in her faith.

I tried to get closer with her for some time after that, but Sharon kept her distance. She was not allowing me into her inner circle.

I decided to try and ask her out on a date. She worked in an office where our guys would stop by and ask her for water during hot summer days. Most of us just wanted to see her, but she did not know that. I was working just outside her office one day in this house that had caught on fire. We were given the job of cleaning out the fire damage and repairing the house. I was covered in black soot and ashes and was soaking wet from sweat. I decided to make my move.

I rushed into Sharon's office and asked her if she would do me a huge favor. She said yes, thinking I was going to ask for water. I said, "Great, sit with me in church tonight?" I then said I would send word what time I would pick her up at her dorm and then ran out of her office. I had a date with my girl (she did not know she was my girl yet).

That night was kind of dry. I picked her up, and we went to church and sat together. She wanted to go back to her dorm after church, so I could not make any time with her. I found out later she was mad at me for tricking her into saying yes before she knew what it was I was asking. I spent from June until October trying to get her to realize how good of a guy I was, but she was not having it.

I was praying about her and trying everything I could to get her to start at least looking my way. It seemed that every time I approached her, she treated me like I was bothering her. I did not give up and quit asking other girls out because Sharon was my girl. Finally, on Halloween night, I was working as security around the girls' dorm and the infirmary. They put security around on Halloween because of the bad side of town our college was on. The city guys would try to harass the girls or vandalize the infirmary.

I was put between the two buildings to be security to stop that from happening. It was funny, though, as I was out there by myself without any kind of radio or weapon to stop bad guys from doing Halloween tricks on the Christian girls or buildings. At any point, I stood outside in the cold, all alone and without much light. I was just waiting to see how it would play out, but there I was doing my job!

It was cold, and I was standing there in blue jeans and a t-shirt, freezing. I looked up, and coming my way was the prettiest thing I believe I had ever seen. Sharon was walking my way. I was the only one there, and past me was the bad area of town, so I had to be where she was headed. She came up and asked me if I wanted some hot chocolate. She made it and brought it out for me. That was the breakthrough I had been praying for. Sharon was, after five and a half months, finally realizing she was my girl. She has been ever since that first night in church when she had been so stuck up. But now she was starting to know she was, and I am so thankful she came to her senses.

I Am Going to Test You

B ible College for me was more than an education. It was something God told me to do that I didn't think I could do. I can't
capture in words how many nights I spent in prayer, asking God to
provide huge amounts of money or the ability to pass a certain class
or just food money. Temple was a complete journey into walking by
faith and serving Jesus, trusting in him for my existence. God used
this time to build me up in trust and faith in his faithfulness. It gave
me the chance to see God lead and provide where He did lead. This
chapter is about one of the times when life was not funny; this is a
"sometimes it's not" chapter.

It was my second year at Temple, and our daily chapel times were,
for me, a time for God to give me little words of encouragement
or guidance. I depended on them for help, and God often moved
in my life in chapel. One chapel in particular turned out to be one
of the most influential of my life. God began a change in me on
this day. There was a very strict policy in our college where chapel
speakers had to be finished by a certain time or Dr. Roberson would
get up, cut them off, and dismiss the 3,000-plus students to class.
This regular chapel day, Dr. Roberson introduced a man to speak—
Dr. Dolphus Price.

He was an older man and carried the respect of Dr. Roberson like
few other men. He began his message by talking to Dr. Roberson.
He told him that God had spoken to him the night before and

impressed on him that there were many students that were not believers and that they needed to be addressed.

Doctor Dolphus preached for one and a half hours about hell and that it was real and that the Bible shows the way to be saved. At that time, I had never sat in a message where God was moving that powerfully as the man was preaching. Dr. Roberson did not move when the hour was ending, and Dr. Price spoke well into the next hour. When Doctor Dolphus gave an invitation for people to accept Christ, over 600 people accepted Christ that day, students and some faculty.

Dr. Roberson stood up and called off classes for the rest of the day for the people to have time to think through what God was dealing with them about.

I somehow ended up under the communion table, praying after that message, and did not come out until later when the church lights were out. I was the only one left in the building. It was not on purpose. It was that God spoke to me about my relationship with him. During Dr. Dolphus' message, he shared a story of deep pain in his life. He shared when his son was killed and he couldn't help or stop it. He shared that for God to use a man, he must break that person first. He made a statement that literally changed my life.

It was this: "When I was a young man, I told God I would be willing to go through anything in my life if he (God) would give me his (God's) power on my life!" Dr. Dolphus began to cry and finished his statement this way. "Now that I am an old man looking back, I would not be able to pray that prayer now, knowing what it has cost me. But I am thankful I prayed it!"

That statement was all I heard that whole message. When the invitation was given, I went forward to the front of our church (7,000-seat auditorium). In the front was a communion table, and

I ended up under it as the altars were so crowded that day. I am not sure how long I was there, but it was a long time. I came to a place where I told God that I wanted people to be saved. I wanted him to use me to help people all over the world to come to him. I also prayed that I would be willing to go through anything in my life that I needed to go through so God could break me of myself enough to give me his power on my life. I knew that Dr. Dolphus had said how much that had cost him in his ministry, but I also had given God all of me. I truly wanted God to use me to reach unbelievers everywhere so they could have what I had—Christ!

Shortly after that day, I broke my relationship with Sharon off. I had come to the place where I loved her more than I loved God. Shortly after our break up one night as I was sleeping, God did a work in my life. It was at three in the morning. God woke me up, just like he shook me, and spoke to me (he didn't, but it was that strong). God said, "I am going to shake you and test you."

I got out of bed and took a shower and sat in a chair in my room with the lights out, waiting on whatever was going to happen. My roommate was asleep, so I just sat and waited. About four o'clock in the morning, a dear friend, Bill Simmons, knocked on my door and told me Dr. Roberson was waiting to see me in his office.

I was ready and walked down to Doc's office. He was sitting at the desk I had walked in on him in when we first met. We, by this time, had become friends. Doc told me, "Frank, there's been a fire, and your house was completely burned down. Your dad was burned and killed in the fire. Your family is waiting on you to come and take care of the decisions that need to be made."

I asked Doc what I should do as a lot of my family was not saved. Doc said he could not tell me what to do as he had never been through that. He and I prayed, and Doc asked God to give me help and to guide me. He then told me to go take care of things and he would take care of my class and work absences. He also gave me some money for gas to get home.

I left at 4:30, headed to where my dad had lived. I went straight to the house site before anywhere else. I walked around the smoking remains of what was my dad's house and found the place where my dad's body had been recovered. If you have ever been in that situation, you understand what I'm saying. I found my dad's spot where his body had been, and by the place where his hand was, I found his wedding band that had melted off his hand and was half in a circle and half melted.

I had to identify the body, which was impossible to identify. I ended up making all the arrangements for the funeral because of my stepmom's state of mind. I was numb as I was going through this, but God was helping me. We had the funeral three days later, and I knew God wanted me to speak. I did not have the strength to speak at my dad's funeral, but my brother, Adrian, and others were not Christians. I needed them to know Christ. The day of the funeral was a blur in my mind. When we got to the funeral home, to my surprise, many of my friends from Temple had made the long drive to attend the service. It was a great encouragement.

The morning of the service was difficult for me. I was pressed to share with my lost family the truth of eternity with or without Christ. There was so much strife in my family, and emotions were high. I was under great pressure. I was dressing for the service, and my rib cage on both sides were covered with bruises from the pressure. It looked like my ribs had been beaten. I have never seen that happen since that time.

I sat on my bed, not able to get peace or the strength to do the message. When I got to the service, my brother and sisters and the rest of our family were all on the front row. The music ended, and I went to stand up, but my knees gave way. I could not do it, and that is when God did a thing in me. He gave me a verse. Isaiah

41:10: "Fear thou not, for I am with you, do not be dismayed, for I am your God. I will strengthen you, I will help you, I will uphold you with my right hand" (paraphrased).

God did just that. That service, my brother prayed and gave himself to Jesus as did others. God helped me and our family. The people who were praying and had sacrificed to drive and be there are forever in my gratitude!

Two things about this that I need to say. My father had been a churchgoer before Tim died, and his pastor was at the funeral. Tim is my baby brother who died at eighteen months of age after nine months of serious illness. I did not know the man, but I remember my dad told me something that happened.

After my brother had died, my dad and mom were struggling with bitterness and at the point of walking away from their faith in Jesus. My dad went privately to this pastor's office for help. He told the pastor he was struggling and was needing help (only time I ever heard of my proud dad asking help from anybody) and asked him for guidance. The pastor told my dad that he was having his own problems and could not help Dad with his too. He turned my dad away. He asked me if he could say a word at my father's service that morning.

I did not know this pastor well, but I told him that the time he needed to speak truth was thirty years earlier and that I would rather he not speak.

The second thing is that many people simply think that Jesus is the same thing as the church. Many of the people (family to me) at that service were hurt by Dad's death and in real pain and needed Jesus to help. What they needed was only available from God, not man or church.

What God helped me to share was his word. In John 3:16, God loves us, gave Jesus for us, and wants to fix what is broken. He will if we come to Him and give ourselves to Him. I gave that truth, and several people that day did just that. I now sign my name with that verse God gave me. Isaiah 41:10 is my life verse. I told you about that pastor, because some of you are upset with Jesus because of how a pastor or church treated you. Please go straight to the source and tell Jesus about it. See what he does about it.

Chapels

One of the burdens that Dr. Roberson had was for the mountain communities all over our part of Tennessee. He started a chapel ministry where men in school, training as pastors, could go into these communities and start or work in chapels. They would pastor in a community, and when they graduated from college, another man would take the work and carry on. I was interested in the thought of doing that, so I began speaking in some of the chapels that needed fill-in speakers.

One of these chapels was a small church of maybe fifty people that was located on the state line between Georgia, Tennessee, and Alabama. In fact, the pulpit of this church was in Tennessee and the pews were in Alabama. I preached in this chapel for several weeks while it was between pastors.

I have two fond memories from that chapel I will share. The first being that of an old mountain man who attended Stateline. He was the most faithful and the hardest working person in the church. I was visiting with him one Saturday and was just thanking him for his hard work. I was absolutely amazed at his response. He told me he was not a saved person. He did what he could around the church because he knew when he died, he was not going to heaven. He said that he hoped his work and dedication would gain him less punishment and torment in hell.

Mountain people are different than country folk or southern people. They have a different culture and different ways. I am going to call this man Mr. White. He was kind and smart and had made a good living for himself. He lived alone and had a nice place with land and several animals. I became burdened for him and would go sit with him on Saturdays and spend time. He told me that the church he went to as a boy was a backwoods church that his family all grew up going to.

The church believed in speaking in tongues. He said his preacher told him that speaking in tongues was a sign that God had really saved someone. Mr. White did not go to school and could not read (he signed his name with an X). He never was able to speak in tongues, and after he was older, the preacher told him he was not one of the chosen few. He was destined for an eternity in hell.

I sat with Mr. White several hours on multiple days, showing him scripture that if he would call on Jesus, he would save him. Mr. White would listen and even agree with me that he understood the verses I would share. He would say to me, "Well, that is what it says, sure enough."

I would then ask him to pray with me and trust Christ. He would hang his head in sincere worry and sadness and say, "I'm past all that, and God will not have me." He believed Jesus died on the cross for his sins and he believed Jesus rose from the grave. He asked Jesus many times to save him, but because he didn't speak in tongues, he thought he was damned.

I never was able to convince Mr. White that he could be saved. Mr. White was what the mountain people mean when they say a person is set in their ways. He was. The last time I spoke at Stateline, Mr. White was sitting in his place and just as faithful as always.

I never saw him again after that day. I never heard when he passed, but one thing I know for sure is that Mr. White was surprised.

He closed his eyes on earth and woke up in heaven. You see, his thinking that he could not be saved was brought about from bad doctrine. Mr. White spent his life serving a Jesus he was sure did not want him. Can you imagine how he felt when Jesus met him in heaven with a bear hug? Cool!

The second memory from that chapel was one of a different nature. I worked for the college in order to pay for my room and classes. I didn't have money for gas or books or other things unless I could get side jobs. I would have to pray for gas money to get to wherever I was preaching that weekend. I would then have to pray for a love offering big enough to buy gas for the way home. Always interesting!

One Sunday night, I finished the evening service and was locking up the church. The offerings went back to the Highland Park Baptist Church, but I could put gas receipts in with the offering if there was enough. That evening, I ended up staying and talking with one of the members about a problem they were going through. It was late before I got on the road, and the offerings were not good. I was driving on I59 toward I24, going toward Chattanooga, when I ran out of gas. I was in a black suit and white shirt with a black tie and was walking down the side of the interstate. I was carrying my Bible, and it was midnight. I was forty-plus miles from my exit for college and was thinking that this was going to be a long night.

I had walked about three or four miles when this eighteen-wheeler passed me and pulled off the side of the emergency lane. The trucker got out of his truck and walked back toward me (he did not know I saw the gun in his pocket) and asked, "Man, what kind of nut walks down the interstate after midnight with a black suit on carrying a big Bible? Are you *okay*? I told him I belonged to the car he passed a few miles back and was headed back to college, trying to get there before class the next day. He was going past Chattanooga, so he gave me a lift to my exit.

When I got into his truck, he was interested in me being a preacher. He was not a believer, but he said he admired people who were. His grandmother was a believer. As we talked, he asked my name, and I told him Frank Penley.

He said, "Penley" and repeated my last name a few times. He said that he dated a Penley in Macon, Georgia, a time back. I told him that was my mom. My mom was a very well-known woman with the truckers.

He started laughing and said, "I never would have guessed Louise Penley would have had a preacher in her family." Then he realized how he sounded and apologized.

I told him no apology was needed. I was able to share with him how I had been a person more like he would have expected Louise Penley's son to be, but Jesus had saved me, and now I was serving him. We parted that night without him getting saved, but I was able to share clearly what being saved was, and he listened. He and I agreed it was a small world, and I got out at my exit and made it back in time to get a few hours' sleep before class.

Popular Street Chapel

There was a family who worked in a chapel at the west side bottom of Mount Eagle Mountain in a little town called Cowan, Tennessee. This pastor and his family were driving back from church one Sunday night. He was going down the south side of the mountain on I24 when a truck lost its brakes and hit them, killing some of the family, and putting the rest in the hospital. I went with Brother Chris Mundell to visit them and pray with them.

After leaving the hospital, Brother Chris, the chapel director, shared with me that the chapel in Cowan had shut down, and this guy was trying to get it open again. I did not think that much about it then, but over the next few weeks, I could not get the place off my mind. This town was seventy miles one way from college. I was taking eighteen to twenty credit hours in classes and working full-time to pay for school and class. I did not have money for food or gas to travel. I also had to do odd jobs as often as possible to pay for my truck insurance and needs. It was impossible to do a chapel. The more I kept telling myself I could not do it, the more I realized I was trying to convince myself God was not calling me to do it.

I went to Brother Chris's office and told him I would pray with him about starting a church in Cowan. We drove up to Cowan (sixty-eight-plus miles one way) and looked at the building and the town. It used to be a busy little town but was now a struggling little town with little there but five or six thousand people. The building was an old WWII chapel that had not been painted in years.

It had huge multi-paned glass windows, but twenty-eight of the panes had been knocked out. In the back-left corner of the building (facing the entrance) was a hole in the floor big enough to lose a kid through. It did not have but one working sink and toilet, and they were in the back of the choir loft.

The church had been locked for several months and it was, in a lot of ways, a picture of the town—rundown and struggling. As we were driving back to the college, Brother Chris and I were talking, and I was sharing with him my situation and uneasiness about committing to starting church 130 miles from school and being able to pull it off. We both were called to be preachers and we both knew that part of the call is living by faith and sacrifice. I agreed to pray about it for a week, and then I would let Chris know.

It didn't take a week for me to know it was God's will for me to do it. I just needed God to give me the faith that he would make a way for all the needs it would take to do it. One week later, I walked into Chris's office and became the pastor of the locked church in Cowan Tennessee. Named Popular Street Baptist Chapel, we would meet on Sunday morning, Sunday evening, and Wednesday nights. I would drive up on Friday after school and sleep on the nursery floor and stay until Sunday night. I did not eat from Friday night until Monday unless God provided food or money.

I would visit door-to-door all Saturday and preached in the afternoon on Sundays in an afternoon Sunday school service near town in some government projects. God opened the door to preach on the local radio station on Sunday's at 5:00. I stayed busy the entire weekend, so it was not so bad not eating. I had to bathe in the sink, and it only had cold water. It was funny looking back at it. We fixed the floor, replaced the broken windows, and painted the outside. I got a wall-sized map of the city and used the nursery as my living quarters.

I visited every house in the city in a five-mile radius outside the city, inviting folks to church. I walked the whole time, because I rarely had enough gas to get back to school. Funny how God would provide every Wednesday and weekends to get to the chapel and I would have to beg him for enough offerings to get home.

The neighbor lady was the writer for the local paper, and she hated our church. She would write in the paper bad things about our church. Whenever we saw each other, she would say something insulting and turn away. It was a wonderful time of God teaching me about serving him and serving people. I am so thankful for the fruit God gave our church in Cowan. In the chapters ahead, I am going to share some of the more memorable things that happened in our little church. And yes, after many weeks, I did finally win the lady next door to a friendship with our church.

I'm Taking a Shower Then Divorcing my Husband

I would get to Cowan late Friday night, and on Saturday, I would get up, get ready in the sink, and start visiting. I marked every street and house on the map I had on my wall in the nursery/living quarters. I wanted to invite everybody in driving distance at least once and talk to everyone who would listen about accepting Jesus. I felt like the blood of every person in that town was my responsibility to tell. So I would get up Saturday morning and head out, knocking on doors and meeting people until evening.

As you came off Mount Eagle Mountain, to the left, at the very bottom of the mountain, was a very nice huge house. It sat on what looked to be a couple of hundred acres. It was a three-mile drive into Cowan from the bottom of Mount Eagle. On this Saturday, I was visiting this stretch of road. I started on the right side, walking toward the mountain, and I wanted to visit every house on both sides before dark. When I got to the next to the last house on that side of the road, the next house was a mile away and no houses on the other side until I got back to the point where I was standing. I could cross the street and keep visiting houses back toward town or I could walk two miles to visit the rich people's house. I felt like I was being lazy, so I started the walk to the last house on this side of the street.

It was a hot day, and I was sucking air when I finally got to the front door of this house. It looked like the Clampett mansion on *Beverly Hillbillies*. I knocked on the twelve-foot-high doors and waited. After a little wait, I knocked again. A lady opened the door, wrapped in a towel with a towel on her head. She looked at me in utter disgust and said, "What do you want?"

I told her, "Ma'am, I want to get you and your family to visit church or I want to talk to you about Jesus."

She shot me another look, and then she said that she did not have time for this stuff (not the word she used). She then said, "I am going to take a shower, then I am going to divorce my husband."

I looked at her, and she was waiting for me to reply. I asked her if it mattered to her what God thought about her plans. She changed her expression and asked me inside.

I entered her foyer and into this huge open family living/sitting room, and she asked me to sit down and she would be back in a minute. I sat on one of her couches, and across the room from me, sitting in a lone chair placed away from other seating, was a man. He did not acknowledge my presence and was reading a paper. He never looked up or made any effort to do anything but drink his scotch and read his paper. They had this little dog that kept trying to bite my legs or my shoes. I sat there for a half hour or so, and finally, the lady came back out of her room. She invited me to follow her into the kitchen. I sat on a stool by their island sink, and she started pulling stuff out of the refrigerator for a meal. I was thinking, *Promising!*

She shared that she had been raised in church and had gotten away from it when she went to college. She and her husband met and were married, and he owned a huge car dealership in a nearby larger town. She went on to mention that they had everything people would want and lived the life most dreamed to have. The whole time she was telling me this stuff, her little dog was still biting my pants leg and snapping at my feet. She went on as she was cooking (hopeful), saying that over the past few years, the magic was gone and that she and her husband were drifting apart.

She talked the entire time it took her to cook a pot of spaghetti from scratch. She continued telling me her marriage problems and was setting three spaces at the table (yes). When the table was set, she called her husband, and we three sat down and started eating. I was starving, and it was going to be another day and a half before I could eat again, so I dug in and started eating. God provides in mysterious ways!

Her husband, still not having said anything, was eating, and the lady stopped in midsentence and asked me, "Who did you say you were again?"

I replied that I had not said who I was and that I had only asked if she cared what God thought about her divorcing her husband. Her husband then spoke. "And who are you?"

I told them I was the pastor of the new church in town.

She started back telling me all their issues. I ate as much as I could without embarrassing myself, and we all three went into the living room again. Their dog was still biting on my pants and shoes, and they just ignored it.

I finally asked her husband what he thought about the situation. He said she had become a nag to him and he was tired of the fighting.

She spoke up and said, "He beats me now all the time."

I listened to every part of their marriage problems. I was young and had little experience with couples in marriage crisis. I finally asked them both if either of them cared what God thinks about their situation. The lady did, and the husband admitted he had never really given God much thought. I asked him if he would now. He thought about it and looked at me and said, "Yes, I really would!"

A little time later, they both accepted Christ and not only invited him into their hearts, but they both invited him back into their marriage. They drove me back to the church and thanked me. They did not join my church, but they did join the First Baptist church where his dealership was, and they both were baptized.

I saw them months later, and they were doing well and serving in their church and seemingly happy. That dog chewed holes in my pants and my shoes. But the couple got new natures and heaven and their marriage back on track. I thank the Lord for allowing me to see that and for the meal that weekend!

The Harlot Preached

One Saturday, I was visiting outside of town and came up to a house with two boys, toddler age, playing in the yard. The mom was sitting on the porch, watching them. I walked up and told her I was from the church. I sat down, and we began to talk about her boys and her family. She was the wife of the chief of police, and they were having problems in their marriage. She was sitting there, watching her boys play, wondering if her marriage was going to make it.

We never know what people are going through and what heavy hearts they carry. She began speaking of her fears for her family and for her and her husband. I could tell by listening that she really loved him and was scared for their future.

I asked her about her faith, and like most southerners, she attended church as a child and stopped going when she reached early adulthood (why do so many walk away?). I told her that I would love for them to visit our church, and we had classes for her boys to hear about the Bible and God. She thanked me, and I started to leave when God touched my heart for her. I asked her if I could pray for her marriage and her family before I left.

She agreed, and we held hands, and I asked Jesus to enter her home and help their struggling marriage. As I finished, I simply told her that it was not church that she needed. I shared that she needed to privately get on her knees and return to Jesus's feet where she had been raised. I shared that Jesus was what she needed and her boys and her husband.

The next morning, to my surprise, she showed up with her two boys for Sunday school and church. That morning, after the message, she came forward and gave herself back to Christ publicly. She was very sincere and in tears. God heard that girl's prayers, and she began taking daily time alone with Christ and his Word. It was just a few short weeks, and both her boys asked Jesus into their hearts, and we scheduled a baptism for them.

On the Sunday we baptized the boys, the dad came to the service. I had seen him and spoken with him in passing but did not really know him. After the service, I was able to share a minute with him. He was a good man. I was impressed by his character and good nature. He mentioned that he was glad his boys were coming to church but that his wife was beginning to bug him about him not coming. He told me he did not like the pressure and was not sure he liked her new Bible reading and praying and religious stuff. He had never been a churchgoer.

I told him I understood his fears and that at one time, I was an atheist. I promised we as a church cared for his family. I also told him I respected him as a man and that I was praying for his marriage.

He came to church from time to time, but not regularly. He did stop and talk with me when we saw each other in town. I could tell he was thankful for what was happening in his family with his boys and his wife. I could tell he loved them.

His wife began to pray for her husband privately and not bother him about not going to church. As a result, her relationship with him became less bitter. She had been arguing with him in desperation of what she feared was happening in her family. He was seeing a constant nagging and not seeing her fears or pains. He was sick and tired of the constant fighting, and she was fighting harder, trying to fix their home. It was a rock pushing against a hard object, and both were very stubborn.

She began taking her fear to God in prayer and not arguing with him. She began praying for her husband, and her love for him began to show in her relationship again. I was proud of her as she was getting it. God was doing a real work over time in her marriage.

She started bringing people to church and winning them to Jesus. One of the people she started bringing was her best friend. They grew up together and had been best friends forever. The friend was coming every Sunday for weeks, and her husband was coming occasionally.

One Sunday morning, I was preaching a message on the prostitute in the book of Joshua that hid the spies. I was speaking on how this unsaved gentile whore had more faith in what God was going to do for the Israeli's than they did. I named the message, "And the Harlot Preached!" It was a message about how God's hand was on the Jews and how everyone watching could see God moving. It just so happened that it was a prostitute that spoke faith to the spies. "Your God is going to deliver this land to you."

God protected her and all her family because of her faith. God used that woman and could use any one of us if we believed. That was the gist of my message, and at the end of it, I finished by saying again how God used the harlot to preach to his own people. I dismissed the church, and when I went to shake hands with the people leaving, the police chief's wife's best friend came up to me in front of the wife and several other people. She started shouting at me in her outside voice. "You know! You know! I know you know!"

Mad as a hornet and still screaming at me, I told her I had no idea what she was talking about, and she screamed back, "Yes, you do, you know that I am sleeping with my best friend's husband!" There it was, in front of several church members and her best friend—this girl just screamed that she was having sex with the chief of police, her best friend's husband! They had been in adultery for some time, and this woman was mad at me because when I said the whore preached at the beginning of my sermon, she thought I knew and was getting more and more angry as the message went on. Finally, she exploded in front of God and everybody. You could have heard a pin drop after her outburst.

She ran out of the church and down the street in tears, and the people were left standing by the wife and her two sons, speechless. I finally asked the people to gather around the family, and we prayed and asked the Lord to help this situation. The people left, and I sat with the wife on the front steps of the church.

She was devastated. She had no idea that her best friend was sleeping with her husband. She knew her husband was distant, but they had been doing better. She was crying and said, "I thought Jesus was helping and we were getting better."

I told her that Jesus was helping and that she needed to go home and talk with her husband alone. I agreed to watch the boys at the church until she came back and got them. She left and went home and told her husband what her best friend had done in the service.

Her husband was shocked. Not only did his wife know, but by the time he found out she knew, half the town had found out. I wished every person in church would have the common sense not to speak of what happens in church, but I am sad to say some Christians love to run their mouths about other people.

Her husband admitted everything to his wife and told her that it was his fault. He also told her that when they were fighting all the time, it started out with her friend just listening, and one thing led to another and they sinned. He told her that after time, he was trapped in the lie and could not get out of it. He said that he would not fight her if she left him. He also told her he loved her and wanted them to stay together.

He left her at home and came to the church to get the boys. I was sitting on the steps, and he came over and sat down with me. He asked me what I thought about it all. I told him that I had never in my life had a church service like that one we had that morning. I also told him that I thought he had a good family with good boys. I shared that I knew that his wife loved him, and he loved her. He knew he had hurt her deeply, and I asked him if he had any other secrets she needed to know about.

He said there were none and that he was sorry for being a liar to his wife. I shared with him that he not only was a liar to her but that he lied to his boys and God also. I knew he was not a Christian, but he made a vow before God in his wedding that he would be faithful to his wife, so help me, God!

I told him that he should think long and hard about his betrayal to his family and be completely honest with his wife. I also asked him to listen to her heart and let her talk through everything with him. I prayed with him and told him next week, I was coming to see them to find out what they were planning on doing about it all.

The next Saturday, I went to their house, and I met with them to hear what they were thinking. I was so happy to hear that they decided to forgive each other and ask God to forgive them for living so long without him in their life. The husband asked his wife and his boys for forgiveness, and he later asked God for it too. He and his wife owned up to each of their faults, and the husband asked for time to prove his trustworthiness to his wife. He accepted Christ and was baptized after time.

God took a family in shambles and began working in a mom and wife, brought her back to him, and saved the two boys. He also, because of her prayers, brought out hidden sins in their marriage and restored their love for each other through forgiveness and mercy. He brought the husband into God's family and made their house a home that Jesus lived in. They were able, by God's grace, to be the family they so wanted to be. God does that for all who will come to him and let him have his way.

Burt

Maybe once or twice in our lives, we will meet someone who has a deep and even life-changing impact on us. Burt is one of those people in my life. Trying to put it down on paper is difficult, because it doesn't make sense that she could be so influential, but she was and not just to me; she was that way to others who were blessed enough to get to know her.

I was walking down one of the streets near the town square. This area was a pretty rundown and "the other side of the tracks" type neighborhood. Some of the poorest and least of these type of people lived here. I was inviting people to our service when I noticed a house that was in ill repair, had an unkempt yard, and an old rusty tin roof. Some of the kids in the neighborhood were standing in the street, throwing rocks at the house's roof. As I got closer, I noticed that after the rocks hit the roof, this old woman would come out, waving a long stick and cursing from her porch at the kids. They would run and laugh at the lady. She looked like the old fairy-tale witches in the children's books.

I asked one of the people next door to her house about her situation and was told she was a crazy old woman who had lost her mind. They warned me to stay away from her house because she was violent. Her door was the next one, and I walked up on her porch and knocked on her door. This woman looked to be eighty years old, but she could move. She opened the door with this 2x4 board that she had carved a handle in the end, swinging it at my head, cussing and trying to hurt me. She ran me out of her yard and into the street, cursing some of the most hateful cursing I have ever heard. She would make a sailor blush. Some of the people around the neighborhood stopped to watch me try to visit her and were laughing as she cussed all the way inside her house.

That week, I could not get that woman off my mind. I was haunted by her hostility and how just pure evil she seemed. I decided I was going to go by her house every Saturday until something happened. Looking back at it now, God put it on my heart to care about her, because she was so offensive, no one—myself included—would care for this old witch.

I went by her house five or six weeks in a row, and every week, the same thing would happen. I'm telling you, this old woman could hurt you. I had to run out of her yard or I would have been getting stitches in my head for sure. One weekend, I was speaking in a church in Virginia and had someone else speak for me. No one visited that weekend. The following weekend, I started at Burt's house on my visitation day, and I was surprised to see her sitting on her front porch with her club in her lap, rocking in an old rocking chair.

I stopped at the road (careful not to step in her yard) and said hello to her. First civil words she ever said to me: "Where were you last week?"

I told her I was preaching out of town and was not here last week.

She just sat there and stared at me. I told her if she would put the club in her house and close the door, I would come up on the porch and visit with her. I made her promise not to get upset, and she said I could come onto her porch but I had better hold my manners. I agreed and went and sat down for my first of many visits with this poor, mean, amazing lady.

I sat in another old rocker and told her I was the new preacher in town and was just out inviting people to church. She said she did not like preachers and did not like the two churches in Cowan and was sure she would not like mine. We exchanged names, and I discovered she was not crazy or broken in her mind. I asked her why she was so mean to people. She shared with me her story.

Burt was married and had two sons. Her husband had died when her sons were young. She did her best to raise them and put food on the table as a single mom. She admitted she did not teach her boys as well as she should have about life and people and civility and such. Her boys were rough, and their family had a bad reputation around town. They were often scorned and, in their mind, ridiculed by the townspeople and the church people.

Her firstborn son got into trouble and was put in prison. He was eventually killed in prison. Her other son was trying to do the right thing. His older brother tried to talk him onto the straight and narrow before his death. Her younger son got married and had two kids.

Burt was a grandmother. Burt shared that her son was really trying to be a good dad and even took the kids to the Church of Christ in town. After several times of his wife and the mother of his children messing around on him, she finally left town and abandoned her husband and her children. Burt said that her son went bad after that and ended up killing a man. He was sentenced to life in prison without parole and was in California somewhere.

Burt took the grandkids and had them for a couple of years. She said that she had made them go to school and even let them go to the church, weather permitting, as they walked wherever they went. She talked about those kids as if she was the kindest most loving grandmother a kid could have. It was obvious that her world evolved around those two young kids.

She lived on a fixed social security income of just a few hundred dollars a month. She put everything she had into feeding and clothing those kids, but it was not enough for some people (as Burt put it). Some of the school people asked the state to check on the kids to see if they were being properly cared for. The state started an investigation and took the kids from her home by force. They had a couple from the church foster them while they investigated Burt.

This is what I was wondering about with Burt as she shared the rest of her story. Burt told me that the church people said she was unfit to care for the kids and that they were malnourished. Burt (crying at this point) said her kids never missed a meal and that sometimes she did, but they did not.

After the investigation, the state came to Burt and told her she was an unfit guardian and could not have the kids back. Burt told them she was not a guardian, she was their grandmother, and became very upset. She tried to take the kids back by force and was arrested. She ended up not being able to see the kids again for fear she would flee with them, and there she sat—in her world; her husband, both her sons, and her grandkids were taken from her by the government and the church people. She felt that everybody was her enemy and if there was a God, he was her enemy too.

I did not try to give any words to her after that. What could I say to her after that? She was not crazy and mean. Burt was a loving mom who, in her own mind, failed her boys, and a loving grandmother who had her only people she had and loved stolen from her by force. To her, they were stolen by the government and the church.

I thanked her for letting me sit with her and asked if she would let me come back and visit again. I promised her I would not try to get her to come to church. I just wanted to visit. She said I could come back if I kept God out of it. I promised her I would keep *church* out of it and would not bring church up again unless she did.

That was the beginning of a friendship that I believe God put together and even orchestrated. I learned that Burt was a very smart person and sensitive. She could not read or write, but she was good with numbers and had a good business sense. She could also read people with an uncanny ability. I went by every Saturday, and she would be sitting on her porch, waiting, and we would sit together for an hour or so.

Burt finally asked me if I would be okay with her coming to church. She said not to try to get her to pray or anything, but she would come. I told her I would pick her up on Sunday's and Wednesday nights. Burt came for several months and would never miss.

One Saturday, Burt asked me to explain what I meant about biblical salvation. She had been taught that baptism was salvation. I explained to Burt that Jesus was a living and real person who watched her from heaven. He wanted her to ask him to forgive her sins and enter her life as her savior. Burt was then asking, if Jesus is a real person who is alive, then why did he let those people take her grandkids from her?

I told her that Jesus did not take her loved ones away but that he knew it happened and he loved her and them.

A few weeks after that Saturday, Burt stood up after the message and came to the altar. She stood in front of the pulpit and waited on me to ask her what she wanted. Burt said, "I'm not bending down on my knees!" Her legs were hurting, and I said to her Jesus would listen to her standing. I asked her what it was she wanted to pray about. She said she wanted Jesus. She said she was ready and wanted Jesus in her heart.

Burt prayed a short simple prayer that seemed almost without conviction. She then went back to her seat. A few weeks later, she was baptized. I got her a set of the Bible on tape, and she began listening to scripture and praying daily.

I could write a book on just what God did in Burt's life after she was saved. I will share just a few examples. Burt soon shared with me that she needed to forgive the people who took her grandkids and her son. She also started praying for people and things, and God gave Burt a clean line of communication. Burt told me later that she was going to pray every day for God to be with her son in prison and her grandkids since she could not be with them.

God gave her peace that he was with them. She came to me one day and said that she wanted to share with people about how to be saved but didn't know how. She started getting up in the middle of the night and walking up and down the street where she lived, praying for the people that she hated and that hated her. Burt, in a short time, went from being the most hated person in Cowan, Tennessee, to one of the most loving. The chief of police even came by the church to tell me that his job was easier since Burt got religion.

Burt became a person of compassion and was as loving to people as anyone I have ever known. One Saturday, Burt asked me if she could tithe her bologna and cheese she got every two weeks. She said God told her to tithe it and she wanted to wrap it up in a bag and put it in the offering. I told her she could if she believed God told her to do it. What I didn't tell anyone was that I was coming from college on Fridays with just enough money for gas to get there most of the time. I would eat lunch on Friday and not eat again until lunch on Monday. I would eat that piece of bologna and cheese every other week, thanking God for it. To me, it was the same as manna from heaven.

Burt became sick and died sometime after I had left the church as pastor, and I was contacted. I found out that the family who fostered her grandkids were distant relatives to Burt and had adopted the kids as their own. They were the ones who the hospital called and they made all the arrangements for her funeral.

As her former pastor, I was asked to do the service, but the funeral was to be held in the Church of Christ in town. Her family had arranged to have their pastor say some words, and then I would speak at her service. When I got to the church, I was sitting up front, watching the people view the body. The church was full of townspeople. I noticed two children standing by Burt and crying. I knew they had to be her grandkids, and the kids obviously had missed her as much as she had missed them.

The pastor of that church came up behind them and told them, "Look at her, children, because you will never see her again. She is in hell, and you will never see her again!"

I could not believe my ears! I normally never contradict a pastor in front of people, but this day, I did a new thing. When I got up to speak, I told the people what the pastor said to the kids. I then looked at the pastor and told him he was wrong. I told the children that I was with her when she asked Jesus to save her. I shared that she prayed every day for them and that someday, they would see each other again.

I then asked the townspeople who had come to raise their hand if they saw the change in Burt from the meanest person in town to the woman walking the streets at night, praying for the people to be saved. Almost everybody in the building raised their hand. I then shared with them about her nightly prayer walks and her prayers for them and gave the people a chance to accept Burt's God. I am humbled to be allowed by God to have served Burt as her pastor, and I still tear up thinking of that mean old witch that assaulted me with a bat who ended up showing a small town how to forgive and love! Way to go, Burt!

A Word from the Word

There was a radio station in our little town that had a thirty-minute *Waylon and Willie* program every week. I was able to get fifteen minutes before Waylon and Willie's time to teach on the radio. Everybody listened to Waylon and Willie, so I took the spot and started a radio ministry. I called it, "A Word from the Word!" My thinking was that I could give scripture to some of the doctrinal beliefs in the area that were not biblical. I took questions on church doctrine and people's beliefs and gave scripture for the answers.

I tried to make it not so much a preaching time but an eye-opening time for the people who wanted answers to Bible questions but did not want to speak to a preacher. It became popular. I dealt with several teachings that were false in our community and gave the scriptures to the people for them to search out in the Bible for themselves. I would read people's questions and then address the issues. This made two of the three churches a little upset with the program as people started questioning them on some of their doctrines that were questionable.

One of the pastors would come into the studio and do a live program in the fifteen-minute spot before mine. He did a live healing and deliverance show where he would take open calls and heal people or deliver them from various illnesses. He came on most Sundays but would often not show up at all. I would get to the station early so I could read any questions that came in and gather my thoughts. This pastor would walk in and shake my hand and say, "God bless you brother, I'm praying for you," and then get on the air and tear me a good one over the radio.

It was funny as he would call our church by name as well as call me by name, saying all kinds of crazy stuff, and then finish and walk out and look at me and say, "Bless you, Brother."

My intent was not to promote our church as much as promote sound Bible truth. I pretty much ignored the other guy and just addressed the questions that came in or addressed the common errors in the community. One Sunday, I was sitting in the waiting room, preparing the questions for the day's program, and my pastor brother was speaking on the hellacious doctrines of the Popular Street Baptist Church. He was scalding us a good one. I could hear him, and I must admit this old boy was good at crucifying people.

The open phone line rang while this old boy was tearing us up, and he answered it and asked if the person needed healing or deliverance. My eyes perked up as I recognized Burt's voice on the other end of the phone. She spoke on live radio that she was listening to his speaking about the Baptist church. The pastor said, "Yes, ma'am, how can I help you?"

Burt then said, "I hear what you are saying, but the best I can remember, the pastor you are talking about never left his wife for another woman in the church and moved away, then came back a few months later and opened his church again." There was a short pause, then all you heard was a click and a dead silence.

The pastor hung up the phone, turned off his mic, and walked out of the studio. He walked past me without his normal "God bless you" and was gone. The radio manager put on a song and gave me the extra time. I felt bad for the old boy but could not help but laugh at Burt doing that.

That night at church, when Burt came in, she was smiling from ear to ear. She said, "We told that old boy, didn't we?"

I think back on that time and think about how scripture affects a community and how spiritual powers work in places to steal God's truth from people. I am not saying the other pastor was of the devil. I don't believe that at all. I am saying that much of his teaching was not according to proper biblical doctrine and that the devil uses that to combat God's Word throughout our world. That is why every Christian should study the Bible for themselves and not follow any man too much. God and his Word is our authority.

Mrs. Payne

I received a call from the local hospital asking me to contact them. I called from the radio station and found out that they had started playing our program on their sound system along with *Waylon and Willie*. In one of their rooms was a patient who had listened and wanted to know if I would come see her. I went by after the program and met Mrs. Payne. She had some type of surgery and was in the hospital for a prolonged stay. She was an older woman who was very shy and soft-spoken. She was going to get better, but the ordeal had left her with life questions about her eternity.

I ended up visiting Mrs. Payne several times, and she began attending our church. She was a religious churchgoer but had never repented personally of her sins and accepted Christ. Soon on a Sunday morning, she came forward after a message and asked to accept Christ. She did so and was baptized a few weeks after that. Burt and Mrs. Payne became good friends and prayer partners.

Mrs. Payne had a very rough life. Her husband had left her with two kids, a boy and a girl to raise on her own. They were very poor, and her children were always in and out of jail. The one burden on Mrs. Payne's heart was that God would get ahold of her children. She and Burt would pray together constantly for their kids and grandkids. I was humbled by Mrs. Payne's faith and her strength of character. She was a truly good person and not a mean bone in her body.

Mrs. Payne's two children lived in Cowan. Her daughter was married and in her late twenties, and her boy was just out of prison and in his mid-twenties. Mrs. Payne prayed so much for her kids. I tried to talk to both of them anytime I could catch them. Neither one of them wanted anything to do with Jesus, and they both were wild and very mean.

One Sunday, Mrs. Payne asked me to promise her I would speak to her children about Christ, and I promised I would. Her son was just home from prison and was staying at her house. I was walking toward her home one Saturday when her son came around the corner in a pick-up truck and veered toward me, trying to hit me.

I jumped into the ditch or he would have run me over. He did not know it, but I was walking to his house. When I got there, Mrs. Payne's son was working under the hood of his truck. I stopped at the door and told Mrs. Payne I was going to talk to her son. As I went around back of her house, her son started cussing at me and told me I had better leave him alone or else he was going to jump on me.

I told him that I had no intention of trying to get him to believe something against his will. I stated I didn't want trouble and was trying to talk with him because his mom had asked me to do so. I told him that if he ever wanted to talk about what it meant to trust in Jesus, I would be glad to share that with him. I also told him he was welcome in church anytime.

I will never forget the boy's answer to me. He looked at me with hate in his eyes and he said something I have never heard anyone but two other people say, even to this day. He said to me, "Preacher, you and the Holy Spirit can both go to hell! If I ever decide I want Jesus, I will let you know, but until then, you and the Holy Spirit leave me alone!"

I told him, "Fair enough" and walked away. Chills went down my back as I walked away. I have heard people take God's name in vain. Even now, people who go to church take Jesus's name in vain too. I am shocked when I hear people break that commandment. But I have only in my life heard three people blaspheme the Holy Spirit.

I heard an old preacher, Dr. J. Harold Smith, preach that God never lets a person live long after they blaspheme the Holy Spirit. I know that the Bible says it is the only unpardonable sin. But sure enough, Mrs. Payne's boy told me and the Holy Spirit to go straight to hell! I was shocked as I have rarely heard such spiritually damning words from anyone.

I didn't say anything to Mrs. Payne about what her son had said, but my spirit was rattled by his words. I just told her that we needed to keep praying for him.

I left for school, and on the following Thursday, I got an emergency call from Cowan, Tennessee. I called, and it was Mrs. Payne. Her son had been driving his truck, drunk, and came around a curve too fast and flipped his truck. He was thrown out the window, and the truck had rolled over him and broken his neck among a few other things. He was dead.

We had her son's funeral the next weekend, and only a few people were there. I never told Mrs. Payne what her son said about the Holy Spirit. At the funeral, I spoke with Mrs. Payne's daughter and husband and invited them to church. The next day, there they sat with Mrs. Payne in church. I thanked them and invited them back and asked if I could visit them. They said I was welcome to stop by anytime.

I went by their house a few weeks after the funeral. I wanted to give them a little time to process the death. Mrs. Payne's daughter and her husband, a former Marine, were a tough couple. They were very honest and told me they were not interested in church or Jesus.

They both partied and were not willing to give up their drugs and their lifestyle for religion. They told me they did not mind me coming by from time to time but not to bother them too much.

Over the next few months, I visited them one or two times and just kept praying for them. They were not only doing drugs, but it was obvious they were dealing in drugs as well.

One Sunday, Mrs. Payne's daughter came to church and asked to speak with me afterward. We sat together, and I shared with her how much God wanted to help her carry her problems. She listened and even asked me to come by and see her. The next week, I went by and talked with her about her need for Christ. She didn't accept Christ, but she did start coming to church for a few weeks. I was thinking for sure she was going to come to Christ.

After a few weeks, she stopped coming. I waited a few weeks to see if she would come back, and she did not. So one Saturday, I walked to her house, and her and her husband were sitting together on the couch. They invited me in, and I sat down. She told me that she was coming to church because she was so upset about her break up with her husband. Now that they were good again, she didn't want to come back. I left there, thinking how typical that was with so many people.

It was three months or so later that I was visiting door-to-door again in her part of town. Her house was the next one, so I knocked on the door. She and her husband were there and both high. They said for me to come in, and I did. When I got inside, the husband began speaking with me about bugging them. I told them not to worry, I wouldn't come back unless they asked me to. Then the husband said, "You can leave and never come back, and you and the Holy Spirit can go straight to hell!"

I was shocked. One, because I had not visited them in a while and all was fine the last time. Also, he said the same thing to me that

Mrs. Payne's son had said before he was killed. Her daughter did not say it, but she was sitting there and did not say anything after he said it. I walked away from their house, but my spirit had that same rattled feeling as before. Again, how strange was that wording? I did not mention to Mrs. Payne about that visit.

About two (it may be three) weeks later, again I got a call from Cowan, Tennessee. It was Mrs. Payne, and she had bad news. Her daughter and son-in-law were both killed in their home. Someone walked in on them and shot them both sitting together on the couch. Money and drugs were sitting undisturbed on the coffee table. No motive and no complaints from the neighbors about hearing shots or seeing anyone. It was a complete mystery and, as far as I know, never settled.

We did their funeral the following weekend, and they were buried next to Mrs. Payne's son. I was amazed at Mrs. Payne's strength. I tried to comfort her, but she knew her children were both lost and in hell. I asked how she was dealing with their deaths. She just told me that she could not bear it. She just gave the pain to Jesus every time it got too great to carry.

I cannot think of Mrs. Payne without thinking of her kind, sweet-natured disposition. Her children were so different than she was, and she never gave up on them. She always loved them and prayed for them. I am at a loss for words at the pain that woman endured throughout most of her life. I also remember how much she loved her Bible and her prayer time. She truly found peace in her walk with Jesus and in the harshest circumstances.

Mrs. Payne died with very few people at her funeral, but she was a giant of a Christian, and God has wiped every tear from her eyes.

I have never, since her two children, heard of anyone openly blaspheming the Holy Spirit, except for one night on a late night Netflix cheesy movie. This actor took the Holy Spirit's name in vain. When I heard it, the same chills went up my back as when both of Mrs. Payne's kids did it. I wondered how long the actor lived after that scene.

One-Armed Lady

One Saturday, the chief of police drove up to the church (same one I wrote about before) and asked if I could come with him. I got in his car, and we started toward Burt's house. The chief shared that he had some trouble with Burt and that he needed me to visit her with him. Burt had been a totally new creature in Christ for some time and was not a troublemaker anymore. Chief said he needed to arrest her but was afraid to because of her age. He told me she had assaulted a one-armed woman with her walking cane.

When we got to Burt's house, she was sitting on the porch, waiting on us, and she looked just like a little kid sitting in the principal's office. I asked her to tell us what happened to get her to do that to the woman.

Burt said that the one-armed woman started it. She was at the post office and was giving out gospel tracts from our church. The one-armed lady came up to her and started talking badly about our church and about me as the pastor. Burt said she told her to be quiet, and the one-armed lady asked what she was going to do about it, and Burt said, "So I hit her in the head with my cane."

The chief had come up at that point and had seen her hit the woman. He told Burt either she could go to jail or meet with him and me together and talk about it. Burt agreed to apologize to the lady and not hit her again. I also told her not to worry about what people say. She agreed and promised not to do it again.

Here is the rest of the story. I had visited the one-armed lady door-to-door and invited them to church. She had a boatload of kids, and I told them about our classes for the children their age and asked them all to come. The mom let it be known that none of her family would darken the door of the church. She was a bitter woman. Her arm had been pinched off in a coal mine accident. Somehow, after everything had settled, she was alone with a house full of kids and her settlement money gone with her husband. She blamed God for all that had happened and was very outspoken against God.

We had classes for children on Wednesday nights at the church. Alice and Bill Simmons (good friends of mine) came with me and helped. One Wednesday night, we were very low in attendance and had just locked up the church for the long drive back to school. Outside the church was a boy, maybe six years old, and his sister, four years old, walking up the sidewalk toward the church. They were both filthy and shoeless. The boy was wearing a suit and a shirt with a clip tie on, and the girl had put on a dress. They were holding hands and asked if they were too late for church.

It was after nine, but Alice Simmons and Bill took them by the hand, and we went back inside and did the entire service and class over for them. Both of those kids prayed that night and asked Jesus into their hearts and lives. It was a sweet experience. It was late after we were through, so we told the kids we would take them home.

As we were driving to their house, we found out they were the one-armed lady's kids. They had dressed themselves and came on their own. We pulled up to the house, and I went and knocked on the door. The lady came to the door and was upset when she saw her kids with me. I explained what had happened and that we had a service for them and that was the reason we were so late.

The lady was happy that the kids had prayed and asked Jesus into their hearts but was not happy about them coming to church. She became very outspoken against us because of that night. She made a comment that she thought we were trying to turn her family against her. It was that incident that brought on the situation at the post office. The one-armed lady never visited our church (probably afraid of Burt) but her children came from time to time and were good kids. Funny how people blame God for their problems rather than call out to him for help when he wants to be there for them.

Jump Off Baptist

I was interim pastor for a short time at one of our chapels in Tennessee called Jump Off Baptist Church. Legend had it that people jumped off the cliffs close to the church to commit suicide. So the church was named after the location that was known as Jump Off. Sort of like naming a church after the street it is on so people will know where it is and how to find it.

It was a church of about eighty mountain people. Mountain people are different than country people. They have their own culture and are precious and fun people to get to know. One would be mistaken to think these folk simple or unlearned. They are incredibly gifted in what is called horse sense, and I enjoyed our time together at this church and became really close to the people.

There was this guy at college who had just been called to preach and had never yet had the chance. Gary, I'll call him, asked me if I would help him find a place to preach. I asked him to get a message ready, and I would take him to Jump Off to preach. I need to tell you that Gary came from a city—Boston, I think—and had never been around southern country folk, much less real mountain people. Herein is where the story gets interesting.

I shared with the church that we were going to have a guest preacher coming next Sunday and that it would be his very first time preaching the Word. I built it up by reminding them that it was important for everyone to be here and that we, as a church, would do everything possible to encourage the new preacher. It became an exciting day for the people, so the next Sunday, the church was crowded.

Gary and I made the sixty-seven-mile drive into the Tennessee mountains to the Jump Off Baptist Church. I was trying to prepare Gary that the people were a little different than he was used to and to not be surprised if some of the younger people didn't wear shoes and so on. It was an exciting thing to be part of, and Gary was excited to have his chance at his first message.

One of the families in our church was a precious couple in their early twenties. The husband did not attend much, but the wife was a faithful, hardworking, dedicated church member. She had a toddler and a newborn who was just a few months old. One thing about this area was that the people did not use a modesty blanket when they nursed. They just opened up and took care of business right out in the open in front of God and everybody.

Another thing about this young mom was that she was, with no exaggeration, one of the prettiest ladies I have ever seen. I kid you not, this girl could have been a model and was gorgeous. Her husband was just as country bib overhaul ugly as they come, and they were deeply in love with each other. They were a fun family to watch and happy and as carefree as they come. Back to the Sunday morning.

The church was packed and only a few places on the very front row were left for seating. We had just started the service, and I was making announcements. This lady and her toddler came in late (very rare) and marched up and sat right in the front row closest to the center aisle, just a few feet from the pulpit. I finished the announcements and we had our songs and a choir special. The time came for me to introduce Gary for the sermon for this day. It was a full house, and the church did not have air-conditioning (not many mountain churches did back then) and it was getting a little stuffy.

I welcomed Gary and told the church how important it was for God to call people into his service and that we, as a church, were honored to have Gary begin his public ministry with us at Jump Off. Gary got up and walked to the pulpit and set down his notes and his Bible. He was struggling with it, being his first time ever speaking in public, much less a sermon. This church did not like preachers to use notes as to them, a preacher who uses notes is not truly God-called (not true). They were willing to overlook this as it was Gary's first time preaching.

Gary also had a big city Boston accent, and most people in these parts did not trust city folk at all. I was sitting just behind Gary on the platform to his right, facing the congregation. This young Mom was on the left. Gary had just moved from his introduction into the first point of his message about ten minutes into it. I noticed that the mom's little baby started fussing. It dawned on me that Gary had not ever seen a baby feeding like he was about to, and I had not prepared him in advance about this possibility. Gary had already been looking at this lady in an innocent way as possible for a nineteen-year-old single man in church and this close to a very pretty young lady.

As I said, Little Bit started fussing, and Mom reached up and started unbuttoning her blouse. Gary noticed her and kind of lost his place but recovered well enough as Mom kept on undressing. Gary was trying to act like he was not watching and to keep preaching and watching all at the same time? A hard thing for a new preacher to do.

When Mom finished unbuttoning her blouse, she pulled down her bra and pulled out her baby's meal. One of the prettiest lunch buffets any baby could want. Gary froze. He stared at the mom, then at the church, then back at the mom. His forehead broke instantly into a cold sweat, and all his notes fell on the ground all over the floor. Gary looked at the church and the mom and then at me and just walked over and sat down on the chair next to mine. I got up and did my best to finish his thoughts as I understood them and closed the message.

The whole time, Gary sat behind me with his head in his hands. I was just about to close the service when I asked Gary to go to the back and stand by the door. In these churches, the people will wait in line to shake the preacher's hand and let him speak to the kids or touch their heads. I told the church Gary was going to do the handshaking, and then I closed in prayer.

The first one up and to Gary was the mom and her toddler and her baby. She grabbed Gary's hand to shake it, and even though she was the same age as Gary, she said to him, "Sir, don't you dare let your getting embarrassed and stopping keep you from preaching! God is going to use you, and you keep on preaching!" She had no idea that it was her—or more accurately, her breast—that had caused Gary's embarrassment. I was so thankful that she didn't know and was reminded that God has a sense of humor!

Spirit of Christmas

My last year at Temple University, I was the student body president of the university. One of our jobs as a student body officer was to create, organize, and carry out a student body project for that year. Usually, that came in the form of a fundraiser or campus improvement type project. That year, I wanted to do something different. I wanted to energize the student body with a project that would take great effort and hard work, ending in helping our community. Something that when we finished it, we would not benefit from it, but people in our community would.

Shortly after taking office, some of our well-meaning faculty leaders from the college were trying to get us to commit to doing a walk-athon to raise the money to give the university an Olympic-sized pool. I was pressured harshly to commit to it but did not get peace that it was what we needed. Our college boasted of being "distinctively Christian." But as a Christian college, we were that in motto, but not so much in practice.

One reason I accepted the office of president was because of our need for revival in our school body. I wanted to do a project that would get our student body thinking about others, not ourselves. To me, the pool (as nice as it would be to have one), was not that type of project.

It was our fall semester and was early October. Our student body council finally agreed to do something for the city of Chattanooga.

We called and asked the city what was one of their greatest needs. The person I spoke with shared with me that the biggest need was helping families with their Christmas needs. Every year, the city had families that could not provide any type of Christmas for their children, and the city struggled with getting community involvement to help. We heard that and knew immediately that we had our project.

I asked the social worker to give us 200 families that needed help, and we would provide for each family. We found out immediately that whenever you want to do something that God is pleased with, there will be a battle along with it. Our student council decided that we would give every family for Christmas a turkey meal, big with fixings, a Christmas tree (decorated if need be), one big present for each child or teen in every family, and the main need that the family unit had. We wanted to meet each family's entire needs for that Christmas.

When I contacted the social worker, she informed us that the city did not wish to work with us on such a project. Some of the leaders of our college said they would not support us if we did that over the pool. Several members of the student body complained that we should be helping our struggling students rather than strangers we did not know. I was shocked that as soon as we knew what we needed to do to help 200 hurting families with every need they had for that Christmas that we would get attacked from every side. It was crazy. We prayed about it. God gave us a clear word that we should do just that—help those families.

Here is what we did. We set up a meeting with the main social worker responsible for that part of the city's need. I invited them to come speak in chapel on behalf of the city to our college and explain the size of the need. We invited them to take part in the planning and put their name in front of the project so they could be involved in the process. We invited them to give us a contact person who could watch our progress and report to them so they would know the project was in good shape. That way, they could take the credit for it with the city when we did it.

They agreed to let us do the project on those terms, and the mayor's office even got involved. Next, we met with Dr. Roberson and shared with him our plan to ask the college student body and faculty to do the project. Our goal with this project was to do something that would take prayer, faith, and sacrifice, and in return, we would touch our city for the Gospel. He agreed, and the following week, he asked the student body and the faculty to join in a project that would take faith, sacrifice, and prayer to touch people for Christ. He advised the leadership to get behind it and do whatever was needed to help the students succeed.

We then had a chapel service and explained that we were doing this to "the least of these" in our city from a biblical point of view and that we were not ignoring our needy. We asked God to help our needy while we helped the forgotten needy in our city in the name of Christ. We called it "The Spirit of Christmas."

We were informed that the city had a total of 168 families that had made requests asking for assistance. We took each of the 168 families and randomly divided the student body between them. The spirit of our student body was divided, and strife was everywhere. We decided to assign people who did not know each other into family groups, hoping to bring a unity back into our student body.

The day came when we presented the details of the project to our student body. In our weekly chapel service, we told the students our goal. We were going to give 168 families for Christmas a meal, a tree, a big present for each child or teen, and meet the biggest need the family unit had. We then gave our plan.

We divided the entire student body into groups with the family's name and address. We laid the family names out and had diagrams telling every student where his/her family could be located. We then had everyone move to their family team and sit together. We had some of our students who refused to take part, but we ended up with 168 groups with ten to eleven in each group. As most did not know each other, we asked them to form a team and choose a captain.

We asked them to work as a team over the next ten weeks to provide for their family everything we promised. We asked our student body to pray for the money, the food, the tree, and ask God to show himself to their team. I asked each group to reach out to their family that week, and by the next chapel, we could get started.

The next ten weeks was a true God-thing to experience. We had people from all over the country praying with us for the team that their student was working with to get their needs met. Students who did not have money for their own stuff were seeing God send in money for their family in unexpected ways. God got in the process, and we saw people who did not know each other working together to help hurting people they did not know. It was one of the best things our university did for our city in years.

On the week before the Christmas service, we had our teams share their needs and their answers to prayers and the things God had done so far. We prayed as a unified body of believers, asking God to provide the remaining needs for our families, and we asked him to touch the parents in his name. The following week, we had a "Spirit of Christmas" chapel. Our chapel could seat 5,000-plus people. We had a building that was in a circle with doors along the back half of the auditorium. The front half was the platform and choir loft. It was a huge auditorium.

We had each team bring their gifts into the auditorium and line them in piles for each family unit. We started bringing in the stuff the night before, and well into the night and early morning, people were bringing in the Christmas needs for these families. We had people bring in their gifts all the way up into the last minutes before the service. The gifts were three rows deep, all the way across the front of the building, seventy-five plus yards in a circular shape. There were thousands of dollars of Christmas gifts. This was prayed up, sacrificed for, trusting God to provide gifts that for ten weeks we asked God to send us, and he did. By the time the service began, every family had everything we asked God for with many having extra.

We invited the families to come, and many did. The news came as well, and we made the front page and the six-o'clock evening news. We had Dr. Roberson and the mayor speak. We then took pictures of each team with their gifts. We sent the teams out to each family with their gifts and had each group get a picture with their families. We gave them their gifts in the name of Jesus.

We offered them the Gospel, but with no expectations or strings attached. We had bunk beds for kids sleeping on the floor, three month's rent paid for one family, several refrigerators—all kinds of needs! We took the gifts to the families, and God did a thing in the hearts of everybody. It was amazing. Not one single family was left out. God did it! I was absolutely amazed at his provision for these poor people.

The headline in the news was "Putting Christ Back into Christmas!" The mayor wrote a letter to the university and stated he had witnessed a truly Christian moment in our city. One-hundred and sixty-eight families received for Christmas a turkey dinner, a tree, every kid and teen their one big wish (many more presents), and the family's biggest stated need. It came from students who did not have extra money, some faculty, churches from back home praying with their students, and all over. The Highland Park Baptist Church had over twenty-one people baptized the next Sunday, and many families started worshipping with our church.

After it was finished, the leadership that was against it, the students that would not help, and the people complaining about us helping people we did not know, instead of our own, were silenced. God worked in our student body that Christmas. I have to say that we had a "Spirit of Christmas" that would have inspired Charles Dickens and Ebenezer Scrooge.

How Did He Get Here?

Sharon and I were broken up for eighteen months. We both loved each other, but we argued too much. During that time, God was doing his work in both of our hearts. I lost my dad in a fire just after our breakup, was student body president after that, and way too busy for my own good. Sharon was working full-time, taking a full load of classes, and working in the bus ministry on weekends. During that period, God was changing things and helping us mature in ways that we both needed.

Sharon felt called to missions' work. One of our friends, Martha, went to India for the summer and came back to school telling Sharon how badly she wanted Sharon to go. Sharon felt God leading her to go and contacted the missionary family to set up the dates.

Solomon Peters was a pastor and director of a big mission in his part of India. He helped many churches and ran a discipleship ministry out of his local church. Sharon wanted to move on past our relationship and therefore asked God to let her go to India. Once there, she wanted time to focus on just her and God and his will for her future. Her plan was that God would help her use this trip to take away her love for me and replace it with a love for missions.

She hoped God would show her where she should serve after college on this trip. She raised her money in a short amount of time and soon traveled, by herself, through multiple airports from

Chattanooga, Tennessee, to India. Through the course of this trip, her plan was to heal, getting over, once and for all, our relationship and for her to start moving toward her future work.

When she arrived at Solomon's house, his family greeted her and welcomed her into their home. They took her bags to the guestroom and told her to rest before dinner, if she liked. Sharon went into the room to do just that, and when she looked up on the wall, she screamed. Solomon and his family ran into her room to find out what had happened. Sharon was standing by the bed, looking at the picture on the wall with her hands over her mouth. "What is he doing here?"

On the wall was a picture of Martha and I. Sharon told Solomon that she had just traveled halfway around the world to get away from me, and here I was on her wall at the missionary's house.

As student body president, I needed to have dates at events we did throughout the year. Martha and I were good friends, but not dating, so she came with me to the events. We had our pictures taken at these events, and neither of us wanted them because we were not a couple, just friends. Solomon had asked Martha for a picture, and she sent them a picture of her and I at one of the events. Solomon shared with Sharon he did not know who the guy in the picture was, but he had it there because it was a picture of Martha. Solomon's wife took a picture of Sharon and cut her face out and taped it over Martha's face.

While Sharon was in India, I was finishing the last of my classes before graduation. I had seen Sharon several times during the year, and we knew the same friends. Just before she left for India, we prayed together. I still had feelings for her but did not think we were going to get back together.

A few weeks into my last semester, my brother died, choking on food. He had a disease that covered his body with tumors. He had several tumors in his spinal cord, and as they grew, they were causing some of his body functions to stop working.

One day at work, while sitting at his desk, he was eating lunch, and his food became lodged in his throat. His muscles were not strong enough to swallow it, so he laid his head down on his desk and died. I went to his hometown to preach his funeral. It was just a short while after my father died, and I was having a hard time. After the funeral, I was sitting in the hotel room and was angry. As I sat there, I became mad at Sharon. That made no sense to me, so I was trying to work it out in my mind. I realized that the only person I wanted to be with was Sharon, and she was halfway around the world, and I needed her with me. At that moment, I realized I needed Sharon to be by my side as my wife.

The next week, I wrote Sharon a letter and told her I was praying for her. I signed it, "Love, Frank." I did not tell her that my brother had died. I also did not tell her that through his death, I realized I needed her and that I planned on asking her to marry me as soon as she came back from India. I wanted to talk with her in person.

I signed the letter, "Love, Frank," thinking she would notice and realize I was wanting to get back with her. It was my attempt to kind of break the ice. The funny thing was that when she got the letter and read it, she thought it was from the devil trying to get her mind off Christ and missions. But every day there was a picture of Martha and I with Sharon's face taped over Martha's looking down at her from her wall.

When Sharon came back to the States, I visited her in Milwaukee. I had set it up with her dad to ask her to marry me. He took me to the place on Lake Michigan where he asked Sharon's mom to marry him. That evening, I took Sharon out to a nice meal and then drove her to the spot. We walked over and sat on the grass overlooking the lake. Sharon mentioned that her parents had become engaged at this same spot. I handed her a box with a ring and asked her to marry me. She did not answer, and I was getting really nervous when she looked up and said, "Yes!"

I am so thankful she did!

Fifty-Thousand Tulips and Daffodils

After I asked Sharon to marry me and she agreed to do it, we set our wedding for December 28, and I had a little over three months to come up with enough money to do so. Sharon's dad told me if I wanted to marry Sharon, I had to pay for the wedding and pay off her school debt. Sharon was well-worth it, and I started praying for the money. I was working with my friend, Bill, planting tulip and daffodil beds around business signs. We both were in school and had full-time ministries, so we sold tulip beds to businesses and planted the bulbs around their signs to make money.

I rented a small apartment, and we had an old junker for a car. I was trying to pay off my and Sharon's school as well as our wedding and honeymoon. Bill could sell anything, but I was not a salesman. God helped us, and we did manage to pay our bills and do our ministries. I managed to pay in advance for our honeymoon. Our wedding was at the school, and many of our friends helped with all our wedding needs. People did our cake and reception, Dr. Roberson did not charge us for the church, and Bill officiated the wedding. It was two weeks before our wedding, and I needed a little over $3,000 dollars to break even with everything I owed. We had fifty-thousand tulips and daffodils left to plant by then. We needed to sell them and plant them in two weeks.

Bill and I met together and prayed for God to open a door for us to be able to sell all our flowers and get them planted. Bill and I both needed the money in a bad way. Bill headed out one way, and

I headed out another way, looking for businesses we had not already pitched to. I was in another town, not far from where we lived, and had talked to a few places, but it was not happening. I was really starting to get discouraged.

I was driving down this long country road, not really knowing where I was or where I would go next. I started crying out to God, telling him all my needs and the short time I had to make the money. It is funny how we pray to God sometimes when we are pressured, telling God what we need, like he does not know! I was doing that. "Lord, if I don't sell these, I won't be able to pay for the wedding…"

I caught a breath of faith and started praying for God to lead me to a place that could buy all the bulbs. I was out in the Tennessee backwoods, and nothing was close. I was just about to turn around and go back when I drove around a curve, and there was this gigantic silo and building complex. There were fences and armed guards with razor wire all around, and it was massive. My first thought was that this place is big enough to sell all our bulbs to.

I pulled up into the parking lot in front of the building that looked like it would have the offices. The entire complex was surrounded by high fences with razor wire on top. There was a guard gate that each person had to walk through to get in, and armed guards were everywhere. I found out it was a nuclear power plant. I had never seen one up close.

I was wearing a nice suit and carrying a leather briefcase. I pulled my car into a parking space and bowed my head. "Dear God, help me sell these people our bulbs." I got out of the car and started walking to the gate to try and pass security. Just in front of me were four other men in suits and with briefcases headed for the gate. I stepped behind the last guy and walked into the gate house with the other four. The guards handed us clipboards and asked us to sign in and wait.

I filled out the paper and was noticing the four other guys were staring a hole through me. I just stood there and waited. Shortly, another guard stepped into the room and told us to follow him but not to step off the sidewalk. All five of us followed the guard through the door, into the courtyard, past the reactor building (I found that out later), and into the office buildings. We passed another guard desk and got on the elevator to the third floor. These guys were not talking, but they were obviously not happy with my being there with them.

The third floor was the director of the plant's office, meeting rooms, a giant receptionist's desk, and a waiting area. We all just walked in and each spread out and sat down. The secretary for Dr. Abercrombie (not sure of spelling) was working and watching each of us at the same time. Shortly, she stood up and said, "Gentlemen, Dr. Abercrombie is going to be delayed, and it cannot be helped." She asked that we make ourselves comfortable and that they would serve drinks shortly.

I was still getting the stare from all the men I came in with. I figured this Dr. Abercrombie was the man I needed to speak with, so I just sat and waited.

After a while, each of the men separately approached and asked the secretary who I was and why I was there. Everyone spoke in a whisper. I came to find out these men were there at Dr. Abercrombie's invitation. The reactor needed a part that only a few companies in the world was able to produce, and the companies represented by these four men were there to bid for the contract. They all knew of each other's invitation, but they wanted to know who I was and why Dr. Abercrombie had invited a fifth bid without their knowledge. I was just sitting in my corner, sipping coffee, and praying, "Dear God, let me sell this guy my flowers."

The secretary came over and asked in a whisper who I was and what company I represented. I was not yet aware that I had just somehow completed a major national security breach. I was an unknown man with a briefcase in the office of the man that controlled the nuclear reactor which was less that a football field away. I just so happened to step in the line of men expected for a meeting with the plant director, and none of the guards knew I was not part of the team. I was not trying to be secretive. I was just wanting to talk with some-one who could say yes to fifty-thousand tulips and daffodils. "Who are you with again?" she asked.

I told her I was with myself. To this day, I remember her face.

Very confused, she said, "I'm sorry?"

I told her I was with myself.

She said that she did not understand.

I said that I was not sure what the problem was and that I was with myself.

She then asked why I was there.

I wish I could capture the look she gave when I told her my busi-ness. I said that I was there to ask Dr. Abercrombie to buy and let me plant fifty-thousand tulips and daffodils at the plant.

Her composure was such that I began to realize it was a serious issue with me being there. She was trying to act like it was not a big deal, but it was clearly a big deal. She informed me that Mr. Abercrombie was a very busy man and that she would take my card and have him call me. I knew if she had me leave, any chance I had to sell my flowers was gone. I also knew that the seriousness of my presence could possibly get me a few minutes with Mr. Abercrombie.

I told her that I understood and would not waste his time and would be fine waiting as long as I needed in order to speak with him. She went back to her desk and did not call security, so I was still good for the time being. So far so good.

It was over three hours later when Dr. Abercrombie walked in (more like ran) and said, "Gentlemen, sorry for the delay, it could not be helped."

The secretary stopped him and told him something and pointed to me. Dr. Abercrombie walked over to me and said, "I am sorry you waited," but he continued that he was much too busy to see me. I asked him to give me forty-five seconds and I would leave.

He turned and walked into what I found out was his private office and sat down and said, "Time is ticking." Behind him was a window with a view to a big patch of grass just outside the building.

I looked him in the eyes and said, "Dr. Abercrombie, I want to plant fifty-thousand tulips and daffodils outside your window there. Tell me to leave or sit down."

He paused, looked a little shocked, and then said, "Those are my favorite flowers in the world. Do it. My secretary will take care of whatever you need. Thank you." And with that, he signed my contract that I had written up while waiting and praying. He bought fifty-thousand tulip and daffodils without asking my price (45 cents each). The secretary smiled at me, and I told her we would be back the next morning to start planting.

The bed would be fifty-thousand daffodils and tulips with the plant monogram in the middle for $22,500. I asked her to copy the signed contract, if she would. As I left, I was able to see just how crazy it was that I just walked in, uninspected or questioned, into Dr. Abercrombie's office. I spent five hours there, but God answered my prayers and he sold the flowers!

I went back and told Bill and we made everything ready to plant the flowers the next day. We figured it would take three to four days. We got to the plant the next morning to drive to the spot where Dr. Abercrombie's window view could see the bed. It took us two hours to pass security. There were armed guards watching us as we worked.

We began laying out the bed, and a man walked up who was the financial director for the plant. He introduced himself and joked about how everyone heard the story of the flower bed and told us that we were becoming famous. He then said that the plant was a government facility and that if we wanted to finish the job and get paid, we had better not leave until it was done.

Our process was to cut an outline the shape of the bed in the ground. Then we would dig out the dirt ten inches to twelve inches deep. We took all the dirt out of the bed and spread it on these large rubber mats. We would then mix bone mill with the dirt. Next, we would place the bulbs every six inches from each other by color and pattern for the desired effect. This bed was to be a solid yellow field with red and other colored tulips blooming in the middle in the shape of the plant's monogram.

After placing the fifty-thousand tulips in the bed, we sprinkled the dirt over them carefully at first so as not to turn them over and causing them not to bloom. After the bulbs were covered with enough dirt to keep them in place, we filled the rest of the bed with dirt and spread it out evenly. We then covered it with a thick layer of pine straw. The flower bed was the size of a small parking lot and the dirt was rock hard.

After thirty-plus hours and four shovels broken, we finished. The financial guy came out and watched while he was there. The next day, it was past four o'clock, and Bill and I were dead tired, but we were finally finished. The financial guy came to us and took our invoice.

It was a week and a half from my wedding and I needed $3,000. The financial guy asked us if we were Christians, and we told him we were. He said he thought so because the Lord had spoken to him. He shared that he would process our invoice before he left that day, but we would not be paid for five or six months. He said the government pays when they want and he said they probably will not pay you the full amount. He told us not to expect but 60–80 percent. Then he took out his own checkbook and wrote us a check for the full amount. He said that was what the Lord told him to do. He asked us to please send him the check in the mail when the government sent it, and we shook hands and he paid us in full.

That guy had no idea how important that money was to us and that we couldn't wait five to six months for it. God spoke to him, and he paid us on time and for the total amount they owed. He took our word and a handshake on paying him back as the check would come in my name.

It came eight months later, and it was 65 percent of what they owed. I took the check to him and told him I was sorry they cheated us out of the rest. He said he knew that would happen, and I signed the check over to him. I thanked him for his willingness to do what God said and for his sacrifice.

After we finished that job, we both slept for a day and a half. We paid all our overhead, and I was able to pay all my debts. I paid off the college, my other debts, the wedding expenses, our honeymoon, and had $28 left over. I look back at that and am amazed at how much God works in our lives as we trust him and pray. That man that paid us was doing what God told him to do, but God used that man to meet our needs on top of everything else that God did to help. I am thankful for his obedience to the voice of God, and I pray I do the same thing every time he speaks to me.

If You Play, You Pay!

S haron and my first ministry after college was at a church in south Georgia. We took the assistant pastor and camp director position. Our church had a summer camp. It was a good little church, and we saw a lot of teens make decisions to follow Christ at camp. We lived in a little apartment in the gym, and my responsibilities included working with the teens, bus ministry, and camp as well as being the church custodian. Our pay was just enough to almost pay our bills, but God always took care of us.

Sharon was pregnant with our first child, and we did not have insurance. We found a little hospital in a small town twenty-eight miles away that agreed to let us have our baby there by making payments. I was always gone working in the church or at the camp. I'm sorry to say Sharon was left with many lonely hours; too many.

As we were getting closer to Donald's delivery date, Sharon would ask some of the moms in our church questions about what giving birth was like. I know you ladies say we men are rude and crude and mean sometimes when we talk. There is nothing in this life as cruel as a woman telling a first-time mother what she is going to go through having her baby.

Sharon would ask a woman about what labor pains felt like, and the woman would say stuff like it felt like you are passing a forty-pound watermelon. Or the ladies would share a story about the woman who was in labor for sixty hours and died just as the baby was born.

Thank the Lord my wife is tougher than most women and was not afraid. But some of the stories the ladies would tell her was just plain wrong.

We had an old car that was on its last leg when we got it. The hospital was a forty-five-minute drive from where we stayed. I just wanted to make sure we could all get to the hospital in time, including the doctor.

We came to the due date and were nervously watching for any sign. This one night, we were just going to bed, and Sharon had a little bit of indigestion. Nothing bad or suspicious. I was trying to sleep, but I kept noticing that Sharon was constantly getting up and going to the bathroom. I would ask her if she was okay, and she would say she was, but she just felt like she needed to throw up. She did not feel any pressure or pain but just like she needed to throw up.

This went on for a few hours, so I began to think something was happening with the baby. Sharon was like, "No, it's not the baby, because I'm not in death pains."

At about three in the morning, I couldn't sleep, and I noticed that Sharon's need to throw up was happening at the exact same intervals of time between each one. It was every fifty-seven seconds that she was having the same type of need to throw up. I suggested to Sharon she may be in labor, but we were not sure. I called the pastor and asked him, "Pastor, how do you know when you are in labor?"

He said he didn't know and we hung up.

The afternoon before, Pastor left his new car at the church and had asked me to pick him up in the morning to go to the camp. His car was a 5th Avenue with a 318 motor in it, and it would move. Anyway, Sharon was in the bathroom, trying to throw up, and her water broke. She started getting the urge to push. We were forty-five minutes from the hospital, and it was 3:00 in the morning.

I called the hospital and told them we were on our way and Sharon was having pressure every fifty seconds and wanting to push. I laid her in the backseat of Pastor's car and told her to relax (but not too much). The drive was thirty miles to the hospital, straight country road, with one little red light in a small town halfway there. I opened that 5th Avenue up, and we were clicking 140 miles an hour toward the hospital. It was after three in the morning, and the roads were empty.

I was coming up on the little town and could see a car with lights on, but it was not moving. I blew through the red light with horn blaring and pedal still to the floor. I could see way behind me blue lights after that, but I was faster and too far ahead. We pulled into the hospital in just over thirty minutes.

I pulled up to the emergency room entrance and ran in and grabbed a nurse to help. She came out to the car and asked if this was our first baby, and we said yes. She said it was probably a false alarm and that we were probably overreacting. She asked if she could check and see, and Sharon told her that she felt the need to push constantly. The nurse checked Sharon and felt Donald's head. She started screaming orders, and they came out got her on a stretcher, grabbed a doctor (who had never delivered a baby before), and twenty minutes later, Donald was born.

The police pulled in behind us after Sharon was already inside and said he figured I was heading to the hospital. He said he wanted to give me an escort but couldn't catch up to me. Donald was born, and Sharon was the only one in the maternity ward except a little field mouse Sharon saw from time to time.

A few weeks after she and Donald came home from the hospital, a funny thing happened. It was my job to put the little saying on the sign at the church so people driving by could read. One of the sayings I used all the time at Temple University was that "if you play, you pay." I had put that up on the sign at the church. Sharon wanted to send a picture of that to our friends back at school.

Sharon went out into the churchyard and was taking a picture of the sign when she decided that she needed to send them a picture of the baby. So Sharon rolled Donald over to the sign and parked his stroller where they could read the sign and see Donald in the same picture. She took a couple of pictures and sent them to our friends. They got her letter, and when they opened it, there was a picture of a sign saying, "If You Play, You Pay," and a newborn baby sitting right there under it. They laughed so hard! Sharon never put the two together until they called her over it, and we all had a good laugh. It's true; in life, "if you play, you pay!"

Camp Cat

One of my jobs in south Georgia was taking care of the camp that our church owned and ran. It was a small camp with about 200 kids a week and around 1,000 kids per summer. When I say one of my responsibilities was camp, I mean I was directing, running each week of camp, as well as being custodian and taking care of all maintenance. The camp was thirty miles back into the swampland between Georgia and Florida just above the Florida state line. It was 150 acres of land that was composed of fifty acres of camp and 100 acres of swamp and marshland. It had a small lake and several buildings and cabins for speakers, visitors, and us when we were there. The camp had a pool with a surrounding privacy (modesty) fence. There was one more thing that the camp had; it had a feral cat.

This cat was wild, but it would let you feed it. Our pastor's wife fell in love with this cat, so I had to put up with it. It was mean unless you were Pastor's wife or had food for it. This cat would cause problems by chewing into the insulation of the buildings, making messes, and damaging the screens protecting the crawl spaces of our buildings. One other thing this camp had was ridiculously large rattlesnakes. Whenever I was working at the camp, I carried a pistol in a holster to kill the snakes. These things were six feet long.

We had a weekend pastors' conference coming up, and I was having to live at the camp in order to wake the camp up for the coming summer season. My job was to prepare the sleeping quarters for the preachers coming in the following weekend for the conference. During these days, I was very seldom home to see my family. I pulled into the camp on the Monday before the coming weekend conference. We had cabins, but our trailer was reserved for our speakers, which was a double-wide mobile home. It had three bedrooms and was fully furnished. It was nice enough and beat having to do the forty-five-minute drive one-way from the closest hotel.

I stayed in one of the rooms while I was working at the camp. I was there all week trying to get everything ready, not to mention make any repairs needed and do the ground maintenance.

I pulled into the camp and was already missing my wife, Sharon, and my newborn, Donald. It had been a few months since anyone had been in the guesthouse. So when I opened the door, I expected a musty closed-up smell. What I was not expecting was thousands of those huge blowflies. They are big nasty flies that are always surrounding dead things. The double-wide was swarming with thousands of these flies which were in every space in the house. The place smelled like something had died in there a while ago, and the place was toxic.

I searched the entire trailer for whatever poor thing had died and did not find anything. I noticed that flies were coming in and out of the vents (all of them) in the floors. The mobile home was on a two-foot crawl space with skirting around it. I had to lay on my back and crawl backward into the entrance with a flashlight to check out the insulation under the trailer. There was insulation between the floor joists and a thick felt-type paper stapled to each joist to keep out moisture and any animals that might want a warmer place to live in winter.

When I looked under the trailer, I quickly became aware of the problem. The camp cat had made a way into the crawl space of the trailer and had clawed or chewed her way into the floor space. She had managed to pull enough of it off the staples so that the felt hung down into what looked like a giant hammock that she had been living in. As I looked closer, she decided to start a little family under there and had a big litter of baby kittens. Either she had them and abandoned them, or she had them and the insulation killed them. But her litter of kittens had crawled all over the area and in different directions and died.

The cat had chewed some of the flex duct from the AC, and the flies were in and out of the ventilation system. The cats had been there long enough to where they were almost withered and dry. However, they were not yet too dry for the flies to move on.

Pastor did not want to spend the money on the fumigation of the trailer and removal of the dead kitties. I was given the burden of the job. I had to shut up the trailer and put bug bombs off in the different rooms throughout the trailer. I then washed everything in the trailer from all cloth items to everything in the drawers and cabinets. I had to steam clean the carpets and clean the floors. My last thing was to crawl under the trailer and find every dead cat and remove it. It was a huge amount of work.

I got a knife, flashlight, and plastic bag and crawled under the trailer on my back. I would crawl back and forth, tapping on the felt, listening till I heard a kitten bounce, and then I would have to cut the felt and reach in and grab a very dead and gushy stiff kitty and pull it out and into the bag. It was a hot day, and I was extremely hot when I had just found the eighth kitty. I was crawling toward the back end of the trailer and was about three-quarters of the way toward having the job done when I heard a very large rattle start sounding off just a few feet from my head behind me. I had been under there for three-plus hours, crawling on my back, soaking wet with sweat, playing with dead animals. I was at a point where there was not much room between the floor and the ground. I was almost stuck and cramped.

When the rattle started, I had no way of turning and seeing where the snake was or its size. I could tell he was big by the number of rattles that were rattling, and he was much closer than I wanted him to be. He had to be close enough to strike my head. No sudden moves were my thought, and I very slowly started crawling forward toward the opening. I could not turn around to crawl out backward because I would have to move closer to the snake to do it, and he would have bitten me. I kept waiting for the strike and kept moving awkwardly away from the rattling.

After what seemed like hours (a few minutes), I was far enough away for the snake to calm down and stop rattling. I turned around and was able to crawl out a lot faster.

When I got close to the entrance, I hit my head hard on the frame of the door. That was it. I was wet, covered in dirt, smelling like dead kitty, and had a big knot on my head after having to run from a snake. I looked up and did see one thing but did not see the other thing. The one thing I saw was that stupid cat that had caused all this (plus much more in the past), standing over by the dining hall watching. She looked like she was laughing at me for having to clean up her dirty work. I thought, *That's it.*

I walked into the dining hall and got a can of tuna from the food closet. I walked to the toolshed and got a shovel. I walked to the trailer and got my holster. I went over and picked out a lovely spot just under a tree in the shade. I dug a hole about three feet deep and two feet wide (perfect fit). I opened the tuna and called, "Here kitty, kitty, kitty," and I put the tuna can in the bottom of the hole. The cat ran over and jumped in the hole and started eating the tuna. I drew my pistol and sent mommy cat to go meet her little kitties. I covered her up with the shovel. I still had a third of the trailer to search for more dead kittens and a big snake to get rid of, but I was feeling much better about things now that justice was served.

159

That is when I found out what I did not see when I came out from under the trailer. Over across the field from the trailer was the pool. The privacy fence was so the ladies could lay out in the sun without being seen by unwelcome eyes. What I did not see, because of the fence, was the pastor's wife's car parked on the other side of the fence, out of view. As I already had the pool woken up, she and one of the church women came for a swim and to get some sun. I did not see her.

As I had put the last bit of dirt over Miss Kitty, I heard Pastor's wife shout out, "Brother Frank, did you do what I think you just did?"

I just went back to work and acted like I didn't hear her. I finished the kitty hunting, got rid of the six-foot-long rattlesnake, and stapled the felt back in place. I patched the chew holes in the felt with a smile and finished "de-deathing" the trailer. I felt much more relieved, and after several curtain and carpet cleanings, the trailer was livable and fly free.

Pastor called me later that evening and asked if I killed the camp cat. He said his wife and one of the deacon's wives heard me cursing, then they heard a loud, "Hear kitty, kitty, kitty," and then a loud boom. Then they thought they heard what sounded like a shoveling sound. I told the preacher that the cat would not be putting dead kittens in anymore of our building's floor spaces. It was some time until Pastor's wife would have much to say to me, but that cat needed killing!

Snake Hunting!

South Georgia and the surrounding areas are known for their huge rattlesnakes throughout that part of Georgia, rattlesnakes thrive and grow to become large long snakes. In my experience with snakes, rattlesnakes are not as mean as moccasins, dry land and especially cottonmouth moccasins which are mean. Rattlesnakes will warn you, and unless they are shedding or sitting on a nest with babies, they prefer not to bite. If you step on them or surprise them, they will get you.

In the swampland of our camp, rattlesnakes were pretty numerous. We had to keep a watch for them during camps or meetings with so many people walking around. I kept a pistol on me while working at camp, just for the snakes. The camp was also home to gophers. In the fields and woods around the camp, gopher holes were everywhere. You had to be careful because you could trip or drive the lawn mower tires into them. Cows and horses could hurt their legs stepping into them. One of the best ways to catch snakes was to find old gopher holes, and as often as not, one would be down in there.

If you poked a piece of garden hose down the hole and poured a little gas in the end of it and then blew on it, the fumes would bring the rattler right out of the hole in a hurry, then you could catch him. It does not take many holes until you find one. The ground was so sandy, and if the snake was big enough, it's weight would leave tracks, showing where it went in and out of the hole. You could look and tell which holes were occupied and which were for rent (in the snake world).

One of the guys in our church was a great guy. Terry was a singer, a musician, a good preacher, and my friend. We would often work out at the camp or be there at the same time, and I invited him to hunt rattlesnakes with me many times. One day, Terry decided he was ready to hunt with me, so we got our stuff and took off through the backwoods of the camp, looking for a good gopher hole. It did not take long to find one.

Terry was a big old boy at the time, well over 350 pounds. I told him that we would slip the hose down the hole until the hose hit bottom. We pushed this one down and poured about an ounce of gas down the hose. I told Gary to get on his hands and knees and blow on the hose. I said for him to stay on his hands and knees and keep staring into the hole, so he could see when it came out.

Gary was afraid of snakes and was very nervous. He had never hunted snakes and did not know what to expect. I told him to stay on his knees and keep looking down the hole because I knew the snake was coming out fast, but Terry didn't know that. I also knew that the snake would be stretched out, coming up the hole, and not likely be able to strike without Terry being able to move (hopefully).

The snake was stubborn and waited longer than normal coming out, so we were just about to move on and look for another hole. Just as Terry was starting to get up, the snake came out hot. I was staring, ready to catch the snake before it could bite one of us, when it came flying out of the hole. It popped out, face-to-face with Terry! In my life, I have never seen a 350-pound man move from a kneeling position to an upright and running position going in the opposite direction that fast. Terry saw that snake coming right at his face and, in one instant, was up in the air, running away from the snake before the snake got to him. I was amazed.

It was the funniest and most acrobatic thing I have ever seen. In fact, I was laughing so hard, the snake came all the way out of the hole and slithered away while I was laying down, laughing my hardest. It was great. We did not catch the snake, but I got a good laugh, and Terry got the chance to get up close and personal with a six-foot-long rattlesnake. Good times!

Knee Deep in Poop

S ome of the things we do in the name of ministry is insane. I was working at the church as teen director, bus ministry, children's church leader, custodian, visitation, and anything else that the pastor needed done. I was also director for the camp, groundskeeper, maintenance for church and camp, and anything else the camp needed. I was supposed to have a day off once a week but never got it. I was paid $95 a week and not allowed to do side jobs for extra money. It got to a place where we barely paid our bills on time. I was always gone, often for days at a time, sleeping at the camp. I seldom saw my wife or new son except on rare occasions when I had the day off, and then we were so broke, I could not do anything with my family.

One day, I was at a pastor's meeting, sitting at a table beside my pastor with other pastors from our area. My pastor spoke up to the others, suggesting that he wanted to have a special three-day conference at the camp for assistant pastors. He said, "We need a conference training our assistants better, because my assistant is not doing a good job, and none of yours are either."

I was the only assistant pastor sitting at the table as he said this. I did not say anything there because in our group, pastors didn't listen to assistants. But I thought about all the things I was responsible for but with no say on the money for any of it. I was the one blamed for everything that was not up to expectations but with no power to make decisions about any of it. I was his whipping post.

164

I promised God when I was called that I would do whatever he told me to do. I spent the weeks after that lunch, asking God if he was the one I was working for, or was it for a man? I was struggling in my marriage and in everything I was doing. I finally decided that I was not going to lose my family working at our church. I told my wife I was going to resign, and a few days later, I told the pastor I was leaving as soon as camp was over that year.

He could not do it at his age, and he would not be able to get someone else in this short of a time. So I told him I would stay on the next few months until after camp, then I was gone. He had just scheduled the assistant pastor's retreat and asked me not to mention my leaving until after that.

Before the conference, we needed to add to our men's restroom at the camp. We added two more toilets to give us four total, two more urinals, and one new shower. All were needed. I had to break up the concrete floor with a sledgehammer and run a new drain line to the septic tank. The pastor had a plumber set the new lines, and I was to mix and fill in the floor with new concrete. I asked the pastor to run six-inch lines for four toilets and six urinals. He decided to save money and ran three-inch lines to the septic tank. I filled in the floor and set the toilets and urinals.

A few days before the conference, we had a work day at the camp, and during lunch, the toilets and urinals backed up from overuse. We had fifteen men that day and would have eighty-plus in a few days and 200 boys a week after that.

Pastor decided to dig out the place where the feed went into the septic tank and bust the pipe and then hand-feed the septic tank through the top until after the conference.

So as you can imagine, the conference came and we had over eighty men, both pastors and assistants in attendance. During the first session, I was sitting in the service, and my pastor was speaking. He mentioned that he required me to take a day off every week with-out fail and that it was important to pay your staff enough. I was furious. It had been months since I had a day off, and I was behind on every bill I had. But I did not say anything.

We had a thirty-minute break, and Preacher came up and told me the toilets were backed up and I needed to fix it. I changed into my janitor clothes and went behind the guy's dorm to the septic tank and dug out the top and side of the tank where the line went into the tank. I dug a pit about three feet deep and four feet around and cut the pipe. I do not need to tell you what came out of the pipe and filled the pit. I had a scoop on a pole and was scooping and emptying the sewage into the tank opening on top. I spent the rest of that day servicing the septic tank by hand.

That afternoon, my pastor sat at lunch with Dr. Faulkner and Dr. Price (the two speakers). He mentioned to Dr. Faulkner that I told him I was leaving and asked him if he would try to talk me into staying. I was not at lunch or dinner as I was trying to keep the septic tank pit from overflowing into the yard.

After dinner, and the guests had finished showers, I was able to finish my duties with the septic tank and went to the trailer where I was staying. I took a much-needed shower and was sitting on the porch, trying to calm down from being mad all day. I was not in the best frame of mind for fellowship.

Dr. Faulkner came out and joined me, and we caught up on the past few years. He was assistant pastor to Dr. Roberson at Tennessee Temple, and we were good friends. After a few minutes, Dr. Faulkner mentioned he knew I was resigning from the church. He asked me what it would take to change my mind. I thanked Dr. Faulkner, because I knew he was a man of character and cared about my family. I did not mention my reasons and just told him my mind was settled and no more discussion was needed. He shortly went back to his flyless room.

The next day, after breakfast, the septic tank problem grew worse. I, by necessity, had to get into the pit where I was knee to waist deep in raw fresh sewage, feeding it into the tank with a bucket. I had been doing this for several hours, and Bradley Price walked around the corner. He asked if I would take a shower and sit with him for a minute. I did not know him other than by reputation and had no idea what he wanted. I was also at my breaking point with anger and was not in the best mind to talk with someone I did not know. I did, however, agree to meet with him, and I ran and cleaned up and changed.

Dr. Price said he had talked with Dr. Faulkner and knew I was leaving. I told him to mind his own business, and I guess I was staring at him in a not so friendly way. He said he was not trying to talk me into staying but wanted to talk with me about coming to work at Central Baptist Church in Panama City, Florida. I looked at him and told him I was through with ministry and was planning on leaving where I was and doing something else.

He asked me how long it had been since I had any time off, and I told him over four months. He said the he wanted to talk with me and took out his church credit card and told me to bring my family down the next week—for a week—and they would pay expenses and put us up in a nice room. He got my phone number and got in his car and drove away.

I did not know him, but I had his credit card and an invitation to Florida to visit. Dr. Price told my pastor he invited me spend the next week with him about possibly working for him. He said it would make up for all those days he insisted I take off in the past four months.

I was at a place where I was ready to quit serving God. I felt like I was a complete failure to God and to my wife and in my ministry. I just wanted to make enough money so my wife could pay our bills and get a new dress every once in a while. I was through. I spent the next day finishing the septic duties (no pun intended) and getting ready to go home for Sunday as it was Saturday night. I did not have a chance to tell my wife until the next day. On Sunday, I told my wife we were going to Florida for a week and leaving the next day.

Looking back on it now, I wanted so badly to serve God, and I thought doing whatever my pastor asked me to do was part of serving. I had damaged my family, pushed my wife past reasonable limits, and drove myself to near exhaustion. I should have never let myself and my wife endure such things.

I went down to Panama City and, by the end of the week, was soon to be working for Dr. Price at the Central Baptist Church. God opened a door that I needed him to open, even though I did not ask for it. God took me from the miry pit and put my feet on dry ground! Literally!

Central Baptist Church

We finished the summer of camp at Valdosta as I had promised to do. Central Baptist Church waited for me, and to do so as was very kind of them. We needed a house, and the church needed to sell a house, so we agreed to buy it sight unseen. It was an old military housing small brick home with one bath and two bedrooms. It was old, but my wife made it a home.

We had our next two boys in that home. Our church was running about 300 in services when we got there, and it was home to a large private school. I was the lowest paid person on staff but was thankful for it compared to my previous church's pay. God blessed us, and I had one of the best church experiences of my life at that church. We grew to over 1,200 in attendance and had many people come to Christ during the six years we were there. I have many friends and fond memories to this day from Central.

One of the funny things in my early days at Central happened on my way to work one morning. Our house was a little more than a mile to our church and on the same street the church was on. It was a straight shot. My wife and I had only one vehicle, so on days she needed the car, I would walk to church and leave her the car. It was on such a morning that this funny thing happened.

We had been at Central just barely a month when one morning, my wife needed the car, so I decided to walk the mile to my office. I have always been terrible with remembering new people's names and their faces. It's terrible for a preacher to be this way, but there you have it. I was just down the street from my house a little after seven in the morning. It was a nice and sunny but not too hot a fall morning.

As I was walking, this Cadillac passed me on the street and stopped next to the curb near where I was walking. As I kept walking, the driver started blowing her horn. She was a little way down from me. I looked through her back window and did not recognize her at all, so I just kept walking. She blew her horn again and again. I looked but did not recognize her face. She blew her horn a fourth time, and it finally dawned on me. She was one of the older ladies in our church and recognized me walking and decided to pull over and give me a ride to work.

I was enjoying my walk and really did not want a ride, but I did not want to make some old lady who may be some deacon's wife mad. So I walked up to the car and opened the front passenger door and sat down. I shut the door and looked at the lady to thank her.

When I looked at her, she had a horrified look on her face. She was ready to pass out. She was so afraid. I calmly looked at her and said, "Ma'am, I don't know you!"

She screamed at me, "Who are you and why did you get into my car?"

I said that I was walking to work when she pulled over. I was new to the church, so I did not recognize her but did not want to make her mad. She blew her horn four times at me. I jumped in so I would not upset her. She looked, still wide-eyed and said, "I pulled up to pick up my ride for work and she is late. That's why I am blowing the horn." She pointed to the house next to where she had stopped.

When she got through telling me that, I looked right at her and said, "Well, miss, in that case, you have a great day!" I opened the car door and got out and started walking away. I was a little down the road from where it happened when I looked back, and she was just sitting there, staring at me as I was walking away. Angels unawares!

You Cuss Just Like a Marine

One of my duties at Panama City was to visit door-to-door, inviting people to our church. Our staff spent a lot of time visiting, and we mapped out our county, devising a plan to invite every family to our church and to Christ each year. It was a very hard but rewarding task. People don't like to be bothered at home, and I don't blame them. When they see you coming, they automatically think you are a Jehovah's Witness or Mormon or salesman. I know that God will, from time to time, work out a situation where you are at the right place at the right time, and then God does a thing in the person's heart.

On one such day, I was visiting, and there was this house with a huge yard and long sandy driveway. They had a posted sign on the gate and a very unwelcoming presence with the property. I opened the gate and began walking up the driveway to the side door, under the garage. I noticed about five holes in the screen when I approached the door.

From inside, I heard a loud voice asking who the blank I was and why I was on his property, followed by a long few sentences of cussing. I could see through the screen there was a woman who had her back to the door (me), sitting at a small kitchen table. Facing her and now me was a very drunk and very mad man pointing a carbine rifle over her head and out the door right at me. I soon found out the five holes where just put there as the man was shooting over the woman's head through the screen. I was looking down the muzzle of his rifle.

"Who are you?" he asked, pointing the gun with intent.

I was a little caught off-guard, and the woman had turned her head and looked as if she had been through hell and back. I spoke through the door and said, "I am Frank Penley, and you, sir, cuss just like a Marine."

He came to the door and opened it, grabbed my hand to shake it, and rattled off his rank and division he served under in Vietnam. He invited me into his house and into his living room and we sat down on the couch. He started telling me stories of being a Marine. His wife looked exhausted and was almost afraid to move. She could see us plainly as we sat on her couch, and fear was all over her face. The man had set the rifle down, and it was safe enough for her to relax for a minute.

I asked the man if he had any coffee, and he yelled at his wife to make me some. He pulled out his photo album and began showing me all his combat and Marine pictures. When the lady brought me the coffee, I thanked her, and she was looking at me nervously as her husband was hanging on my arm, showing me his life. I winked at her with the eye that her husband could not see and thanked her as I sipped the coffee.

Within the hour, the man passed out sitting beside me with his head slumping over on my shoulder. She said if he stayed asleep for a little while, he would not wake up but that he could come right awake any minute. She whispered that her husband was a Vietnam vet and that he had seen a lot of action and lost a lot of friends. She said he was a hardworking friendly man that very seldom did this type of thing. She continued that he had been having bad dreams lately and that something else happened (I don't remember now) that had got him in a bad frame of mind. She said that he had been drinking for three days and had turned mean. He forced her to stay up with him.

When I came to the door, she was afraid for her life. He, a little while before that, forced her to sit at the table, and he sat in a chair across the table from her. He was shooting over her head anytime she moved. She said she had never been that afraid with him before and that he had never been that violent.

I told her that if she needed to, she could lay down for a few minutes and I would sit there until she felt he was passed out for good. I sat there for over an hour, and she lay her head down for forty-five minutes or so. Then she got up and went into her room and cleaned up. She called a friend, or it might have been their son, and he came over and carried Sergeant to bed. When I left, the wife hugged me and thanked me for coming and said she was praying for God to save her when I knocked on the door. I assured her that it was God and that he had a plan and a will for both her and her husband's life. She said she was a believer, but her husband was not.

I went back to visit them a few days later and had a long talk with them at their table. The man was, in fact, a very kind and soft-spoken type of guy and was very ashamed of his actions. He thanked me for what I had done and agreed to seek help so he would not put his wife or family in danger again. I was also able to witness him accept Christ, with his wife rededicating her life back to Christ. They were baptized and came to our church for several months. It was fun watching the work God did in that old veteran and his wife's lives.

I have lived long enough that I don't judge a person for their sins. God and Jesus are the only ones who can do that. I believe that any person that is in a relationship that is dangerous or abusive should protect themselves. I also think that as badly as that old boy was behaving, he could have shot one of us. He was also a veteran. Not an excuse for his actions, but a man I chose to respect and forgive. God did and worked in their lives and entered their lives right where he found them. Thank you, Lord!

I'm Asking You Outside

One of my jobs at Central was to handle the ten buses that picked up the kids for our Christian school. I was responsible for the routes and the stops for each kid. It was not that much work, except a few times a year and at the first of each semester. I had an office in the back of our pastoral offices. It was down the hall, a right turn, then past Brother Jerry's office, and then my office. Past that was a door that opened into the elementary school hall where a right took you to the dining hall and school, and a left took you outside on the side of our office building. It was just a few steps and through two doors, and I was outside. Brother Jerry was our music pastor and a very great man and friend!

A forty-five-minute drive away from our church was an air force base. We had several kids coming from the base and one kid who rode the bus. It was an hour and half some days with traffic before the kid would get home. It worked out well for the parents, because they both did not get home from work before then. It also helped the bus driver, because they made a little more money driving the longest route.

One school year, just after the kinks had been worked out of the new bus routes, the state of Florida passed a new mandatory law that no kid could be on a bus route over one hour in length. It was not a big deal for anybody else, but it was for the one kid just mentioned. It was twenty to thirty minutes from the last stop before this kid got to his house. There was no other route going anywhere close

176

to his home but the one he was riding. I had to either have a school van drive him home by himself or find a solution the parents could live with.

I could not have a van drive forty-five minutes one way, two times a day, five days a week given budget restraints. I asked around and found a mother who would be willing to watch the kid until his parents came and got him. It was the best I could do given I had two weeks to implement the new law. I wrote a note home to all the bus students stating the law and stating the changes in policy.

Again, the only family really affected was this one kid who lived on Tyndall Air Force Base. I asked some of the other parents who picked up their kids if they could take him, but no one wanted the responsibility. It was down to him getting off at the one-hour stop and being watched until he was picked up (which the family that would watch him was willing to do) or not riding the bus. I had no other choice.

The mother called me, as expected, and explained that they did not get home until 5:30. I explained that this was a new state law and could not ignore it. I also informed her that I could not have a van drive one and a half hours, twice a day, for one rider. She understood and mentioned her husband was going to be upset. I told her about the family who was willing to watch him for a fee.

A few days later, I was working in my office when I got a call from a distraught parent. I took the call, and it was this rider's dad. He introduced himself and then began telling me I had better come up with a solution better than that I offered his wife or he was coming to see me personally. I told him the same thing I told his wife and said he had one and a half weeks to decide. He said that he had paid the year's tuition in full and that we had a signed agreement that we would provide transportation for his child for the year.

I referred him to the letter informing them of the changed state law, and that law forced a change in his contract. I mentioned that I had a family who was willing to watch him for a price. He said that the school had to pay for the family to watch their child. I told him that he had one and a half weeks to decide if he wanted to stay on the bus and let that family watch their son. He cussed at me and said he would be talking to his lawyer. I told him to have the lawyer explain the state's letter to him, and he hung up. I did not think a thing about it.

The next week, I was in my office again and was told I had an upset parent on line one. I picked up the phone and was greeted by the dad of this rider, cussing at me in a very loud voice. He cussed and called me everything but a Christian. He kept cussing at me, not letting me get a word in edgewise. After four or five minutes, I was through with being cussed out by someone on the phone. I finally stopped the guy and told him that I was not going to listen to his cussing me from behind a phone. I told him if he wanted to cuss at me, he was going to have to be willing to do it to my face and hung up. Jerry, in the other office, told me he could hear the cussing from his office.

About two hours later, this guy walks into my office, without knocking, in an Air Force uniform. He was a middle-aged man who was obviously a weight lifter. He was cut and very angry. My office was small, and if a person walked in the door, there was just enough room for two chairs and my desk and my chair behind the desk. So this guy barged in without knocking and started cussing very loudly and pointing his finger at me.

I was startled, at first, at his rudeness. I sat there, determined not to lose my temper with him. In the other office, Jerry told me later, he was just waiting to see how much I was going to take. He tried to console me with, "I did much better than he expected."

This guy cussed me and would tell me to shut up if I tried to respond. "Shut up and listen, I'm talking now," he would say. He was an officer and had some rank, but I didn't know how much. After what seemed like ten minutes or so, he was still going strong, but I had enough of this and was about at my limit of being nice and understanding.

The man took a breath and then said the words, "And now that I am through with you, let me tell you what I think of your pastor." He then started cussing about Dr. Price. Pastor gave me a chance when I was at a low place. He also was a hard man to work for, but he was fair and taught me a lot about leadership. He also was family to me and my pastor.

When the old boy started on Doc, I stood up and took off my suit coat and started taking off my tie. The guy, still cussing, got this confused look on his face as I was taking my tie off. He stopped and asked me why I was taking my tie off. I said I was taking it off so he could not try and choke me with it as I kicked his butt.

He stopped cursing and asked, "What do you mean?"

I said that I had been as kind as I possibly could with him and that I was done with him cussing at me. I continued, "But when you said what you did about my pastor, you violated one of my principles." I said to him that now I was going to whip him. I asked him if he would step outside as a gentleman or did he want his butt kicking here in my office?

Then the guy started making excuses and trying to apologize. I got mad after that. When he started crying and giving excuses, I lost it and came around the desk after him. He took off down the hall and into the front office, screaming, "He's crazy! He's crazy!" and he ran out the door of the church office.

I came through the doors from our offices, trying to catch the guy, and there was an office full of church people and our secretarial staff staring at me. I stopped chasing the man at that point and walked back to my office. I was so mad, I had to sit there for a long while before I spoke to anyone else.

Directly, Brother Jerry (whom I respected) came over to my office and said that he had heard everything. He said that he was surprised that I took it for as long as I did. He said he also knew the minute he started on Dr. Price, I was going to get him. In any case, he said he was proud that I did as good as I did and that he was getting to the point where he was getting upset.

Every Thursday, we had a pastor's staff meeting for the first half of the day. It was mandatory, and the only non-pastor person allowed was Sheila (Pastor's secretary) who had to attend. It was in this meeting that Dr. Price would deal with any issues he felt needed to be addressed. It got hostile at times. The next Thursday, Dr. Price started the meeting by saying we had an issue to deal with as a staff. He went into how tight our budget was and that we did not have money to lose because of pastor's being incompetent in their duties and lacking self-control. After saying that, he asked the question, "Can anyone explain why an Air Force officer came screaming into the school office about somebody being crazy, saying he wanted a full refund for the year? He said he was taking his son out of this place. The school had to refund over $3,000 dollars." Then Dr. Price looked at me and asked again if anybody wanted to answer.

I sat there, not saying anything, waiting for whatever came next. Preacher asked several other staff, and Sheila said he came through our office too, yelling the same thing, but she did not know anything else. Finally, Preacher looked at me and said, ""Do you have any idea about this?"

I finally told him the situation and that I had tried but that the guy had just pushed me too far. Preacher was just about to tear into me and possibly fire me when Brother Jerry spoke up. He and Pastor were close, and Jerry was able to reason with him.

Jerry said to the preacher, "I was in the next room, and I heard everything that happened." He said, "Pastor, there was no way to work with that man and you, yourself, would not have been able to have it end any other way."

Preacher looked down at his notes and was silent for a few minutes, then looked up and said, "Okay, let's move on." I praise God for Jerry!

I'm Going to Kill His Kids

One of the things about working with people is that sometimes you end up upsetting people who are unstable or mean. This happened at Central with a transient guy passing through.

This young guy, twenty-three or so, was homeless and sitting on the side of the road with a "will work for food" sign. One of the young girls, sixteen, in our school talked her parents into giving him a place to stay until he got on his feet. They were advised against it but did it anyway.

The family had money and was also experiencing their share of problems. After a short time of living with them, this guy convinced the girl that nobody loved her but him. They stole some things from the parents and they ran away together with no indication of where they went. It was found out later that the girl was also pregnant. It was heartbreaking for her family and a sad situation.

A few weeks after she ran away with this guy, I found out that the guy was working for one of my good friends who was a brick mason. I asked him about the girl, and my friend said he didn't get involved with his employee's private lives. I asked him to get me an address of where the girl was so I could give some peace of mind to her poor mother who had heard nothing for weeks. I did not hear from my friend and forgot about it.

One day, I was visiting in a local trailer park, going door-to-door, and I came to this rundown trailer that looked almost abandoned. I knocked on the door, and to my surprise, the girl who had run away answered.

She had a black eye and swollen face where she had been hit several times. The trailer was cold and without electricity. The girl was pale and in poor health and looked like she was in prison more than a home. I asked her what was going on, and she broke down weeping. She told me that the guy soon began slipping into her room at night when they lived with her parents. He convinced her that nobody cared for her, but him, and that he loved her and wanted to marry her and have a family together.

She ran away with him and they rented this trailer. He started being aggressive and angry and hitting her. She told him she was going to leave him, and he told her he would kill her and her family if she did. He beat her up bad a few days before. There was no electricity or food in the house, and she was not allowed to leave without him or she would be beat. She was showing her pregnancy by this time and had no doctor visits.

I told her to get her clothes and get in my car. I took her home, and while she was still sitting in my car, I went to the door and told her parents that I had her, and if they would let her, she wanted to come home.

I sat with the family, and after a few hours, the dad and mom and girl prayed with me and rededicated their lives to their faith in Christ. They committed to pulling together as a family and working out the issues. A week or so later, the mom and daughter were sitting in church during a Wednesday night church service. Just before the service started, the guy who ran away with the girl walked in and came down to where the girl and her mom were seated. He sat down by the girl and the mom, causing the girl to start crying. The dad was out of town on business.

During a song at the beginning of the service, we had a time where we shook each other's hands. I walked down off the platform, and stuck my hand out to shake the guy's hand. When he reached his hand out, I grabbed his hand and pulled him away from the girl and moved into the seat by her and her mother. He sat down beside me. I told the girl and her mom not to worry, it would be okay.

When the church service was over and everyone was standing up to leave, the guy spoke past me and told the girl to come with him or else. He then reached out to try and grab the girl's arm. I grabbed his. I told him that the girl was not leaving and that he had better leave. He threatened to beat me up. I told him I would be a little more difficult for him to beat up than a pregnant teenager. I again asked him to leave or we would call the police, and so he turned and left. As he was leaving, I informed him the family was going to take out a restraining order. I let him know that I was going to the police about her bruises the next day. I warned him to stay away from their house and family.

The following day, Dr. Price called me into his office and informed me that the guy, while working for the brick mason, was running his mouth on the jobsite. He told the guys he was working with that he planned on coming by my house and throwing a gas bomb into my three boys' bedroom window, killing my kids. Ted fired him and called Dr. Price to warn him of what he heard. Dr. Price handed me a pistol and said I could hang on to it for a few days. The next few nights, I slept in the living room in a rocking chair where I could watch my front yard and my boys' window. I had something for that old boy if he came visiting.

On the fourth night, I got this feeling that something was going to happen, and I was edgy. It was about 1:30 in the morning, and I heard something coming from the bushes on the opposite side of the house. It was the only place I could not see if someone was coming up to the boys' window. I got up and went out my side door and inched up to the corner of my house, facing the boys window. I listened and heard the noise again, so I turned the corner with the pistol drawn down to shoot. There I stood in my underwear, gun pointed at John Russell, our church's teen director and my closest friend at the time. He was pointing a 12-gauge shotgun at me. I almost shot him as he said he almost shot me.

John said he knew I had not gotten much sleep the last few nights, and it being Friday night, if the guy was going to try something, it would probably be this night. He decided he would come over and wait in the bushes for the guy, just in case I was asleep. We agreed it would have been better if he had called. How funny would it have been if John and I shot each other in the bushes of my front yard in the middle of the night? The old boy never came, and last I heard, he had moved on down the road. The family made it and became a closer family from the trial.

Mr. Harsey

There was a man who lived in our area who had three sons and an old man living with him. His name was Mr. Harsey. He was a decorated Florida State trooper and one of the toughest men I have ever met. His boys were mean, and Mr. Harsey had that same reputation with those who did not know him closely. He was shot eleven times and killed thirteen men so far in his career, all in the line of duty. He was known and respected by everyone in law enforcement, and the governor or any other politician sought his endorsement when seeking election.

Mr. Harsey was not politically correct and spoke the truth, no matter what his circumstances. If you proved to be less than honest, he would tell you to your face (no matter who you were). He did not like liars or cheats and would walk away from you if you seemed to be either. If you went to his house, he would not answer the door, even if he was on the other side of the screen in sight of you. If he did not feel like talking, he would not talk. Even looking at you, he would not answer. The only hobby he had was bear hunting.

He hunted bears in the Florida swamps with his dogs and killed two every year using his service revolver. His wife left him when his boys were very young, and he never dated around his boys, all the way up to their college days. His wife who left him had her dad living with them as her dad's health was bad. After she left, Mr. Harsey took care of him until the old man died. He loved his boys but raised them rough.

One story about Mr. Harsey that I remember is there was a multi-state car chase with a wanted and dangerous felon. He was spotted by a police officer and grabbed a random little two to three-year-old girl as a hostage and jumped into a car and sped away. The chase was coming into Bay County at high speeds with multiple cars of law enforcement following from every place he had run through. It looked like a police car NASCAR race with a civilian car as the pace car. They were coming up a northbound two-lane highway with a median in the middle and two-lane southbound highway to their left. The highway was wooded on both sides.

The radio announced their position with speeds of well over 100 miles an hour. The man had killed multiple people without hesitation or preference. He had a three-year-old (estimated age) girl as a kidnapped hostage. The fear and thought was that even if he got away, he was going to kill the child. The highway had very light traffic at the time, so the man was speeding recklessly and unhindered.

From over the radio came Mr. Harsey's voice. He stated he was southbound on the highway, heading toward them, and would intercept the car. Mr. Harsey drove through the median and pulled his state cruiser into the two lanes blocking them both. He got out of his car, walked in front of the cruiser, and drew his service revolver and waited. Just a few seconds passed, and about three-quarters of a mile away, the felon came around the curve, speeding straight toward Mr. Harsey who was standing in front of his car, pointing his revolver at the man. The police cars behind the man all instantly hit the ditches and median when they saw Mr. Harsey.

Officer Harsey waited until the man, heading straight for him without slowing down, got as close as he wanted, and then he shot the man with one shot. The car veered of the highway into the brush, just feet from where Mr. Harsey stood. He had already called for an

187

ambulance that was en route for any wounds to the girl from the wreck.

The girl was recovered with a few scrapes and bruises, but nothing life-altering had happened. Mr. Harsey walked to the wrecked car and soon appeared walking out of the brush with the little girl in his arms. The man was no longer going to hurt anyone else. Mr. Harsey was rewarded for saving the girl's life.

His boy played football for the local high school and was all state in his position with several big colleges wanting him for their programs. The son was at a spring break party on Panama City Beach when a college guy came up behind his girlfriend and pinched her behind. Harsey's son turned around and confronted him, and the guy swung at Harsey's boy who then punched the guy one time, killing him. It was a freak thing, but the fact is the other guy who turned out to be a college football player died.

As a result, Harsey's boy was arrested and kicked out of school. The jury found Harsey's boy not guilty and he was free to go. Dr. Price visited Mr. Harsey and talked him into letting his son play for our school's football team.

After that, I got involved with the family. Rusty Price and I led Mr. Harsey's boy to the Lord. Rusty was Dr. Price's son and was good friends with Larkin (Mr. Harsey's son). It was Rusty who brought Larkin to a place to where he wanted to put his life in Jesus's hands. I ended up visiting their house from time to time.

They lived out of the city and in the county backroads. Mr. Harsey kept his house doors open with screen doors shut. I would go to the door and knock on it with Mr. Harsey standing by the stove four feet from me. I would knock, and he would look up at me and go back to whatever he was doing. Nothing said, not "Come in" or "Go away," he would just ignore me and go about his business. If one of the boys were home, they would open the door, but even then, I would go in and speak to Mr. Harsey, and he would go in the other room; not acting mean or rude, just acting himself. He answered if he felt like it, didn't if he didn't.

One day, I drove up to their driveway, and Mr. Harsey was chopping wood and loading it in a trailer. I asked him what he was doing because he had plenty of wood for himself. To my surprise, he answered me. He told me he was thankful for our school and church's ministry to his son. He liked Dr. Price, he said, and then turned away.

I again asked him where he was taking the wood. He said that there was an older black couple who lived far from town that had a wood stove, and the man was too old to chop wood, but he kept trying. Mr. Harsey was afraid the old guy was going to give himself a heart attack chopping and putting up wood. He was doing it for him.

I helped with the wood until the trailer was full. As I was leaving, I told Mr. Harsey that his son had prayed and accepted Jesus. He said he was glad he did. I asked him if he was saved. Mr. Harsey turned mean in his face and said, "I used to go to church, but it does not work for me." He said that he respected the Lord but that he was too far gone for that stuff. He gave up on God sixteen years ago when his wife walked out on him and left him with the kids and her dad. He turned and got in his truck and left.

Over the next several months, I ran into Mr. Harsey from time to time at football games, in town, or at his house when his boys would let me in. I found out that Mr. Harsey loved his wife a lot and had never loved another woman since she left. He loved his boys but was not much good with emotions and stuff like that. He took care of the old man because no one else would. He kept a picture of every man he had killed and was not proud of what he had to do. He did not see himself as a hero (he was) or a big man. He was a state trooper and did his job or would die trying to do it. I got to the place where I started treating Mr. Harsey as a friend, and he didn't mind.

I was praying for Mr. Harsey and began getting a real urgent burden to speak with him about his eternal state and his need for Christ. Mr. Harsey had let me know he did not want to discuss his religious state. I don't believe in pushing anyone into a decision for Christ or forcing someone to listen. I became more and more burdened for Mr. Harsey until I finally decided I was going to confront him about his need for Christ. I am not sure I mentioned that Mr. Harsey was about six foot four and built like a solid rock. He was older, but he was ready for whatever came his way. He was tough.

I drove to his house one night on church visitation. I had another guy with me and I told him we were going to visit the Harsey's. The guy with me became nervous. When we got to his door, Mr. Harsey was finishing his plate of dinner and looked at me and turned and walked into the living room, leaving me standing there. I was so burdened for him, I decided I was going to talk with him or he could throw me out of his house. I opened the door and walked in uninvited. The guy with me was freaking out.

I walked into the living room and sat down on the sofa beside Mr. Harsey. I started talking with him, but he just kept staring at the TV. It was like I was not in the room. I have never done what I did next nor have I since that time. I stood up and walked over to the TV and turned it off!

The guy I was with was looking for the door, and Mr. Harsey looked dead in my eyes and said, "You just walk in my house, interrupt my dinner, start talking, and you just turned off my favorite TV show!" He looked like he was going to kill me, and he could.

I looked back at him and said to him that he was right and had every right to throw me out of his window if he wanted, but that was what he was going to have to do. I said, "Either listen to what

I have to say or throw me out your window or door, but I am not leaving until you listen or you throw me out." Then I said, "You decide."

He looked upset, and I thought I was going out the window, but he said, "Sit down," and I did.

I told him that I respected him more than he realized and that I was worried about his soul. I was afraid he was going to die without Christ and I couldn't let that happen without standing in his way and making him move me out of it. I said I would leave and turn his TV on if he asked.

Mr. Harsey said that he had been faithful with his vows to God and his wife ever since he had made them, even though his wife had not. He mentioned how many people he helped and how many times he had been shot helping people. He stated that every time he shot someone, it was when he had no other option, and he took no pleasure in doing it. He said that he lived as good of a life as I did and that he did not care what any man thought about him.

I opened my Bible and showed him the scripture where it says "there is none righteous, no not one." I looked at him and said, "Mr. Harsey, you need to admit you are a sinner and that you cannot get to heaven on your own good works." It was like cutting him with a knife. He started to raise his voice, and I stopped him and said, "You know you are a sinner. Now admit it to God."

He was quiet and was looking at me with a fearful hurt bear type of look, and I knew the next few seconds were either going to be good or bad. After what seemed like a long time with him deciding, and us both staring at each other (it looked like we were in a staring match), Mr. Harsey hung his head. He put one of his hands over his face and said, "I know I am!" He then started crying and admitted he knew he was a sinner, but he was just mad—mad at life, mad at God, and mad at himself!

I asked him to ask Jesus to take it all from him and for him to give his heart to Christ. I stuck my hand out and said, "Take my hand and pray with me." And he did. He prayed the most straightforward and meanest prayer, but one of the most broken and earnest prayers. When he finished praying, I prayed for him and got up to leave.

He stood up with me, and I told him he needed to tell somebody he had accepted Christ so he would not be ashamed of his faith, and we shook hands, and me and my partner left.

The next week, Larkin came in my office at church and asked me what I had done to his dad. I asked him what he meant. He said that Mr. Harsey had told the boys and the old man living with them to come to the living room and sit down. He had to tell them something. Mr. Harsey then said, "Boys, I prayed and asked Jesus to take my sins away and come in my heart." He told them if they had not, they needed to do so too.

Larkin said his dad had been different, and he wanted me to tell him what happened. I told him the story, and he looked at me like, "Man, it's a wonder Dad didn't kill you."

I thought the same thing.

A few weeks later, Mr. Harsey came to the church and met with Pastor Price and told him what had happened and that he had accepted Christ. They became a part of our church family and God saved and changed Mr. Harsey into a true friend to me and a kind man to everyone but felons. God worked in his family. I am thankful for getting to know and befriend Mr. Harsey!

Please Do Not Harass the Wildlife

I began playing golf in Panama City and became pretty good at it. I kept a weekly golf day early Friday mornings. I often met with people during these golf games to discuss whatever business we had, and from time to time, I would play with church staff or church leaders. One day, one of the deacons in our church invited me to join him in a game against two of his friends at their private member's only course. It was a very nice course with strict dress standards. You could only play the course if you were invited by a member, and then only a few times a year per visitor.

It was a wealthy man's private course and very selective about who did or did not join the club. Basically, you had to have deep enough pockets to be allowed in their club. I did not have deep enough pockets to join nor did I desire to join, but I played enough with this deacon, and we made a good enough team that we felt we could win this challenge by the other guys.

We got to the club early and were hanging out in the clubhouse, waiting on the other guys to show up. We had coffee, and I was introduced as one of the pastors of Central Baptist to other guys at the club. I knew a few of them, and it was a neat time of meet and greet.

Our guys arrived, and we warmed up, hitting a few practice balls and putts, then we got our game going. It was team play with each man playing his own ball. On each hole, we added the total team score and low score won the hole. No mulligans or handicaps.

There was some money on the line between my friend and the other team, but I was not sure how much. I was not part of the bet and was not going to benefit from the win as far as part of the winnings. I was only able to help him win money or be the reason he lost if he needed someone to blame—win-lose type of thing.

We teed off on the first hole, and each of us was close in our ability to play. Before long, the game was getting intense. We were even after the first few holes, and it was going to take our best game to beat these guys, but the same was proving to be true for them. The course was on one of the inlets to the ocean, and there were private boats at the club's marina in the distance. The course was a difficult one with challenging pin placements. The landscaping blended in and out with the bay waters, and on dry holes, small ponds were in play. It was a beautiful, challenging course.

I was a long driver in those days and was always ahead of all three of our group. I would drive and go to my ball and wait for the others to shoot next. We were on like the sixth hole that was a long par five. It had a little stretch of trees, bunkers, and ponds separating it from the seventh hole that was running alongside our hole but back the other way. It was a busy course with close boundaries, so you always had to be alert to stray balls coming from other fairways. People were watching each other all the time.

We were up by one, and I drove a long straight drive into the fairway. However, on the right side of the fairway, next to the rough where my ball landed, was a pond big enough to be a hazard for both holes it lay between. It was a pretty big long pond and quite deep. My ball was in the fairway, but I parked my cart in the rough next to the pond, so I could watch out for incoming balls if any were heading my way. As I was sitting there, I noticed on my side of the pond, and quite close to where I was sitting, an alligator. It was not that big, maybe four to five feet in length.

It was not uncommon at all to see them in that area wherever fresh water was found. Some people would wake up to find one in their pool from time to time. This gator was minding his own business, sunning with his back to me, sleeping (it looked like he was sleeping).

I started staring at the gator, and I had ten minutes or so before I could address my ball, so I was not pressured for time. I got to thinking how easy it would be to catch that gator. I was just going to grab it and roll it over and rub its belly and put it to sleep. It would be fun. I looked around and had plenty of time, so I climbed out of the cart and started sneaking slowly toward the gator who was maybe ten yards away, right on the bank of the pond. I was getting close, and there was no movement from the gator, so I thought, *I'm going to get this guy.*

I got completely into the mind of the hunt. I was hunched over, slowly closing on this gator, three feet from its tail, and just about in position to snatch his tail and flip him over. You must be careful with the tail of these gators, because they can get you with their tails! I was inches away from being able to grab his tail, and the gator, with one instant burst of energy, dove into the pond. He dove at the same time I was reaching for his tail.

Without thinking, and in the spirit of the hunt, I dove into the pond, right behind him, trying to grab him from behind. Did I mention the dress code? I was wearing my best slacks with expensive golf shoes and shirt and hat. I dove into the pond after the gator and I touched his tail but did not get enough to hang on. He was faster than me, and I came up for breath with the pond too deep for me to touch bottom.

I had to swim over to the bank and climb out of the water, hat in hand and clinging to the grass because of the steepness of the bank of the pond. It took some effort to get out and on my feet. When I did, I looked around, and every person within sight of this pond was standing completely still, staring at me. I did not mention that most of the members I met were very condescending and uppity. Not the kind of guys you could enjoy a cigar with, unless it was a Cuban and on your own private boat. I was standing there with the entire course watching me, including the guys I was playing with, and especially the deacon who had invited me to the course.

I picked my hat up and put it back on my head. I walked over to the cart and took each shoe off and poured the water out of them. I put my shoes back on and went to the back of my cart to dry my face with my towel. I picked my second club out of my bag and went and stood by my ball and started staring back at our guys, waiting on them to shoot so I could make my next shot.

I never acted like I was wet or that any of the alligator thing had happened. I acted totally normal around everyone the rest of the round, like I was not soaking wet and muddy in places. No one in our group said a word nor did anyone else. My partner never mentioned it, and most people would not look at me directly as if trying not to notice that I was wet.

We went into the clubhouse for drinks and a snack at the turn and finished the eighteen and had lunch at the clubhouse again. No one ever said anything about the little gator thing as if it did not happen. We won the round (close) and were turning in our carts and heading to the parking lot for our cars when one of the marshals for the course casually mentioned as I was leaving, "Please refrain from harassing our wildlife in the future."

I said, "Absolutely," and walked away, knowing as he did that there would never be a next time playing that course. The victory was mentioned, but my little extra adventure was never mentioned between my deacon friend and myself. We enjoyed many rounds of golf after that day, but never at his private course. They take their wildlife seriously, evidently.

Just in Time

M ost Saturdays were spent visiting the homes of our bus kids. We had twelve buses that went all over our county, picking up any and every kid that wanted to come to church. We had 800 children a week with some days having 1,200. We had classes for every age and one big assembly. There were forty-one people who helped us, reaching out and loving on these kids for Jesus.

On Saturday's, Rusty Price and I would visit any kid's homes who had previously made us aware of any issues they were having. We would answer any questions about God or follow up on first-time visitors. We had fun and games and singing on the buses and always challenged the kids to bring more kids. We also were able to get to know the parents of many of our kids. Most of our bus kids were low-income families from broken homes. Many of the parents were single and carrying a lot of baggage that filled their lives with hardship and pain.

Rusty was a teenager who was a great football player. I asked him to help out with my bus kids, and he jumped in full force. He soon became a big piece of our ministry to the special needy families that had so much to benefit from Christ. We visited together most Saturdays, and God gave us a lot of converts to Christ.

On one Saturday, we were visiting in the government projects close to our church where some of the kids who rode Mr. Bogg's bus lived. One of the teens who had been coming was wanting to talk to someone about accepting Christ. Rusty and I went to her house. She came to the door and said she was ready to come to Christ but was more worried for her grandmother who was in a coma in the hospital. She asked if we would go see her grandmother and pray with her.

We agreed to go. I received a call from one of the ladies in our church who was a nurse for this same woman. She asked if I would come because the woman was in an absolute panicked state of mind and needed someone to talk to. Rusty and I got to her room a few hours later.

Once there, we found out that the woman was terminal and dying. The lady had already coded (died) once, and they revived her with a shock to her heart. She was in a terrified state ever since she came back from her near-death experience. We went in and told her who we were, and she grabbed my hand and told us her story. The lady was wealthy and had been very active in her church. She and her husband (who had already passed) paid for one of the buildings their church built.

She felt comfortable in her faith until her first episode with death. She passed out at home, and while the ambulance was coming, she stopped breathing and her heart stopped beating for a short time until the paramedics shocked her and started her heart again.

The lady told us that when she fainted, she felt herself falling into a deep pit. She said when she hit the bottom, she could hear screaming people and felt intense heat. She was in a deep pit and said that coming toward her was this giant wall that was like something she could only call the blackness of darkness, and it was giving off this burning heat. She said she was so afraid that she turned around and started trying to climb the walls of the pit to get away from this wall that was coming closer to her every second. She said she finally started screaming out to Jesus for help, and she woke up on a stretcher.

They got her to the hospital. Her doctor told her she was dying and needed to make peace with herself and anyone else she felt was necessary. So she asked for her priest to come visit, and he did. She told him what had happened, and she asked him to help her not to have to go back to that place. Her priest gave her, what she called, her last rights and anointed her with holy water. As he left the room, he told her the next time she felt like she was falling to relax, and Jesus would take care of it. She said she was still a little afraid but felt better.

The day after her priest visited, she had another episode where she passed out and her heart stopped. "I was falling into the same pit again," she continued, "and I could hear the screams again." This time, though, when she hit the bottom of the pit, a little man was standing beside her. She asked him who he was, and the man told her he was all the works and money that she and her husband had given to the church during their lives. It was what she was trusting in to get her to heaven in a bodily form. She then said the little man started laughing at her, and she looked up, and that giant blackness started coming toward her. The little man was laughing louder and louder.

She dropped to her knees and just started begging Jesus, "Help me, please!" The next thing she knew, she woke up in her hospital bed, having just been shocked again.

She asked us if there was any way she could find and have peace in her death. She was terrified and exhausted but afraid to go to sleep, fearing she would not wake up. I took her hand and started telling her how she could have peace. I asked her if she would pray to Jesus and confess that she was a sinner and that she knew nothing she had done would earn her place in heaven. She could not trust in her money she gave or her works she did. She needed to confess that she was putting all her faith in Jesus and his shed blood for her and his resurrection from the dead. She also needed to confess her guilt and ask for forgiveness.

She said she believed it and wanted to pray and tell Jesus. She asked if I would help her, and I agreed, and we started praying.

As soon as we started praying, she cried out that she was starting to fall again and that she could not hear me. Rusty started praying for God to keep her alive. I was speaking loudly in her ear what she needed to pray. In just a few moments, Rusty was spread out on the floor, begging God to keep her alive. I was up on her bed, bending over her face with my hands cupped over her ear, shouting for her to just cry out Jesus's name! The nurse was outside the room, guarding the door and praying she would get saved and hoping the noise would not cause an interruption to what was happening.

The doctors and the family had signed a no revive clause, and the agreement was to keep her pain free and let her pass the next time she lost her heartbeat. Rusty was still on the floor, praying, and I was still with my face cupped over her ear, shouting, "Just cry Jesus's name!" when she lost consciousness. Rusty and I were gathering ourselves and hoping she had cried out to Jesus. She was unconscious but still had a heartbeat, so I leaned over to her ear and asked if she cried out to Jesus to just squeeze my hand. I felt a weak squeeze, and Rusty saw it.

We both held hands and prayed for her to be at peace while she passed. She no longer seemed tense or in a panicked state. She looked like she was resting. The nurse came in and checked her, and the doctor agreed that she was passing. A few hours later, she stopped breathing and passed as peacefully as if she were sound asleep. I know that dear lady will be standing in heaven when I get there.

So many people want to trust their own goodness or their good deeds to get them in heaven. After all, God is loving! Yes, God is loving, but our sins must be punished, and no matter how good a person is, they are not perfect. That is why each one of us must come to God by trusting totally in Jesus, his punishment on the cross which he took for each of us, paying for all our sins with His blood. I am so thankful my dear lady friend came to that understanding and called out to Jesus just in time.

"AttI"

Everybody I visited knew about the truth of Jesus, his death, burial, and resurrection. Most of the people who did not believe had heard it most of their lives and just did not think it true or necessary for them to accept it. I began praying for a chance to visit where people had never heard the truth about Christ. I didn't tell anyone what I was praying, because I could not afford the trip, the time off work, and our church was so wound tight, I would not be able to get off for the time if I asked. It looked impossible for me to get to go, but I started praying about it. I asked God to let me go to a place where people did not know him and to take care of the issues if he wanted me to go.

A few months later, one of our school teachers who was a retired missionary was asked by his mission board to return to his field and spend some time with a family that needed some help. Wilford Neese was the man's name. He was a missionary to the tribal people in the Amazon jungle. He had been raised in the jungle as a missionary kid and went back as an adult missionary. Wilford mentioned it to our pastor and told him to pray about going with him. In turn, our pastor mentioned it to our staff and asked if anyone wanted to go. I told him I wanted to go, and a few weeks later, I was getting on a plane with three others, heading to Caracas, Venezuela.

Our trip was to take us into three different villages of tribal peoples. We were to spend three days and three nights in each village with our last one to be with the family Wilford was being sent to help. It took half the day and all night driving to get to the river. We spent several hours on the river until we got to the place where we hitched an eight-hour ride on the back of a delivery truck. It took us to the airport where we caught a single engine Cessna and flew 800 miles or so to our first village.

The deal was that we were to observe and assist the missionaries but not try to initiate any interaction with the tribal people unless they began it, and only then with the missionary's permission. The people were very primitive, and the tribes we visited did not have contact with outsiders except the missionaries and river traders. They did not trust outsiders because of the treatment by some of the river traders. We were told that the natives would be very leery of white men they did not know! I began praying that God would give us an open door so we could interact with the natives.

Our first tribe was a tribe that had already developed a church and school and had a native pastor. The missionaries there were second generation missionaries. They had a school started and were teaching the kids how to read and write. The church was sending out natives to take the gospel to other family tribes down river. It was amazing seeing how one family's life could change so many people.

The first family came to the village early in the 1940s. They moved into the village and started studying the tribe's language. They spent years working with this single tribe, learning their language and customs. They had to have total command of the language without any doubt. When they knew the language well enough and were positive they could give the true explanation of the Gospel, they would call a village meeting and share the message that took them years of sacrifice and hard work to give.

Wilford told me that what would normally happen is that after as many as eight, sometimes more years, the main population would accept the Lord when they heard the story of Jesus. He explained that the missionary only had his village and that after years of learning their language and living with the people, they were almost family. The people would begin to understand that the missionary had an important message to give them, and when the time they could share the message got closer, the natives would know that hearing it was closer.

By the time the missionary was able to give the story in their language, the tribe would have been anticipating the story and were hungry to hear it. This first village was a clear picture of three or four families giving their lives to one village with a few hundred people in it to hear the gospel. Then the village learned about Christ and grew into a village that, in turn, took the message into further reaches of the jungle, tribes of distant families, and shared the story with them.

It was soccer and Ted that God used to open the door of acceptance to the first village. Ted was one of the men of our church and was in his late twenties, like me. The missionary was a soccer player and had the village clear a soccer field out of the jungle. It was a clear flat field with four walls of jungle all around it. The tribe was composed of small men, but they were tough. They played soccer almost daily, and when we got there the second day, they asked us to play with them. The missionary said it was okay, so we went at it.

Ted and one of the natives ended up bumping heads and split Ted's eyebrow open badly. All the natives thought Ted would quit playing because of the blood (he needed a few stitches), but he didn't get them. We taped the cut back together and kept playing. Him not quitting made Ted welcomed into the village men's circle. The men invited Ted to their homes to meet their families. They told the missionary they liked him because most white men were soft like women. Ted was tough, so they liked him.

I do not know the name of these people, I think it was Panatti, but I am not sure. They were kind and very gentle people. I would not want to go to war against them if they had to fight for their families, but they were kind people. They did not have any cuss words in their language. They had one word they used. It was *Atti*, and it meant "my heart is very frustrated." In any situation where they became aggravated, they would shout, "Atti."

I learned this because I was in good enough shape to run with them, but I had never played soccer and was a little too aggressive when trying to get the ball. I would run in to take the ball and bump the guy out of the way. He would shout, "Atti" at me and keep playing. The missionary told me I was upsetting the men because they were trying to be easy with us, and I was being too aggressive. So I started running at the guys and then just grabbing them and pushing them away. I would scream "AttI" at them real loudly, and it would scare them.

They finally started pushing me back and hitting me out of the way, screaming "Atti" at me as they did. By the end of the game, we were all just hitting and pushing and screaming "Atti" at each other. We all became buddies, thanks to Ted's hard head, and a few pushes and "Atti's." When we took off from the airfield to our next village, I will never forget watching the men waving goodbye and the picture of a perfect soccer field in the middle of the rainforest.

Six-Foot Iguana

We flew for a few hours to the next village who were Yanomami people. This tribe had a missionary who had been with them for eight years. The tribe had a good relationship with him and trusted him but did not like strangers. When we arrived, they gave us a hut that had a straw ceiling and sides with two cots and two hammocks. The tribe was a pretty good-sized tribe of people, maybe 200-plus. The kids followed us all around. If you woke up at night, you would see little heads watching us from the door and windows.

The kids in this tribe played until they turned thirteen. On their thirteenth birthday, they had to endure a testy initiation and pass it to become a man. When they passed, they no longer played. They were given a red loin cloth and began hunting at night and fighting when their village was attacked.

We spent the first day there exploring the area around the village. It was a very heavy jungle, and the men carried long blowguns with poison darts. They could disappear at will in the jungle right in front of your eyes. Unbelievable survival skills.

The village had a chief who was the law and the jury, and no one argued with him. I was able to greet him, but that was all. I wore bib overalls and boots, and it was very hot and humid or raining. I kept my pockets full of pieces of candy, and occasionally, I would throw a big handful of candy into the jungle, and the bushes would shake like crazy. The little kids were following us in the jungle, and we could not see or hear them, but they always were around. These people were very hard, fierce-looking people. They were kind to you with a twist of suspicion. They were fighters.

The missionary told us to keep an eye out for something that was killing his chickens. He had a pen in his backyard, and something was sneaking out of the jungle and eating one of his hens every few weeks. He asked that we keep a watch out and let him know if we saw anything.

It was ninety degrees at night, and 100 percent humidity, and I was always wet with sweat. I woke up early and decided to go down to the river and take a bath for the day. I put my soap in my coveralls pocket and walked down toward the river, just as it was almost sun up. As I was walking behind the missionary's house, between it and the chicken coup, I saw something moving in the grass. The grass was almost knee-high, and about ten yards ahead of me, moving toward the chicken pen, was an iguana lizard. I could only see a little of its head, but it was an iguana. I thought to myself, *I should catch this thing.*

There were three native men with spears standing over against the river, but everyone else was asleep. I started sneaking up behind the iguana and was getting almost close enough to grab it when I stepped on a stick and the lizard stopped, stood up on his two back legs, and turned his head around and started hissing. That thing was huge! It was almost four feet high, standing on its feet, and it was mad.

The three natives looked over and saw it, and they started chattering away, holding their spears. I looked at the little demon-possessed lizard and was thinking about my best options when the lizard twisted and leaped toward me, hissing. Growing up in government projects, I learned that you did better attacking than you did running when you are being attacked. I ran toward the lizard and kicked his body like a football. He flipped through the air and hit the ground, coming right back at me. I kicked him again, and this time, he went over the knee-high fence into the chicken pen.

I jumped over the fence in the pen with him. He was tearing me up with his tail. It was like a whip and it was starting to draw blood. He was trying to bite me, and I was trying to knock him out. It was crazy for a few minutes, and chickens were flying everywhere. The three natives were still holding their spears and chattering, and people were getting up, running toward the fight. The whole time, the lizard and I were fighting it out.

I had my one knee on his midsection and was trying to punch him in the head to knock him out, but he wouldn't knock out. He was whipping my other leg and arm with his tail and had his head turned around, trying to bite my fist.

The missionary came running out of his house in his underwear, and I saw all these people watching me, but no one was helping. The fight could go either way for a while, but finally a few of my head punches had effect and I was able to reach away and pick up a stick and bust my little lizard friend one good time on the head, and he went limp.

I rolled off him, bleeding from my punching hand, my other arm, and my leg from my ankle to my knee because of it hitting me with its tail. But I beat him. The three natives ran away and told the chief I was in a fight with a lizard. It was limp and looked dead when I picked it up. We measured the lizard, and he was a few inches longer than six feet from nose to tail. His head was as big and wide as a grapefruit, and his teeth were needle sharp. He could have easily bitten my fingers off.

I have seen these boys in the zoo that were big, but this one was lean, mean, and cut. I got Ted to get the camera and take a picture. I was holding a six-foot lizard that I had fought and killed. Ted and Wilford took pictures holding it, and we had a teenager with us who wanted to hold it. We took his picture with it in his hands, and just as we took it, the lizard woke up and looked up at the teen boy. The lizard hissed at him and the boy started crying, "Momma!"

I wanted to skin the thing and save the skin, but the chief of the village would not allow it. He and the natives thought that if I skinned it, I would offend the demons because it would not be respectful to the lizard. I had the right to kill it, because it jumped on me first, but since I was not hunting for food, I could not skin it. I threw it into the river and let it float away. God answered my prayer through that fight.

The chief asked the missionary to bring me to his tent to meet him and his wives. I was able to take Ted, and we had two days where we got to get to know the men of the village. I have kept that picture and often think back on how God answers prayer. He made a way for us to get to know the village, and he saved the missionary's chickens with the same prayer.

Anything They Serve...

The chief's name was Pooka (spelling guessed), and after the fight with the iguana, I was invited to his tent to talk. The tribe was Yanomami, and God answered our prayers by creating an opportunity to be invited into the natives' lives. I took Ted with me, and the missionary translated the conversation.

We went to the chief's hut, and it was a larger grass thatch hut open in the front and back. It had no doorways, and people came and went in his hut as they wanted. As we were walking to the chief's place, the missionary told us he had never had this happen before—white visitors being invited to his hut. He asked us to be very careful to treat the chief as a king. It was important that we did not hurt his years of work by offending the chief in any way.

We got to Pooka's tent and sat down to talk. He told us that he was the chief of the village and that his tribe and their village were a great people. He also boasted that he was the best hunter in the village. The men hunted at night and slept during the day. During the day, the women cleaned and cooked the kill. Whatever game the men killed, the women would prepare it and dish it out evenly so that every family in the village got an equal portion. They took note of who killed the most and was the best hunter, but every family ate from the previous night's hunt. They had smoked monkeys and fruit from the jungle for those days when the hunt did not go well.

I had a very expensive knife on my side in a sheath. It cost $150 back in the '80s. I had it with me when I went into the chief's tent. He showed me his knife which was an old but sharp kitchen knife he had traded for with the river traders. He asked to see mine, and I let him see it. He kept his eye on my knife from that time on.

He took us out to the river where the ladies were preparing the food from the hunt the night before. Pooka had four alligators from his hunt, and he shared how he crept up on each of them and stabbed them between the eyes with his spear. Each of the alligators had a big round hole right between the eyes in the same spot! We went back to his tent, and I was walking around, looking at his odds and ends he had on his walls. Just like we have pictures and what-nots, they had little things they kept for the same reason we do.

As I was looking around, I saw an old coal miner's lamp sitting on the floor in the corner. Beside it was a banana leaf full of 12-gauge shotgun slugs, and under a mat was an old single shot 12-gauge shotgun. I picked the gun up and started shaking it over my head and pointing to Pooka. I had found out his secret. He was shining the alligators on the bank and shooting them between the eyes. Everybody was laughing, because he was telling tall tales of his hunting with a spear. It was an eye-opening thing to sit and talk with him and his men and to listen to their stories and hear of their families. They were no different than any one of us, and they were anything but primitive.

As we were leaving, the chief called the missionary to the side and spoke with him privately. We were walking back to our hut, and the missionary said that the chief wanted to honor me for killing the iguana lizard. He asked if my friend and I would sit with him at a special meal they were having that evening. Every year, they celebrated the beginning of some type of season for their fishing or something like that.

They took this poison root they had and they would go up the river just a little way and beat the root with a rock over the side of their canoe, and the poison would drip in the water. The other men would be down river and would scoop up the fish as they would float to the top of the water, paralyzed. This was a very special celebration for these people like Christmas or Fourth of July would be for us. The men would gather all the fish that were taken and throw them live into the fire as we all sat around it.

After a minute, if you were lucky, they would pull out a fish, chop it in pieces, and you were handed a banana leaf with a piece of the fish as your meal. The missionary was very clear about a few things. He told us he had never been invited to sit with the chief and that the natives considered us doing that as a great honor. He told us we could refuse the invitation and no offense would be taken. But if we accepted the invitation, we would be fed the same thing they ate and would have to eat it, or it would offend them and hurt the missionary's work with these people.

He went on to share that the village did not eat like we do in America. They eat for survival, and they eat everything they kill and every part of everything. I thought I understood and told him I wanted to attend this once in a lifetime chance to eat a celebratory meal with the Yanomami Indians. He told me again, "You have to eat whatever they serve you!"

Ted agreed to go too, so just about an hour before sundown, the men got in the river canoes and beat the poison, and the other men grabbed up the fish, and then they all gathered around and lit the fire. The circle of men was large, and the wives and children sat behind their men. After the ceremony, the men started grabbing fish and chopping them in pieces and putting the pieces on banana leaves and handing them out. By this time, Ted was on one side of the chief, sitting on the ground, and the chief was in his chair, and I was sitting on the other side of the chief.

They brought the chief a banana leaf, and everyone started celebrating. Then they brought Ted his banana leaf, and it was a giant fish head with the mouth wide open—about a pound plus of raw but scorched fish head that Ted had to eat, everything but the bone. I looked over at him and was laughing hard, and the people were all looking at Ted and began celebrating his meal being given.

It was now dark enough that even with the fire, the night in the jungle almost ate the light and it was hard to see. They came over and handed me a banana leaf, and again, everyone started celebrating when they gave it to me. I nodded to all and looked at my leaf. It weighed about a pound and a half and, in the dark, looked like an eight inch by eight inch by five-inch thick piece of raw fish meat. It was still wet and had the skin and scales on it, but compared to Ted, I was feeling pretty good about raw fish fillet.

I stuck the raw flesh to my mouth to take a bite, and a funny thing happened. I bit the corner and the piece collapsed on itself to just skin, then when I took it out of my mouth again, it expanded back to normal size. I opened the leaf a bit more, and it all made sense. Evidently, the person of honor at this celebration gets the best part, just like the chief. We were both given the gut pouch of a big fish full of raw fish entrails.

I had the entire village and the chief watching as I was blessed to eat, beside the chief, a pound and a half of raw fish guts still in the wet skin, scales and all. Ted looked over and started laughing, and we ate our Yanomami fish special (I got the deluxe). Not only did we eat it, but God gave us grace to keep it down. We finished the celebration with our little brown brothers and were treated as friends, and in my mind, we *were* friends.

On the next day, as we were leaving, the chief asked me to his tent. I went to thank him for the honor of last night. The chief said he had a greater honor than last night. He took off his necklace (monkey tooth) and told me he would honor me by trading me his chief's necklace for my $150-dollar knife. The missionary reminded me it was not negotiable. I have it on my wall as a reminder of old Pooka, my Yanomami Indian chief brown brother and our fish dinner we shared together.

Heroes

The last village we visited was 1,500 miles into the jungle. It is in a village that had a language that used guttural sounds to make the syllables. No other known village had a language or relation to this people. It was one of the longest distances to get to, and at times, they had trouble getting supplies. They had a ham radio they used to call each night, checking in with home base to let them know they were safe.

It was a relatively new mission, and two teams had been there five going on six years. The native village had 408 people and were a hard people. They did not have any words for kindness or caring in their language, and the people were hard, harsh, and totally nude.

Ron and Sue Rodman were there, and the other team that started with them had left. The other family that went with them to help in the work, the wife had caught malaria and died there in the village. It took three days until they could retrieve her and the family from the site.

The Rodmans had decided to stay rather than shut down the work. Ron and Sue had been there three plus years, alone, trying to learn the language.

The purpose for our trip to their village was for Wilford to evaluate Sue Rodman's health (mentally). As far as the Rodman's knew, we were just the third leg of a team mission trip. We went to the other two villages as a team mission trip. This visit was set up for us to spend three days with them to give Wilford (veteran missionary) a chance to watch and see how they were holding up. Also, Ron needed to return to the states for furlough to report to his churches.

Some of the churches were going to drop their support if he did not come report to them. He was close to finishing the language and did not want to leave without giving the Gospel to these people. Some of the older men in the village were short for this world, and Ron wanted them to have a chance to get saved before they died.

This village was a bear to get to for the pilots. To land, they had to circle into the valley to line up with the runway and then land downward on a runway running upward. The end of the short runway was a cliff. I was enjoying the excitement of it until I saw the pilot's face after we stopped. He said that runway was his biggest challenge as a bush pilot.

When we got there, it was a larger village, but the villagers would not even look at us at first. They were very standoffish. We met Ron and Sue. They were a couple in their thirties and had gone to Temple, the same college as I had. We stayed in the house where the first missionary couple had lived, and it was just down the trail a bit from the Rodmans. We carried our own food for our stay as supplies were hard to come by here. We found out that they had not been able to get their monthly supply flight of staples in three months and were running short on almost everything.

The first day was spent following Ron who was having some of the men cut the landing strip. He took us into the village where we visited several old people who were bedridden, and we prayed with them. Before the Rodmans came, none of this village had ever seen white people or any other people for that matter. They had no idea about Jesus, but they had come to trust David and Sue and would do anything they asked and, for their part, seemed to care for the Rodmans.

They understood Ron, and Sue cared for them and trusted them. They were prone to stealing. If you left anything laying around, they would take it and not give it back. Sue had to watch her laundry when she hung it out to dry or they would take it. They were bad liars as well. One of the men in the village had stolen one of Ron's t-shirts a while back. The second day we were there, we were fixing something on his house. The four of us and Ron were standing outside their house, and the guy comes walking up the trail with Ron's tee shirt on. Ron told him that it was his shirt, and the native told him it was his own. He found it and he owned it.

Then he said he was smarter than Ron. Ron asked him why he thought he was smarter, and he said because of how he wore his shirt. He had put the shirt on upside down and stuck both legs through the arm holes, and his private parts front and back were hanging out the collar. He told Ron, "See, I can wear clothes like you, but I don't have to take them off when I must go." It was quite funny seeing the man bragging about being smarter than Ron.

We went over to the Rodman's house that evening, visiting, staying up most of the night, sharing stories and laughing. It was a time of refreshing for all, but we hoped it was for sure one for the Rodmans. The two evenings we spent sharing made me realize that I had met him at Temple. They were athletes and were married their last year at Temple, which was my first year.

Ron and Sue were always in trouble for being on the edge of the rules and being "too worldly" as the leadership at school would tell it. However, they were spending their lives trying to figure out a language that no other known language was like. He was racing to figure the language out before some of the older people in his village died of ill health or age. He had several of his churches threatening to drop him if he did not leave and come back and report to them. He knew if he took a year off and went back to the states, it would put him years behind in his studies for the finished language.

He was under great strain to get it, and his wife was about to suffer a complete mental breakdown.

They were giving their lives for 408 people that nobody had ever heard of, and the tribe had no known relatives. We spent the first two nights telling our stories and laughing, and it was very much like a medicine.

On the last night of our visit, Sue asked us over for a home-cooked meal. We accepted and set the time to be there. Sue had not had a visitor before we came who spoke English in over three and half years, and therefore, she was forgetting some of the words we use. She had brought with her to the jungle a set of china but had never brought it out and used it with visitors. She had forgotten how to set the table and was much too nervous for just a meal. It was apparent to us that this meal was much more for her than for us. She was trying to be American and have a normal night with us but had forgotten how.

We went to her house, and she had her table set with candles and her china and she went all out. The issue was that they could not get supplies for months. She did not have any American food. She had the natives hunt for her and bring meat to eat. She did not realize that what they brought was not something we ate. She was mentally one step away from breaking down, and it was obvious she was straining to appear normal.

We sat down, and she began serving the side dish and the main course, which was something they had on a regular basis. She had baked an eight-pound rat. It was a river rat that lives on the Orinoco River. It was huge, but it was a rat. She had baked it, and there it was, lying on its back, legs sticking up in the air. It was the biggest rat I have ever seen.

She leaned over and cut the rat and placed a healthy portion of rat breast on my plate. She was watching each of our faces very closely.

219

She was watching to see if we reacted to her doing something wrong. So we all knew what was happening, and we acted like all was well. The meat was gray with a lot of veins running through it. I took a bite, and it was the most disgusting thing I had put in my mouth since the fire a few days ago. It tasted like spoiled puss with giblets. It was repulsive.

I ate it like it was steak with Sue watching everything we did. After we had finished, she was noticing none of us had asked for seconds. I leaned over and said, "Sue, can Ted and I please have some more of that meat?"

She smiled and served us both a double portion. We ate it with pleasure.

After I got outside and was walking back to our place, I asked Wilford about all the veins in the rat. He told me they were worms, not veins. The reason you bake rat five hours is so you do not get worms when you eat them! Ron and Sue Rodman are heroes for our faith, and they gave their lives and health for 408 people nobody else cared for. I thank God for them!

My Children

I am amazed at the wife God gave me and the five children he blessed Sharon and I with. Sharon has a college degree to teach through high school age. We determined to have her stay home with our children instead of putting them in daycare. It would mean surviving on one income, but it also meant that we would be able to raise and train our children as we saw fit. We talked about it and agreed that Sharon would stay home and raise our kids, and I would provide for them. Sharon is the best mom and teacher and prayer warrior that any family could hope to have. I am so proud and thankful for her life of sacrifice and selflessness.

When I was growing up, I had a brother die in my family. I know firsthand the pain and loss and devastation that a family suffers when a child is lost. Many families are not able to weather the storm of a child's death. They seem to die themselves through the pain and by the bitterness along with the child. I am just saying I know the effect of this and have seen it. And yes, my family was one of the ones that did not weather the storm of my brother Tim's death.

In our church, we do not baptize babies for biblical reasons. When we have a child, we do often have a dedication ceremony (not mandatory, but encouraged). It is where the child is brought in front of the church and the pastor anoints the child and parents and prays over them, asking God to take them in his grace and guide and help them raise the child in faith. We pray for God to help the child when it is old enough to know his need for Christ and that it will believe. It is a very serious and important part of a child's life. We ask God to put his hand on the child and keep him from the world and the devil.

Sharon and I were wanting to have each of our children dedicated as soon as they were able to be carried to church. With all five of my children, but individually, God dealt with me in my prayer closet for a deeper commitment. As I was praying for my family and my newborn child, God put it on my heart to put each of them on the altar. What I mean is that God came to me with each child and put it on my heart to be willing to let him have them, no matter what that meant, even if God wanted to take their life and call them to heaven. He was asking me to lay them on the altar of God's will without any control or say in what God wanted for each child.

I lived through the death of a newborn child and witnessed firsthand what it did to my dad and mom and us kids. I know God is a loving God and can and should be trusted. I also knew that if God was asking me to give them to him as a sacrifice, he was free to take them if it was his will to do so.

I could not do it at first, but finally, with Donald, Joshua, John, Levi, and Heather, God brought me to a place where I was willing to lay them on the altar just like Abraham did with Isaac. So when we took them to church and the time came to bring them forward, each just after they were born, we went to the altar for the pastor to pray a dedication over us. Each time I gave each of my children completely and unreservedly to the Lord. I tell them that they belong to God, and each one of them do!

I mean it when I say God is a God of love. So many people blame God for the death of loved ones or blame him when tragedy strikes. Why is God so cruel? God explains all of this in the Bible, and people choose not to learn it for themselves. They do not seek God or pray or learn of how much God loves every single one of us. God loves every single human being and wants to have a friendship relationship with us, even though our world is full of death.

My brother, Tim, who died at eighteen months old a very sick and painful death was/is loved very much by God. God allowed Tim's death. God loved/loves my parents and my brother and sisters who endured the pain of death just as much. God is a God of love and he could have stopped Tim's death, but he did not. But he did send his Son, Jesus, to die on the cross, so even in death, Tim, my family, and anyone else can know God's love and find strength in him to help and strengthen them until God does end death. Just because pain and death happens does not mean God does not love those hurt by it! He is the only one who can help in these times.

God asked me to give each of my children to him, even if he wanted to take them home, and I did. It was not easy, and I am not telling you so you will think me some spiritual giant. Not the case at all. I am sharing it with you so you will think about your own life. How much of your life, loved ones, possessions, dreams have you given to God on the altar? I knew in my heart God owns my children anyway and holds them in his hand. I guess he just wanted me to decide, no matter what, who I was going to love most—them or him. I love my family more than anything, but I choose to love God more than them!

Dalton Heath

After our trip into the jungle, I was so excited to be able to see people who had never heard about Jesus getting a chance to hear how they can know him, just to get to see it and learn a little bit of the sacrifice and hard (often seemingly impossible) challenges that had to be overcome to do so. Years of hard work, and finally, a church is birthed and many of the people saved. It was amazing.

I had a lot of responsibilities at our church and was always busy. I shared Jesus with people every day, trying to see them come to Christ. Some did, but the thought of telling people that did not know and who wanted to hear was thrilling to me.

One Sunday, soon after my return, we had a visiting speaker named Dalton Heath. He was a kind of ugly looking, short, skinny, road-hard, and put up wet type of guy. I was not too impressed with the man at first glance. Dr. Price had scheduled him to preach and I sat back to listen, wondering what this old boy had to say. I was not prepared for what God was going to do in my heart through that man.

Dalton Heath was a missionary in an Asian city on the coast of somewhere. He had been a missionary there for a long time and was getting older and thinking of retiring. His story, as he shared it, is as follows:

Dalton was invited to speak on an island to a group of people who lived there. All he knew was that it was a small island, and nobody ever spoke about it, and seldom did anyone visit to or from the island. Dalton had only heard about it in passing.

Dalton was speaking in a meeting for other preachers, and a man he did not know came up to him after he spoke. The man invited him to come to his church and speak. Dalton accepted, and the man told him that his was the only church on the island. They set up a date for him to pick up Dalton in a boat with the agreement he would go to the island and speak for three days. Then they would bring him back. Dalton mentioned that something seemed funny about the situation, but he could not put his finger on it.

A few weeks later, Dalton was waiting on the dock, and the brother pulls up in his boat to pick him and his gear up for the trip. When Dalton boarded the boat for the hour or so boat trip to this secluded island, the man started thanking Dalton so much (too much) for being willing to come.

Dalton asked the man, "Why would I not want to come preach? You asked me."

The man's face suddenly grew very serious, and he was looking at Dalton.

"What is it?" Dalton asked.

And the man said, "You do not know, do you?"

Dalton asked him what he was talking about, and the man had the driver stop the boat. The man then told Dalton he thought Dalton knew or he would not have invited him without telling him. Dalton was still asking, "What are you talking about?"

The man said, "The island. You don't know about the island, do you?"

Dalton looked at the guy and said he had no idea what the guy was so excited about. He had only heard a little about the island and nothing about its people.

The man told Dalton, "Well, it will be okay if you do not come. I have told everyone you were coming, but they will understand if you do not."

Dalton asked the man, "Why on earth would I not come speak to your people?"

The man told Dalton, "The island is a leper colony. No one comes or goes except under certain circumstances such as you coming to speak."

Dalton said his heart dropped when he heard "leper colony."

The man continued, "People come whenever they are diagnosed with leprosy, and they stay there until they die." At one time the island had a church, but it had been a very long time since anyone had come and spoken to them from the Bible. This man had a family member who was on the island, and he did what he could to help by delivering supplies and running errands. They asked him if he could find a preacher to come teach them as it had been years without the church being used and someone teaching. So he heard about the preachers' meeting, and when he heard Dalton speak, he felt led to ask him to come. He assumed Dalton would know about the leprosy when he said he was from the island. He also said that it made sense as to why Dalton answered so quickly that he would come.

He was starting to tell the driver of the boat to turn back, not waiting for Dalton's answer. Dalton said that he felt like God had set this up, and it seemed to him that God wanted him to go, so he told the man he would do it.

When they arrived on the island, Dalton said the people were all at the dock waiting on him. He was met first with the smell of the leprosy. He was taken back by it and the appearance of the crowd. The islands population was a few hundred. They had people from the first to the last stages of leprosy and all ages. The group had become one big family of dying people with adults taking in kids, and everyone watched out for each other.

He was surprised by the huts that the people lived in were well-kept and clean. They had a small clinic where, from time to time, nuns would come and treat their wounds and bandage them. Dalton said he was scared to death and emotionally at his limit just trying to process what he was seeing.

The leader of the colony introduced himself to Dalton and then thanked him for being willing to come to the land of the walking dead. He said that many had been invited and that he was the first to come. The man seemed to understand Dalton's dilemma and emotional state, so he asked if he could show him to his room so he could rest from the trip. They took him to a house made of concrete and brick with furniture and bedding and all the comforts of home. The AC worked, and the place was spotless.

As the man was leaving Dalton's room, he told him not to worry, that everything was handled with care, and that he could eat, drink, and live in his quarters during his stay with no fear of being infected with the disease. He told him that Dalton was scheduled to speak that night, the next day and night, and next day and night after that, and that he would be taken home on the fourth day. He again thanked him for his willingness to come to them.

When the man left Dalton, he confessed he was struggling with his thoughts. These people were all dying, yet they were worrying about his comforts. Everything was just as they said. His food, drink, everything was done to protect him by these people in every way (except for the finger floating in his tea that one time; just kidding).

Dalton spoke the first message, and every single person was there listening. When he finished his message, he was preparing to gather his notes and stuff, and the people just sat there, waiting. The leader of the colony asked him if he was stopping already. Dalton had never, as a preacher, had a group ask him to keep going after a full message. They told him they had waited so long to hear the Word, they wanted him to please keep teaching.

Dalton said he spoke into the early hours of the next morning with the people sitting and hanging on every word. When he finally was not able to speak anymore, he told all to turn in for the night and he went to his room.

Early the next morning, there was a knock at Dalton's door, and breakfast was brought in, and Dalton was informed that the entire village was already back and waiting for the morning session to begin. Dalton taught till lunch, took a short break, and the people were back again until they finished that night, late again. Dalton said the people would have stayed and listened the entire three days if he had not made them sleep.

When Dalton finished, he was getting in the boat to leave, and the people were crying and thanking him, and they had the leader give him a small bag of money that each had collected to give him for coming. The leader asked Dalton if he would pray that God would call a pastor to the island to live and teach to these people. Dalton said he knew instantly in his heart that God wanted him to do so.

Dalton went home and shared what happened with his wife, and they both knelt and committed those people and their need for a pastor to the Lord. Soon after, Dalton and his wife moved full-time to the island, and he began his work with the lepers.

After working there for a while, Dalton was in the city doing some paperwork with the government, and as he was getting on the bus, he had a major heart attack. He lay in the gutter for a few hours before someone scooped him up and took him and rolled him out on the sidewalk in front of the local hospital. They came and took him to a room, unconscious. No one knew where he was for several days, and finally, someone thought to check the local people's hospital, and there he was, eating pork chops. They put him in a bed and waited to see if he woke up or died. When he woke up, they fed him, and it happened to be pork chops.

Dalton and his wife were sent back to the states for rest, and he was treated by doctors. They told Dalton he was through as a missionary. He had heart damage and would need to take it easy the rest of his days.

Dalton and his wife prayed about it. Every person in their church was dying, and some were still not saved. He also knew no one else would go to the church if he didn't return. The doctors told him if he went back, he would probably die there.

After praying and seeking God, Dalton and his wife decided that his wife would stay back home to keep their affairs in order and that Dalton would go back and teach the people while trying to get a new pastor. Once a new pastor was found, Dalton would return home. That was their plan.

When I heard his story and watched the old ugly skinny guy tell of his plans, I was filled with wonder at how God had worked on the island of lost lepers and on a preacher and his wife to give those walking dead people the plan of salvation. I was challenged by a wife kissing her husband goodbye, knowing she would not see him again until heaven. I was also moved by a preacher's heart who chose to return to a church full of dying people, knowing that his going back would mean his dying also. Is the price of a nobody leper worth that? Ask Dalton Heath, but you will have to wait until you see him in heaven to ask him as that is where he lives now!

Go

The night I accepted Christ, God called me to serve him. God impressed me to commit that I would not do ministry as a job or chase money in the name of ministry. I felt him telling me to trust him for my family's needs.

Over the years, my wife and I have done that to the best of our faith. We have followed God's leading in our lives and trusted him to provide where he has guided. There have been times of famine, but also, God has always been faithful. I can say with everyone who has walked this path of faith, God has never failed us or left us alone!

Shortly after my time with Dalton Heath, God began to speak to me about giving my family's needs to him and to serve God on the mission field. We saw a lot of people come to Christ where we were serving, but the thought of being able to reach people who have very little (if any at all) knowledge of Jesus was luring me. I want to see every person alive hear the Gospel. I wanted to be part of that work. I was making good money where I was serving, and I loved our church and our pastor. But God was dealing with my heart, and my wife was surrendered to missions before me. Finally, I went into Dr. Price's office and told him I was going to surrender to missions. We agreed on a date to tell the church, and the journey began.

We went forward as a family and told our church we were stepping away from pastoral staff and going to the mission field. We resigned and started raising support. The way our churches raise support is crazy, but that was our only option. We joined a mission board that was well-known in our church circles. We chose our field, and I started calling churches, setting up meetings so we could go and ask the church to support us financially to do our work. The way it works is you figure how much money you need a month to live on and do the ministry. Then you contact churches and ask them to let you share with them your vision. Your hope is they will promise to support you for x amount of dollars a month until you get enough supporters to equal the amount you need.

Say I needed $3,500 a month to go to Mexico City to start orphanages and schools, training the orphans who will in turn start churches after they grow up. That was my vision, and I thought after doing research that my family could survive with that amount. I then began calling churches, asking if I could come and share our vision and have them be a part of it. The idea is that growing churches will be able to support more missionaries. The truth was that almost without fail, the churches were not growing and could not help the missionaries they had already promised to help, much less take on new ones.

The second issue I ran into was that most of the churches I was going to still thought they were in the forties or fifties. Many of the churches would have you come present your work, and then they would give you this ten-page questionnaire detailing what you believe, and then they would either support you or not for $25 or $50 a month. It took thirty-plus calls to get one meeting, average, and one in seven would take you on for support. It took seventy supporters to raise support if each one gave $50.

On average, each year, you could plan on losing as much as 20 percent of the promised support. So the work of raising support was a challenge, to say the least. I soon realized the brokenness of our churches in the process of giving the gospel. Missionaries would come to churches for a meeting, spend one service with them, and there was a one in seven chance they would get $50 promised a month. The churches began to see the missionary family as a number and a $50 bill due once a month rather than people.

Missionaries hardly know the church, and churches hardly know the missionaries. It was a big numbers game, and good families with real vision would spend three to five years trying to get support, and if they did, they were often worn completely out by time they raised enough money to go. I would call churches that were supporting my family and often had to remind the pastor who I was so they knew we were on their mission's team.

We decided to sell our car and house and use the money to finance our travel until we raised enough to sustain our needs. We got a converted used Chevy van and traveled for four weeks on and one week off to rest. We would sleep in the van and save money when churches would not put us up. It was a time of faith building. We (Sharon and I and two boys) lived on the road, going from church to church, raising money. There were times we would drive 400 miles to a church of 500 people who invited us to come, and after presenting our work, they would thank us and say good night. No expense money or love offering, or maybe $25 and a pat on the back (that happened way too often).

Every so often, we would pull up to a church that had invited us, and they treated us like we were welcome and would listen and commit to pray for us and would give a love offering that helped. It was a blessing when that happened.

We learned firsthand that some churches are fake and dead, and we also learned that God's church is still alive and well. It was a bittersweet eye-opening thing. Deputation, the way our churches do it, is from hell and reflects the selfishness of so many of our churches, pastors building their own kingdom and not God's.

We raised our support in a little over eighteen months and were getting ready to go to language school in Mexico. The mission board I was with insisted I use a slideshow that I had to buy from them, and it required a system they made me rent also from them. I did not use it, even though they charged me monthly for the rental on their equipment. I told them I did not want a slideshow presentation, but they made one and charged me for it. I did not want it, ask for it, and even insisted against it. They made it for me anyway and charged me an enormous amount for it. I did not have the money they wanted for it, and they said we would work something out.

We were at 80 percent of our support amount and traveling through Wisconsin. I was in eight churches in five weeks. I traveled 1,200 miles and had about $1,800 in expenses. Each of these churches had asked me to come and promised to at least pay my expenses. At the end of the eight churches, we had been given $400 total with one church giving $250 of it themselves. I was ending in Milwaukee where my wife's family lived.

We were not able to travel home because we spent $1,800 visiting churches and got $400 total in offerings. I didn't have the money for gas to drive to Florida from Milwaukee. I went to the church that gave us the $250 and asked the pastor if I could borrow from the church enough to get home. Our monthly support was due when we got back home, and I could then send them the money back in a few days. They helped, and we made it home.

When I received the support check from our mission board, instead of the monthly support, I got a letter from them stating they took my support (without asking) to pay themselves for the slideshow they made me buy that I never used. I could not buy food, gas, or pay back the church. They took my support without so much as a phone call. I was devastated. I called some friends and borrowed more money and paid my commitments and then drove to this mission board's office to have a little talk with them.

I ended up in the director's office, arguing the fact that they took my money without asking me. I was told that the board had too many missionaries to call each one when there was a problem. Their policy was to hold the support for the missionary until the missionary called them. Then we would work out the problem and release the money if they agreed with the outcome of the issue.

In my case, they took out a loan in my name without my signature or permission and kept my money to pay off the loan that I had no idea they had forged. I addressed the director about their dishonesty. I told them I would tell my churches what they were doing if they continued to do that. The director told me, "You had better be careful, I can hurt you a lot more and faster than you can hurt me, son!"

He was not kidding either. I changed boards, and shortly after that, a rumor was started that I had an affair and got a woman pregnant in New Mexico. I lost everything overnight. My wife and I traveled together on most of my deputation, and I never was in New Mexico. But the rumor killed our work, and we lost everything.

Just a few weeks after the director telling me, "We can hurt you a lot faster than you can hurt us," I had lost all but two of my churches and was $3,000 in debt. I lost my house, equity, my car, and was with no income and $3,000 in debt over a complete lie that a big named preacher started from the area of the mission board that I had left.

The truth is that churches are not free from politics and dirty dealing. I was still young and was not expecting Christians to be able to do that kind of thing. Our family lost everything and was homeless and unemployed, and my wife was pregnant. Sometimes, life is not so funny!

Robert Tippens

I did not know about the rumor and the damage caused by it until I got back from setting up my family's apartment for language school in Mexico. I lost all of our scheduled meetings, every bit of our monthly support, and was now $3,000 in debt to my home church who paid my expenses until they could tell me what happened. Here is the way it happened.

Sharon was four months pregnant, and we just arrived back into Panama City from six weeks on the road and two weeks in Mexico. We pulled into the church office, and Sharon waited in the van as I went in to get our mail and support money. I thought all was good. I did not know about the rumor or that it was sent to every church that was supporting me, in letter form, and to the churches I was scheduled to preach for in the coming days.

I walked into the office and Sheila (our church's secretary) told me I needed to meet with the financial pastor as soon as possible. I walked over to his office, and he told me to sit down. He informed me that about seven weeks ago, the church started getting calls from my supporters dropping my support. My church had also received one of the letters. He handed me the copy, and it stated that Frank Penley had an affair and had a child with a lady in New Mexico. It went on to say that the board could no longer support such a person and advised that the receiver of the letter make their own mind up as to what to do.

I then was told that the church had supplied my expenses until I returned home in the amount of $3,000 to date. He knew that the rumor was false, and Pastor Price told him to continue helping until we could adjust, however, to the situation.

The situation was that as of that minute, I went from planning on leaving for Mexico in six weeks with full support to no support, no home, $20 in my pocket, one-fourth tank of gas, two kids and a pregnant wife, and $3,000 of debt to my home church. It was a very bad day.

Again, our home church knew I did not have an affair, but other than Dr. Lee Roberson and Dr. King in Ohio, the other churches and so-called friends believed it without checking with me or contacting me. My family was instantly homeless and broke with nowhere to turn.

I went back into the main office where there was a private office on the side that was available for use by anyone who needed it. I told Sheila I was going to use it for a minute. Sharon was outside, thinking all was well, and nobody knew my situation but the pastor and financial guy. I did not have anywhere to go and nothing to go anywhere with. I was completely helpless. I shut the door to the little office and got on my knees and started crying and crying out to God for his help. I confessed to God that I did not know what to do. I was begging him to show me what I was to do next.

While I was in the little office crying, in walks this member of our church, named Robert Tippens. He was a multimillionaire that drove an old truck and wore blue jeans and acted like an old farmer. He owned three trucking lines and two marinas. He did not know I was even in town. He asked Sheila if she knew a way to get a hold of me. She said yes and came over and knocked on the door where I was praying. She asked if I could talk with Robert. I was crying but said yes, and he came in where I was and said he needed to ask a favor of me.

Robert and his wife owned a small house on a little inlet from the ocean on Panama City Beach. It was empty. It was on the water with a shrimp boat tied to the dock in its backyard. Robert shared that it cost him more money to insure it empty than to have someone live in it and him pay for everything. Robert had no idea about what had just happened to me fifteen minutes before. He asked if my wife and I could move our stuff into his house and stay there when we were not traveling as a help to him.

I told Robert what had just happened and that by all practical purposes, I was homeless and broke and unemployed.

Robert said, "Great, then you can move in today." Robert then mentioned that God had put it on his heart to come find me or at best try to contact me and ask us to move into his house. After him finding out what happened, Robert wanted us to move into his house on the water, and he would pay all utilities, and I did not owe him rent. He would pay everything if I would cut the grass and keep the place up.

He gave me a couple of hundred dollars for food and gas and told me he liked my boys and he wanted to do it for them. Robert paid me to paint his car wash. It was enough money to pay the church in full. He allowed me to stay in that house for two years and would not let me pay him anything. He would always say that God told him to let me do it and he needed all the help he could get with God. He would also say he did it for my boys because he liked them and Sharon but did not care much for me. I will never forget Robert Tippens and am forever thankful for God bringing him to my family the very minute we lost everything. Thank you, Robert Tippens!

Sidenote about Robert. He was a very wealthy man who did not show it. He was not a real spiritual man and would tell you exactly what he was thinking. We became friends, and I would drop by his house from time to time and catch him in his yard, drinking. He would get mad and tell me not to drop by without warning him. I would say that God saw him doing whatever he was doing and I did not matter. He was not a believer but attended our church with his wife.

Dr. Price talked him into going on a mission trip into the Amazon jungle with the men from our church, and Robert went. It was on that trip God got a hold of Robert, and he gave his life to Christ. Robert and I became close friends, and we would meet, and I would answer his questions about God and being a Christian. The funny thing is that some of the leadership at our church would try to get me to talk Robert into being more committed (which meant they wanted him to give more). I never tried to get Robert to do anything other than what he wanted to do.

Some of our leadership worried he was not a real Christian because he did not do things they thought he should or he did things they thought he should not. Why do so many Christians judge others so freely? This is what is funny to me. The day I was completely blown away and cried out to God for help, the same men who judge Robert were there as I cried out to God for help. God reached down and used Robert. That tells me who was the closest to God! God says you will know them by their love! Robert loved God and loved my family when I needed God and him to!

You Let Him Curse Me

A few months after I moved into Robert Tippens' house, I found out who started the rumor. I was working to pay off my debt and thinking that my days of serving Jesus were over. I came to find out a guy, who graduated the same time from our college as I did, did have an affair with a woman in New Mexico and was also a preacher. He was not me, but the rumor was his story with someone putting my name on it.

I did the math and knew that the rumor came from the same man that had threatened that he could hurt me faster than I could hurt him. The difference was that I was threatening to tell the truth to people who needed to know it. He was threatening to hurt me faster, and worse, with a lie. And he did. He destroyed my name and my ministry.

I am ashamed now of my pride, thinking back, but the truth is I was full of myself at that time. I decided to kill the man who started the rumor. He had killed my ministry and my name, and I was going to kill him. I told my wife I had some business to take care of and would be back late. I knew the man and had been casual friends with him, and he lived about six hours away.

I got my gun and started the long drive to his house. I am sad to admit it, but I planned to shoot him and come home. I didn't care who it hurt by me going to jail. I allowed myself to be so bitter that

I was not thinking straight. I was not going to hide it. I would tell anyone who asked me that I did it.

As I was driving toward the house of the man who had hurt me, God began to bring to my mind the times he had worked in my life. He reminded me of some of the promises he had given me. He brought a Bible story to mind.

In 2 Samuel 16, King David was running away from his own son who was taking over his kingdom from him. His son was also planning on killing David. As David was running away, this man named Shimei was throwing stones at King David and cursing him. One of David's men, Abishai, asked David if he could go and cut the man in half. David said to Abishai, "If God has told him to curse me, then let him curse me!"

As I was driving, God spoke to me about the preacher who was destroying my name and ministry. God spoke to me clearer than if it was audible. God said that he was letting that man curse me. He told me that he let that man destroy my ministry. Then God spoke to me in a way that changed my life from that moment forward. God said to me that he never called me to have a ministry that was mine and that he never asked me to build my own name. He reminded me that I was called to do his ministry and to work building his name. I was to build his kingdom, not my own. He said that the man needed to kill my name and ministry and that he was letting him do it. He told me to turn around and let him finish. He let me know that he would punish me if I did not turn my car around. I did.

I am far from the place that I need to be, but I have since that day tried to do what God tells me to do and not worry about what people think. I do care about what people think about Christ. A funny thing is I never made it to Mexico City, but I did end up church planting in Mesa, Arizona. A few years into the work in Arizona, I was invited to a mission's conference to see my buddy, Rusty Price, who was their speaker. When I got there, the pastor asked if I would preach one of the nights, and I agreed.

It just so happened that the night I preached, I sat by the man on the platform I was going to kill—the very man who started the rumor that destroyed my ministry and my name. It was funny, because he was much more uncomfortable than I was being on the same platform together. God did a work in me back in the car that day so I would and could yield my bitterness up to him. I had the knowledge and peace that God used that man to help me learn more about dying to self and serving him. I still, from time to time, run into men who ask me if I ever got things right with God from that affair. I ask them just to pray for me. The only name that matters is Jesus!

Sometimes God Has to Kill You to Use You

Sharon and I worked in a children's home for problem teens in Florida. We took the position to help the director with the workload. Our home was a place where teens who were having problems with their behavior or living in extreme conditions could come for help. They had to agree to come (not forced) and had to agree to the home's rules before we would accept them. We had eighteen to twenty-one girls from childhood to young adult and a boy's home of eight boys aged seven to fifteen.

God put us there as he continued working on my heart about doing whatever he called my family to do. It was a time of long hours and short pay. I did anything and everything that was needed to give these kids a chance to get their lives together.

Sharon and I had three boys of our own by this time, and as I was always busy, I did not allow Sharon to be taken from the boys to work at the home. In that type of place, usually every person is overworked and stressed to the max, but Sharon and I agreed she would raise our kids, not someone else. I made this clear to the director that I worked for him, but my wife did not work for him.

One of my jobs was taking our girl's home to church services and special meetings which we had to do quite often. When local churches had a special meeting, they would always ask the home to come and the girls' choir to sing. It was a sure way to get twenty visitors and free music. I was the driver, and many of these churches were churches that used to support me before the rumor started.

I never answered my critics or defended my name. My close friends knew the truth, and the others needed someone to talk about. I was the guy. One night, I was in a special meeting with our girl's home and choir, and the pastor stood up to speak. He told the church that there was a visitor with them on that night (we were the only visitors there) who was running from God. He said the man used to be a pastor and had fallen into sin and was now running from God.

Sharon leaned over and asked if he was talking about me. We just shook our heads, sat through the service, and left at the end.

God was doing a work in my life, teaching me to trust him and not to be proud. Those pastors were just helping God do his work in my life to get me to a place where it did not matter what people thought of me. Jesus is the one who matters, and he is the only name given whereby men must be saved. I wanted God to use me to do his will, and I was learning that his will and name was more important than my own.

We had been at the home for about two years when the director's wife had a stroke. They took a leave of absence, and I became the director during the transition. I was not willing to take the position because my children were too young at that time. Also, there would be many long hours that I would be away from them. I told the board I would stay on until they found their replacement.

During the time between directors, Dr. Lee Roberson and Mrs. Roberson came by the home so Mrs. Roberson could speak in chapel to the girls. She would never speak if a man was in the room, so Doc and I had an hour and a half to walk around and catch up. God had allowed us a friendship that was a blessing in my life, and his counsel was often a help. Dr. Roberson knew about the rumor and the loss of everything.

While we walked and talked, I mentioned the pastor who used me as an illustration in his message as a man running from God. It was Dr. Roberson who had advised me against answering my critics. He warned me not to defend my own name. He advised me to let God fight those battles for me. When I told him about the preacher speaking about the man running from God, Doc just laughed. We discussed where both of our ministries might take us next, and then it was time for them to go. I walked he and his wife to their car, and as they were leaving, Doc stopped and said something to me that has stuck ever since.

Dr. Roberson said that I was far too stubborn and that God was doing something important in my life. He said to me, "Frank, sometimes God has to kill you to use you!" He got in his car, and that was one of our last conversations.

That statement has proven true in my life and the life of Bible personalities. Many a person God uses will be "killed" through some type of thing life throws at them. After the bitterness and pain settles, they begin to understand God is doing a work in their heart, so their work is about God and not them. God must kill some of us so he can use us sometimes!

Just after that time, the board came to me and told me I had to either take the director's position or move my family off the property. The problem was that we had used every penny of our money plus what they paid me, paying our bills and feeding our kids while working there. It took a little bit more money than we made every month to stay there and serve. By this time, we had pretty much used up our savings in order to make up the extra bills. I was given two weeks to answer and had to move or start the director's position. I did not have anywhere to go or any money to go with. I was completely back to where I had been the day Robert Tippens came to me.

I prayed for help and called my former pastor, Bradley Price, who was now pastoring a church in North Carolina. I mentioned that I needed to move soon and was wondering if he was okay with me moving to his new church. I then called my father-in-law and asked if I could bring my family to his house to live for one month. I could not give him any money but needed him to take care of them until I worked out our next move.

Don agreed, and I gave the board my answer. I shared with them that I had been there for almost two years doing everything they asked of me. Now that they wanted me to be their director, they were putting me in a position where I was almost forced to take the job. I let them know that my children were too young for me to do it, so I would be leaving. I also mentioned that I had used most of my savings to work for them and was leaving empty. All my furniture and everything we owned was in storage on the property. So I asked them to hire me for thirty days to work for $10 an hour, fixing all the things that needed to be fixed. They agreed to pay me cash for my time at the end of the month.

So I took my family to Wisconsin and left them. I came back and moved into a little camper for one person and began working every day and praying about where to go. I took all our furniture and anything of value and sold them on the street in a yard sale (I did not tell my wife I was doing that).

Near the end of the month, Dr. Price called me and asked what my next step was. I told him I was still praying about it. He mentioned that his church had a house for rent and that I could move there, and the church would work with me until I could pay the rent. It was the open door I was praying for.

I accepted, and at the end of the month, I put a box of clothes and one twin mattress in our car and drove to North Carolina to the rental house. I put our things in the rental and drove to Wisconsin, picked up my family, and brought them back to our new home. It took everything I made to do it, and here we were again, starting over with nothing but a promise that God would take care of our family. He has always been faithful.

Home Improvements

At the time we left the church in Panama City for missions, Dr. Price was called to a church in North Carolina. The church that called him also wanted Rusty to come and pastor their bus ministry. Rusty took the bus ministry in Panama City after I left, and God blessed his work. Rusty had a much larger ministry in this new church, and a lot of people were saved. We had buses bring kids and teens from all over metro and inner city Charlotte, North Carolina. Rusty had married Anna, and they lived in the house next to ours.

We had 1,200 kids a week coming to church from all over the city. Most of the kids came from poor or dysfunctional homes. We spent a lot of time in the government projects and down and out areas but ran routes in good areas as well. We went after anyone who would listen and discipled every kid who would come. The need was great, and workers were few, but we had a team of good-hearted people who loved Jesus and cared about lost souls.

Rusty and I began a Sunday school class called Home Improvements. It was named after a TV show that was popular at the time. Our vision was to get into the homes of our kids who rode the buses every week and win the parent or parents to the Lord. Our hope was that they, in turn, would start bringing their kids to church as a family.

We had great success and, in a few months, had thirty couples on average and families being reached. It was a refreshing class, because after these couples got saved, they knew very little and soaked in the teaching like a sponge. It was fun teaching people that wanted to learn and that came to class, ready to hear. It was good for our church as well, because the church was a formal, wealthy church, and our new people stirred the pot a little bit. It was a good time for all involved.

One of the couples we won to Christ was a big-time well-known wrestler named Gary (not his TV name). His wife was named Toni, and they were fun to be around. Gary was huge, and his wife was beautiful. He was famous, and everywhere he went, people were asking for his autograph. He and his wife were the life of the party.

We began visiting them because they were having marriage problems and wanted to talk. Rusty and I both began to visit them, and we started inviting them to class. They decided to try to work out their problems and started coming faithfully to class every Sunday. Neither one of them were saved, and their questions in class were neat to hear and reflected how God was beginning to work in their lives.

One Sunday, they came charging into the class late as I was giving announcements. You could tell from the look on both of their faces that they had been arguing right up to coming into class. Gary had a size sixty chest and thirty-two-inch biceps, and his hair was down to his waist. He was a typical big-time TV wrestler, and his wife the same type wrestler babe. Gary sat down and interrupted me and said, "I have a question." We had a time for questions every class, but I told Gary it was not that time yet. He said, "Well, it is now. This one cannot wait."

Toni was fuming, and he was upset, and our class was wild, so no telling what was coming. I said, "Okay, Gary, shoot. What's your question?"

He looked at me and said, "Is PMS part of the fall?" And then several of the other couples voiced that they had the same question.

I told them, "Most definitely!"

God let us see many parents come to Christ through that time, and Rusty and Anna have been our dearest friends since those days.

Albania

I had not been in North Carolina long when I received an interesting invitation. A pastor in Michigan who I had never met asked me to go to Albania with two other missionaries on his behalf. There was a new ministry that was setting up base in Albania.

Albania had been under extreme communist control for seventy years, and the government had just collapsed a few months before. This ministry had contacted the church from Michigan and informed the pastor that the new president of the country had promised that ministry control of the orphanages all over the country. His ministry wanted to get churches in the states to finance one orphanage as their own with the ministry in Albania, supplying the leadership and organization there on the ground. Their vision was to raise up, through the orphanages, young men who, upon leaving, would start churches all over Albania.

The pastor in Michigan had the money and was interested but did not know children's home ministry too well. He had two missionaries he was sending to Albania to check out the people running the work there. He wanted me to go because I had experience working with children's homes. He gave me a check for $350,000 to give them—with that much coming again for an orphanage—for his church to take over. He asked that we not tell the people we had the money until all three of us agreed the ministry was up to standard. We all were on the same page, and in a few weeks, I was off to Albania with my two missionary friends.

The ministry in Albania was hosting some thirty different people, all of whom were representing groups willing to work with the orphanages throughout the country. We arrived in Tirana, the capital, and were taken by taxi to the main hotel in town. The country was one of the poorest rundown countries I had ever seen. The countryside was covered all over with machine-gun bunkers, and every fence, post, or pole and post of any kind had a sharp spearhead on it. The people looked like they lived in the 1700s. Roads were all over, but no one had cars. The roads were for military vehicles. The hotel was cement walls and floors with an army cot in a room that also contained a table and chair. They had a restaurant, but they did not always have food. The country was as poor as I had ever seen.

We were scheduled to be there for fourteen days. The ministry had planned for us to visit each of the known orphanages in the country and come up with a list of needs for each one. Each day, we would be assigned to a translator and a taxi and given exact locations to visit. We would return each night and meet as a group and report our findings.

The leader for the group told us that the translators were college age Albanians who would work for one dollar a day. They suggested that if you hired the same translator, they would work for one day for free if you told them to so they could get the whole fourteen days of work. The average pay for them was a dollar a day, and the country had collapsed economically. The people were starving.

The head of this ministry was telling us to make our translator work a day without pay for the right to work six days for pay. Fourteen days' work for twelve days pay type thing. I was a little set back by that, but Albania was a lot to take in at first visit.

The next morning, the teams met, and we were given our locations. I was with the two missionaries that I had traveled over with, and we headed for breakfast. I ordered two eggs and potatoes, and the waitress brought me a piece of toast and cheese. I told her that was not what I ordered, and she told me it was all they had to serve.

When I got up to pay, they charged me for eggs and potatoes. I told them I had ordered that but was served toast and cheese. They insisted that I pay for the eggs as it was not their fault they were out of food. I paid it and learned to ask what they had before I ordered from then on.

We went outside, and there was a large crowd of people and taxis trying to get hired, many more than was needed. This group of people who were employed a few months ago were now trying to somehow feed their families. It was almost panic. Our team picked this cute college age girl whose English was good enough to understand. I asked her to pick us a taxi that we could trust, and she did. She told us that the people heading up the ministry told everyone that the pay was one dollar a day without meals, and the day was as long as the trip took. She agreed to the pay, and we took off for our orphanage.

The translator was named Lydia, and I could not say the taxi driver's name. Our first orphanage was three hours from the capital, and we had good roads to travel on. The people were not used to cars, so they would step into the street without looking or run in front of you on bikes or such, so it was important to stay on your toes.

We came to our scheduled orphanage, and when we got there, they did not know we were coming. The city looked like a war-torn city, and people were walking all around in mobs. The orphanage was surrounded by high fences and barbed wire at the top. It looked like a prison, but we were told that the fence was to keep people out, not in. Some of the townspeople thought there was food in the orphanage, so they would break in to steal it if they could.

We were walking around outside, looking at the grounds, and a couple of times, a blanket with a baby rolled inside would be thrown over the fence toward us from the crowd. The workers would scream that their babies were starving too, but still, the townspeople threw them over the fence.

When we got inside, I was heartbroken at what followed. They had about five, maybe six women in nurse uniforms taking care of the kids. All the newborns to two-year-olds were kept in cribs, two to three in each crib. They had fifty-plus, and each baby was wrapped tight in a blanket so it could not move its legs or arms at all. They all were just lying there with almost lifeless stares.

The lady keeping them was apologetic for the situation, but she said they had no choice. They tried to unwrap them and let them play sometimes, but it was days at a time before each one could be unwrapped. The second floor had the toddlers, and they had two women watching them, and the toddlers were naked and walking around. Their arms and legs were stiff and not working properly from the wrappings.

This orphanage did not have many children over three years old. The kitchen was a cement room with a big metal bowl in the center. They had about fifty pounds of powdered milk stirring in the bowl. It looked like it had soured. The kids each got one bowl a day when there was milk to be had, and the babies got one bottle a day. The ladies did not know who owned the orphanage and had not been paid in a long time. They were the only ones trying to keep these babies alive.

We left the orphanage with the thinking that when that fifty pounds of sour powdered milk ran out, those kids were going to starve. On the way home, we stopped at a place to buy sandwiches on the side of the road. The missionaries and I got out to grab something, and Lydia and the taxi driver stayed in the car. They were going to work all day for one dollar without eating because they had no money.

We told them to come in with us and asked them what they thought about the ministry we were with. Lydia got nervous and was trying not to answer. I told them that if they would stay with us every day, both her and the taxi, we would pay her $20 dollars a day and include meals for both. We would pay the taxi extra at the end of the trip. They agreed and stayed with us our entire trip.

When we got back to the hotel, we said goodbye, and I asked Lydia if she wanted to make some extra money. She began to look a bit scared, and I told her that I wanted to street preach to the people walking around the square in front of the hotel. I promised her $20 more dollars if she would translate for me. Lydia said she would if I would let her tell everyone that what she was saying were my words and she was being paid to say them. She was afraid she would be arrested.

The communist government had collapsed, but the army still walked around with guns, waiting to be told what to do. Nobody knew what was allowed or not. A few months before, I would have been shot on sight for speaking in public to any size crowd, and now Lydia did not know what would happen.

I told her she could say her thing and then I would speak, and if anything started to go bad, I would excuse her with pay and make sure the offended party knew she was not part of my preaching. She agreed, and I gave a public message in the main square of Albania, and crowds came and listened.

The next day, our trip was to a city on the border of Macedonia. It was a larger city and had a coliseum in the middle of it. We ended up following a group of our other teams, and this orphanage was 450-plus kids in one building downtown. In the group we followed, they had a medical doctor traveling with his pastor. We got to the building after a several-hour drive, and they knew we were coming. The place was clean as could be under the circumstances, and the workers were very nervous when we arrived.

It was the same situation as the first orphanage with a handful of ladies in nurse uniforms caring for 450 kids. The food situation was also extreme. The kids were wrapped in cloths binding their arms and legs from moving. They got one meal of powdered milk a day. I was overwhelmed by the children in this place because of the starvation. The children almost entirely were hollow and empty in their eyes. They looked with the same stare that the concentration camp Jews had in the pictures. I spent time trying to speak to some of them, and no response came. Blood was coming from their ears and the sides of the eyes on many of them.

The doctor and I went outside and were walking around the block, trying to process the situation we had just witnessed. I asked him what we could do for these kids, and he answered with tears in his eyes. He said if he could medivac every kid in the orphanage that minute to the states, he doubted that any of them could live. They were all starved past the point of no return and were already dead but did not know it yet. I still see their faces and the smells and the look on the workers faces. They knew! Too little too late has a whole new meaning to me.

That night, Lydia helped me preach again to the people in the square, and a larger crowd was there. An army man in uniform was standing, watching but not interfering. I found out from the doctor who had joined me that the ministry we were visiting had received a large shipment of Bibles in the language of the people. Owning a Bible was a capital offense punishable by death for the past seventy years. I asked the doc to check into getting me the Bibles, and we would give them out the next night. He said he would, and we called it a night.

The next day, our team was given an orphanage on the border of Kosovo. This was during the Serbian and Kosovo fighting. It was a long drive, and we left early in the morning and drove well into the day to get to the place. It was in the afternoon when we pulled into the orphanage. We parked on the road and walked up a long trail to a four-story white building on top of a hill. The village was war-torn, and people were very skittish. We could hear gunfire and small arms going off in the not too distant fields just over the hill from the orphanage.

As we were walking up the path, we could see sewage running down the little dirt gutter on the side of the path. When we got close to the building, there was a giant Red Cross flag hung from the roof, draping down across the top part of the building. The smell of ammonia was strong and coming from the building.

Again, the same situation as before with the workers. There were five ladies in nursing uniforms taking care of the four floors of occupants. The biggest difference with this orphanage was that it also housed the mentally ill. The first floor was babies and staff and kitchen and bathrooms. The second floor was toddlers, and the top two floors held the rest.

There were all ages of children and teens and adults. The adults each had severe enough mental issues that warranted them being there. They would not fake it to stay in this place. We were told that the war was thick in these parts and that the kids came from both sides of the fighting. Their parents were killed in the fighting and they would come from all over.

There was a huge hole in the building between the third and fourth floors. The nurses said it was a stray rocket from a grenade launcher that hit the building during one of the battles that had spilled over into this village as the battles often had. The lady said the commander apologized afterward for the damage.

The workers fed the kids powdered milk, and some of the villagers would bring any extra food they could, at times, to help. Many of the occupants were completely naked, and on the third and fourth floors, the workers tried to keep eyes on things, but teens and young adults all slept on blankets on the floors with very little supervision. The children were sleeping wherever they could on the same floors with the older teens and mentally ill adults.

The workers were sensitive to the little children's safety concerns but could only do so much. They did punish any abuses they knew of, but it was impossible to know everything that happened. The babies were left dirty and in need of attention, but they were not bound in cloth so they were using their arms and legs. They were not neglected. It just took the workers too long to attend to every need, so they were often left waiting.

The building had no electricity and the water supply was gravity fed from a cistern that had to be filled by hand pump between rains. The bathroom was three holes in the floor, evenly spaced, and the floor was several inches thick with human waste. The ladies that worked there were the best I had seen as far as trying and caring. They seemed to love each child, and every kid responded to each worker's attention with affection as they looked at us with fear.

The workers were in a war-torn village, caring for 300 plus people, from babies to mentally ill, with little help and nowhere to go. They were very excited to show us something that the international group in that area had given them. They took us into a room that was spotless and empty, except in the middle of the room was a brand-new washer and dryer with a giant red bow tied around each one. They were so proud of those two machines. No electricity and two-thirds of their occupants naked, and their help from the international community was a matching set electric washer and dryer.

We left everything we had with us for those people, and as we walked away, I could not help but think of the irony of the washer and dryer gifts. In my mind, I was seeing the picture of our ministry in the overall scheme of things. I represented a church willing to give $350,000 to an orphanage they could own and control, but I could not give any of it to these dear people who had just taken me to school on compassion, faith, and service. I felt guilty leaving only giving what I had in my wallet. We traveled late into the night with little words. When we got back, it was middle of the night, and we all had an early day coming, so we turned in.

The next morning at breakfast, the doctor told me they had 800 Bibles in their language that a church had paid for and sent for the work. I asked the director to let me give some of them out in the street meetings. He said that he was afraid to because it was so serious of an offense to the past government. He said that the situation there in the city was unstable, and no one knew how the police and army would react to giving out Bibles.

I had a copy in my room of the letter this man had sent to the preacher in Michigan, stating that the country was now a Christian country. The president welcomed churches to come help and the Gospel was welcome. I did not tell him about the money I had, but I said that when I got back that evening, if he did not have some of those Bibles ready for me to give out, I would tell the church that his letter was not true.

We did our trip to the next orphanage with the same situation as before—babies bound in cloths and sour powdered milk and too few workers who were without pay. It was truly a place where every penny would help so many, if the money would get to the children. When we got back, Lydia and the taxi driver agreed to help me get the Bibles to the square where I had been speaking each night. The director was not there, but his assistant took me to the closet where the Bibles were stored and then said he lost the key. It was a sad excuse for trying not to push the issue.

I picked the lock, and we loaded the sixteen boxes into the taxi and took them to the square to give them out. We had thirty men in this group, and I asked for help giving out the Bibles, and the only ones who would help were the two missionaries I had traveled with and the one doctor. There was a risk involved, as just a few months before, owning a Bible would get you killed. On the other hand, we had the opportunity to hand out God's Word to people who had never seen it or even heard it. That risk I will take any day, and so would the three men who helped me.

We walked the boxes across the street and stacked them up in the center of the square. It was 100 yards and sixteen boxes of Bibles. It took six of us some time to do that (taxi driver and Lydia helped). I gave the driver and Lydia a Bible privately, so they each got one. I cannot put into words the reaction from a person being offered the Bible who had, all their life, been threatened with death if they messed with one. They both treated the paperback Bible as if I had given them each a bar of gold.

People were used to me speaking to them every night, so many were waiting, and the others were just out walking and talking. No TV or radios. The people would go to the square and walk and visit with each other in the evenings.

The army guy, who was there every night, was standing to the side with his rifle. I had Lydia interpret for me as I shared that God had given us a copy of his Holy Word and that it was true. I told them that the Words to eternal life were in the Bible, and for that reason, the communist government they had lived under was against it. I then told them that I had Bibles with me. The entire place within my voice range stopped when Lydia said that.

I told the people that I would give each family one if they wanted it. I shared that Lydia was getting paid to help me and that I was doing this on my own because I wanted them to know the truth and for them to be set free from their sin. I took the first box and opened it and held up one for everyone to see it. You should have seen the awe in these people's eyes seeing a Bible for the first time in most of their lives.

When I held up the Bible, the army dude ran over to me and was facing me nervously, holding his rifle. He did not know what to do, and the other police were watching from the back of the crowd (that was growing bigger by the minute). I handed the soldier a copy of the Bible, and he took it and ran off.

The next thing that happened was interesting. The people formed a circle around Lydia, myself, and the boxes, and turned their backs to us and joined hands. Then people would hold out their hand for a Bible without anyone being able to see who they were. We were in a crowd of hundreds of people, and I told Lydia that the Bibles were one for each family. Hands started coming into the circle, and we were handing them Bibles. It was slow at first and never got crazy or out of control. Before long—with Lydia, the doctor, and the missionaries helping—we gave every Bible out to hands with no faces.

When we were down to our last Bible, an old lady (no way of telling) came up to my face. She asked if I would please give it to her. Lydia was translating for her as she told me her story. She was one of the few who were still alive in the day when the communists seized power. She said out loud, "I am not afraid to show my face and I want one of the Bibles." She spoke with a bitterness and said that her sister had spoken of God publicly on the street one day, and the government guards had beaten her unconscious. Her sister took her home and had cared for her ever since because she had never been able to move her legs after the beating. She said her sister did not even believe in God. She just mentioned his name out loud.

She looked around the crowd and spoke loudly that she intended to sit and read every word of the Bible to her sister. I gave her the Bible and she walked away.

We gave every copy of the 800 Bibles out to families who had not been able to see one, much less own one. I am so thankful God let me be part of that.

As I was cleaning up the boxes and getting ready to go back to the hotel, the old lady came back. She asked if she could please have one more copy for a friend who was bedridden. I told her I was out, and Lydia reached in her pocket and took out hers and gave it to the lady. Through Lydia, the lady told me that when she was just a little girl, she remembered the communists calling all the people into the square and telling them that God was dead and that no one could speak of God in any form again. They took all the pastors (thirteen) and lined them and their families up across from the people. The leader then asked the pastors, one at a time, to tell the people God was dead. She said every one of the pastors refused, and in response, the communists took them from their families and shot each one in the head.

All the pastors refused to deny Christ and were shot and piled into a pile in the middle of the square. The leader then told the people to bring out every Bible and all the religious material they owned and throw them on the pile. It took hours, and as the sun was going down, the leader stood by the pile of Bibles and books and papers lying on top of the pastors' bodies. His men were pouring kerosene over the pile as he spoke. He proclaimed that any person found with a Bible would be executed on the spot. Anyone speaking God's or Jesus's name would be severely punished. He then lit the pile on fire.

The lady was now looking past my face into her memory. "When the fire began burning the Bibles," she said, "the fire was circled by soldiers with guns. As the flames rose higher, those strong men were trembling in fear." I never forgot what she said next. "I have always wanted to read that book that was able to make such strong men afraid." She took Lydia's Bible and said, "Now I can."

The two weeks spent in Albania gave me a new understanding of so many things—human suffering, man's need to control others, selfishness, and poverty to list a few. Being able to share Christ with people is the most important thing a person can do, but if I was not a preacher, I would be a soldier and would fight communism anywhere it showed its ugly head.

My last night street preaching, I gave the people, many of whom had come every night, an invitation to personally accept Jesus. I explained what it meant and did not mean and how to do it. I also told them that the person of Christ was watching them and they should pray and seek his hand in their lives. I had noticed this guy, who lived behind our hotel, in a very nice tour bus, standing over against one of the statues in the square, listening.

When I finished, he motioned me over to where he was standing. He had a new Mercedes and was wearing a leather trench coat that went down to the ankles. He was obviously very wealthy. I went over, and he was Russian and about twenty-four years old and spoke good English. He told me he had been watching me and wanted to talk. He opened his coat and offered me some vodka. He knew I was an American, and he mentioned that he thought I really wanted to help these people. He did not believe in God but did not mind that I did.

He said that Albania would not fully become democratic. The Albanian people were just waiting for the Americans to come and give them freedom. He said the people had been robbed mentally from the thinking it would take for them to develop capitalist thinking. He said they would wait until someone else came and took them over again. He also thanked me for caring and shook my hand. I have often thought about that man.

After our final meeting with the ministry, I shared with their leadership that they had not been truthful with the pastors in the states and that they needed to adjust their vision toward the true state of things. I never mentioned the money, and we got ready to leave.

The two missionaries and I had Lydia bring her family to meet us at the hotel. We offered Lydia a college education in the states if she would come, but she turned it down. She said, "Who is going to fix my country if I leave?" We had paid her $20 a day for interpreting for us and another $20 for interpreting for my street messages almost each night. She told us that she liked our type of Christianity better than the ones who made the others work for pennies.

I left my suitcase and briefcase and everything I had but $20 with them. I gave my pastor's Bible to Lydia because she could read it, and she had given hers to the old lady. The other stuff her parents could sell for food. We gave the taxi driver the money for a ticket he got while helping us, and Lydia said it was very important for his family that we did that. We all hugged goodbye and got on the plane to leave.

I have no idea if or who was helped on that trip other than what God did in my life. I do know that we made friends with good people and gave out 800 Bibles to families and preached to many who had never heard the Gospel. God knew each of the babies and kids in the orphanages and held them in his hands and now in his arms. The church in America will one day give an account for how we spend our money and who we spend our money on.

One last story from Albania. We were driving several hours back into the countryside from the capital where cars are rarely seen. The military had not been on the roads because of the collapse in the government. The rules to roadways were not really known, and people and animals, especially children playing, would run out into the road with no warning and without looking. You had to really be on your toes. It was middle of the day and hot that afternoon. The driver and Lydia were in the front, and the two missionaries and myself were in the back.

We came over this little hill, and in the middle of the road was a donkey, sitting. Over to the side of the road was the donkey's owner leaning against a tree, napping. Our taxi driver pulled to a stop and shut off the car and started reading a book he brought along. I asked Lydia what was going on. She said that it was not polite to wake a guy up from his nap to have him move his donkey.

The donkey was just keeping his ground and staring at us, chewing something. I reached out the car window and slammed the side with my hand and woke the guy up. I shouted to him, "Hey, dude, get your dumb ass out of the road!"

The two men looked at me in shock, and I looked back and said, "I have been waiting my entire Christian life to be able to say that to someone biblically. Lydia even got that one.

Jackson Park

One of the places we ran buses into was a set of government projects known as Jackson Park. It was a place where the police would not come alone, only in groups. Drugs and gangs and you fill in the blanks were there. One other thing about Jackson Park, it was filled with kids, none of whom had any say about the environment they were raised in. Rusty had been visiting there for his bus route and had a couple of buses coming from there every week. The complex was huge. It had masses of people.

I began visiting with Rusty, trying to get some of the parents to come to our class. We brought children three to four years old up to older teens and taught them. Some of the teens had their own kids and could not come unless they brought their kids with them. We had teachers for their babies who loved on them every week. One of the things that came with bus work was that you got to know the families you worked with in a very personal way. We also got to know the young men who were involved in the bad stuff very well, and they knew us too.

Often as we visited Jackson Park, we would hear gunshots and fights. One day, Rusty and I walked around the corner of one of the buildings into a drug transaction. The guys with their backs to us turned around, pointing pistols at our faces. The dude doing the deal said, "It's just Rusty and Frank," and they turned around and continued.

Rusty asked one of them if their mom was home, and he said, "Go check, I'm not sure," and we walked on by. It was always that way in Jackson Park.

The city was slowly boarding up apartments in some of the worst buildings in a ploy to shut them down. The boards were then ripped off, and transients and druggies stayed in them. We had one lady, a young woman, twenty-one at most, who came on the bus with her little three-year-old girl. The baby was a sweetheart, and the mother could be a good person but was addicted to drugs. We worked with them until they dropped off the map.

One Saturday, I was visiting for the class and the bus route, and this lady lived upstairs in an apartment building that was all boarded up but her unit. I was walking up the stairs, and the little girl was playing on the back porch area with the door open. She told me her mom was home, so I knocked and said hello loudly and went in through the kitchen. I walked into the living room and the mom, another woman, and a guy were all lying naked, passed out on the couch and floor from drugs. The mom was yellow from her habit with dark sunken eyes. At one time, she was probably very pretty.

I turned to walk out, and the little girl asked, "Mr. Frank, will you play with me?" I sat down on the steps. She jumped up and ran inside to her room to get something and then ran back to me. She put this little baby dead kitten in my lap and asked me to make it play with her. The cat had been dead long enough to stink, and its eyes were not in its head. "Fix it, Mr. Frank," she asked, and then she started petting it in my lap and saying, "Please make it play, it's broken!"

I took the little stinking cat and wrapped it in paper towels and told her it was in kitty heaven. I helped her wash her hands and told her I would see her tomorrow and to tell her mom I came by.

We loved a lot of kids out of that place, and some kids did well while others got caught up in the lifestyle of Jackson Park. I am thankful to have had the chance to teach them God's love and the chance to help those who wanted to find a better way of life. I believe some of the ones who did not find a better life did find Jesus and they are not alone in their suffering and shame. Thank God for loving us!

Goat Face

For years, my mother suffered from schizophrenia. I often would have to travel to her hometown and find her and take her, against her will, to Central State Mental Hospital for help. It would often mean I would have to go from bar to bar until I found her. Then I would have to drag her, kicking and screaming, the whole way.

Sometimes I would have to fight our way out of the places, while carrying her, and even worse things happened that need not be mentioned. When my mom flipped out, she would have super-human strength, and I was the only one that could handle her for some reason. One time, I got a call that Mom was acting up again, and I had to go find and help her. When I got to Macon, Georgia, it took me three days to find her and get her safely into Central State. I had to physically fight her, and a few others, to get her out of the cutthroat bar she was in and to a hospital before taking her to Central State.

By time I got her in Central and was heading home, it had been three days and nights that I had not laid down at all. I pulled into my driveway about ten at night and was a complete basket case mentally and exhausted physically. I walked into the house and jumped into the shower.

No sooner had I finished my shower and had just sat down on the couch when the phone rang. It was Rusty. He asked me if I could come with him on a visit that was an emergency. He knew what I had been doing and that I had just gotten home. He said he normally would not ask, but this was crazy, and he needed my help. I told him I would go, but that I did not think I would be much help.

When Rusty picked me up, he explained that one of our bus kids' parents was having weird problems. The family was a mom, step-dad, and little girl and they were well-off. The girl loved the buses and was one of our regular kids. She also attended our church's private school.

On the way over to the house, I told Rusty that I was emotionally and physically gone and that I did not have any strength to help him, much more than be there. When we got to the house and knocked on the door, the husband let us in. He and his mom were there, and his wife was knotted up in a ball on the couch. The husband told us the wife had freaked out a couple of hours earlier and was acting strange. The living room was several degrees colder than the rest of the house and the family dog was going crazy.

We started toward the couch where the lady was, and her head popped up. She looked at Rusty and spoke in a demon's voice, "I will not speak with you, your faith is strong." Turning and looking at me, she said, "But your faith is weak, and I will have your mind!"

Rusty and I looked at each other, and we knew this was crazy. Some people do not believe in demon possession, but it is a very real thing. This woman was possessed by a demon. I had, at that point, dealt with a demon-possessed person one time before, and I know Jesus is the only way to handle it.

I answered that I was not going to fight with the spirit but that the blood of Jesus was what we would call on to help the lady. We stayed there, praying and fighting that spirit to leave her for over three hours. At one point, we were quoting parts of Psalm 22 about

Jesus on the cross. The demon said, "I was there, I saw the whole bloody mess." Finally, we asked to speak to the woman, and we told her to call on Jesus for help. The demon would throw her around and shout profanities.

At one point, as we were praying and asking God to help, the lady's face popped out of her contorted position, and the bones in her face shifted into the shape of a goat's face. I would not believe you if you told me this, so no hard feelings if you do not believe me, but Rusty and I saw it. We asked the demon its name, and it said it was a lust demon and it was the lady's grandmother's name, Anna. The grandmother had been a Satan worshipper and often used the lady, when she was a child, in her worship practices to the devil. She never told us what they did to her, but whatever it was, it had done great damage to that child who was now a mother.

The lady was a stripper in a high dollar night club and made a lot of money at it. We asked to speak with the woman again, and I asked her if she would be willing to take Christ as her Savior if the demon left her. She said she would.

After that, the woman completely went limp, and in her own real voice, she said, "I am free." Rusty and I looked at her, but it was still cold in the room, the dog was still going crazy, and it did not feel like the demon was gone. We put our hands on her head and started claiming the blood of Jesus, and sure enough, the demon was fooling or trying to fool us. We kept our hands on her head and prayed Jesus's blood over her, and finally the demon left her. It was obvious that this time she was free.

We explained what had happened to her. The lady did confess her sins, and she asked Jesus to come into her heart and save her. Her face was back to normal (for those who are wondering). God did a work in that lady's life and in her home. For me, to this day, I do not like goats.

WrestleMania

"Italian Stallion" was Gary's wrestling name. At the time, he was a household favorite of wrestling fandom. He also had a heart for helping people. I am blessed to call him one of my friends. Rusty and Gary worked with a lot of street kids, teens, and even adults. They flocked to Gary.

Rusty decided we needed to somehow do more for the inner city of Charlotte. We were reaching some families and many kids. We had a teen church for gang members with well over fifty coming (no colors allowed at church). But there are so many in the inner city of Charlotte that needed to hear and be reached with the truth of the Gospel. Rusty had our church rent the Charlotte Hornets Auditorium, and Gary brought in his wrestling crew for a night we called WrestleMania.

We advertised the event and opened the doors for anyone who wanted to come, free of charge. Gary had a group of young and up and coming guys who traveled with him, doing shows all over. On this night, we opened the doors, and about 10,000 people showed up. We were in the Hornet's stadium and used half the seating area for our crowd. It was a crazy time all around with many people at the arena for their first time.

Admission was free, and we had the homeless, down and outers, and every kind of person you could imagine. Many families from the projects came (we ran buses) as well as teens from different gangs. I enjoyed watching security. Although it was a small crowd for them, I am sure it was their roughest. I am amazed at how many people like wrestling.

One of Gary's partners was a guy who wrestled by the name of Gorgeous George South. He was an outspoken Christian in his daily life, and he opened the show by giving his personal testimony. He told the crowd how he came to Jesus and what God was doing in his life. The people listened. I/We were nervous about how the crowd would react to the Gospel, but they listened to George.

The show was a good one, and Gary provided the crowd with a real wrestling experience that had plenty of the stuff wrestling fans expect and enjoy. The last match featured Italian Stallion wrestling for a grudge match and a belt against another named opponent. The match was a good one with cheating, hitting with chairs, bleeding, the bad guy making the crowd crazy. To the audience's amazement, Gary won by coming back from being illegally beat down and almost out. He, in the last minute, stood up and took out the bad guy and kept his belt.

There were a few times that I thought the crowd was going to come out of their chairs to get the bad guy, but Gary got him good enough. The crowd was going nuts, and the houselights went down to just Gary in the ring.

Gary looked at the 10,000-plus of Charlotte's broken and down and outers. He cared—you could see it in the way he spoke and you could hear it in his voice. He simply asked everyone if they had a good time. The house went crazy. He told them he would have lost if they had not cheered him on. Then he asked if they would be still, without talking, and listen to him for a little bit. He said he was not a preacher, like Rusty, and that he did not have much practice at speaking on Jesus type stuff, but he wanted them to know something.

He said that he had a lot of money compared to most of them. He also said that his money did not take his problems away. He shared how he and his wife were about to break up and that he was in a bad place in his life, very unhappy. He then said to the crowd that he took all his life—good, bad, and ugly—and laid it at Jesus's feet. He asked Jesus to forgive his sins and come into his life. The crowd was silent and listening.

Gary continued by saying that the arena was filled with people who had made bad decisions, hurt loved ones, and had committed sins of every kind. Gary said, "Every one of you listening can be forgiven, just like I was forgiven." Gary asked the people who wanted to take Christ and his forgiveness to stand to their feet, and many did.

Rusty came to the ring and led them in a prayer to Christ. He then shared some things that those who prayed should do. It is impossible to know how many or who did what, but I can tell all of us this truth. The biggest wrestling match of the night was not Black Scorpion and Stallion. It was Satan and God wrestling with the hearts of the people there for their eternal souls.

I believe that Gary won a new title that night. It was the title of compassion for the hearts of man! I also believe God answered weeks of prayer and hard work by saving many down and outers who are now saved and inners!

A funny side note. Gary had just been saved and baptized and had just started coming to our church. God did a work in his and his wife's hearts. One of the deacons of our church pulled me aside and asked me to tell Gary to get his hair cut. Gary was huge, size sixty chest and thirty-two-inch biceps. He could pick up 500-pound men and throw them wherever. I told the deacon to go tell Gary himself so I could watch.

Around that same time, Gary had called me to meet him late one night at the Waffle House. When I got there, he was struggling with something God was asking him to give up in his life. The thing was a big deal to him. My point is that this deacon who thought he was God's judge to other Christians was busy judging Gary about his long hair. God was asking Gary to give up something much bigger in his life for himself.

Gary did surrender the thing to God, and God blessed him for it, something every Christian should come to realize. God never called that deacon, you, or me to tell people what they need to give up for God. We need to love them and teach them how to talk with God so they can hear God's Word in their own heart and follow him, not us or man. God is the judge, and we do best at being servants to the people God is reaching out to.

Year of Prayer

During these days of working in the projects and inner city areas of Charlotte, God was doing a work in Rusty's heart and mine. One night, we were out late visiting, and on the way back home, Rusty mentioned that he had been praying about Cuba. I asked him what put Cuba on his mind, and he said he did not know but that he was feeling burdened for Cuba lately.

I then shared with Rusty that I was beginning to feel it was time for me to get back to the call to missions like I had promised God. A few weeks went by, and I was feeling more of a burden, and Rusty seemed like he was too.

We stopped for coffee late one night again, and we both began sharing with each other that we were beginning to feel God's tug on our hearts for something more. Rusty was on staff at the church and couldn't let anyone know he was feeling burdened for some other work or they would replace him. He was just married and needed his check every week.

I was working construction on my own and working for the church as if I was on staff, just without the pay. I also could not tell anyone that God was dealing with me about fulfilling my promise to do missions work. For several weeks after that night, after every message at church, Rusty and I would be led to the altar for prayer. God was speaking to both of us.

Finally, we met one morning and admitted to each other that God was working on our hearts. We still had a heart for our work there in Charlotte and still reaching people, but it was clear God was calling each of us to something. But for our own reasons, we could not tell anyone else other than our wives.

We decided to meet every morning during the week to pray together. We would do this for the next year or until God made it clear what he was guiding each of our families to do. We met for one full year, Monday to Friday mornings, praying for God to make his will plain to us and our wives.

During that year, God continued to bless the buses and the classes and our special days. No one knew that we were praying for guidance. But God was showing each of us his will. Rusty began praying more and more for Cuba. I began being burdened for churches in the areas of our country where there were none. Rusty was praying with me about the needs for churches, and I prayed with him about the need for Cuba to hear the truth.

Rusty was visiting door-to-door one day and came across a Hispanic group of families. He wanted to start a Bible study, and they were open to doing it. He came to find out the group was about fifty strong and they were all Cuban. I started writing articles and placing them in the newspapers of cities in the northwestern part of the country. I was asking for anyone or groups of people who felt the need to start a church to contact me. God was making his will for each of us clearer as each week went by.

By the end of the year, God had given Rusty peace that he was being called to Cuba as a missionary. He already had a group of Cuban's meeting with him in Charlotte. I had not heard from any of the ads out west, but I knew God was speaking to me about the need to start a church.

After one year of praying and waiting on God, we both knew clearly what God was asking us to do. Rusty and I went public in our church. Rusty announced his call to Cuba, and I announced my call to start a church out west. We both began our preparations to go.

Rusty joined a mission board and raised his support money in record time. He also had several businessmen in the church start donating medical supplies to his ministry. They had companies that made medical supplies, and because of the way they were packaged, they were not able to be sold if one of the layers of packaging became broken.

Rusty ended up with warehouses full of medical supplies. United States Senators Max Burton and Jesse Helms together passed the Burton Helms act, making it possible that medical aid could be given to Cuba from the USA. God was opening doors for Rusty to break into Cuba in God-sized ways.

I, on the other hand, asked God to show me a sign that he would take care of my family if we moved somewhere to start a church. I decided to take all our savings, $450, and travel to the northwestern United States, city by city, and pray in each one until God told me where to start his church. I asked God to provide for the trip without me having to tell anyone my needs. I promised God I would take only the $450 and leave by myself with it in cash.

I then asked God to please prove to me his will to move my family by providing the rest. I also promised I would not tell anyone my needs. It was not that I did not have faith in God; I needed God to affirm that he would protect my wife and four young boys and meet our needs! My wife's dad heard about the plans, and he offered his Cadillac for me to use if I let him go along. I told him the test I was making with God and how I was leaving with $450, depending on God to provide, as a sign for my family.

Don agreed that he would ride along, not aid in money, and not tell anyone our needs. He promised to help drive and pray. So, I drove to Milwaukee and picked up Don, and we started out with now about $350 and faith.

I had mentioned in an e-mail that I was surveying the western United States for a possible church planting location. One of our friends who was stationed near a church that both of our families had attended years earlier contacted us and asked us to stop by and see them. He was a dentist with the air force, serving on a base in South Dakota.

We did, and his pastor invited me to preach for him, and I did. The pastor shared his burden for eight cities he felt needed churches. He gave us a love offering of $450 for preaching as we were just running out of money.

We stayed on the road for two weeks, driving and praying. Each time we ran almost out of money, God would do something. We ended up in Washington, in the Kirkland area of Seattle, just about out of money again. I was looking for churches in the area when I found out I knew a pastor there. We met for coffee. He had me speak, and his church gave us a love offering.

A snowstorm hit the northwest, forcing Don and I south through California. God spoke to my heart to start his church as we were just driving into Mesa, Arizona. By the end of our trip, we had traveled all over the northwestern and southwestern United States. God provided every penny, and I knew that we were going to Mesa, Arizona, to start his church.

We did not share with anyone our need and were down to the last few pennies and drops of gas a few times, but God showed his hand each time, providing enough for a few more miles and beans and gallons of gas. My father-in-law and I had the best time together and became much closer friends from the trip!

Thinking back on those days, from one year of prayer, God led both families to different fields with open doors and provision to start his work. God made a way for Rusty's family and for my family. He was and is and will always be faithful. Trust him with your stuff and watch and see what he does!

I Get to Laugh in Your Face!

We set a date for our move and made it public. I had some revivals scheduled and things to take care of with our couple's class that had to be finished in order to go. There was a deacon in our church named Steve Mallory who is a Godly deacon and a good friend. Steve flew F16s in the Navy and was a pilot for Eastern Airlines.

One Wednesday night during church, about a month before we planned to leave for Mesa, Steve came up to me and asked if I was going to go find a place for my family to move into at Mesa before we left. I let him know that I did not have the money yet to move, much less survey the city for a rental house. I told him unless something unexpected happened, I was just going to pack up and go. Steve said he figured as much, and the next week, he and I flew to Phoenix, Arizona, and drove to Mesa to find a rental house.

Mesa was a busy place at the time and was tied with Vegas as the fastest growing city in the country, or so it claimed. Mesa had a Mormon population stronger than Salt Lake City, Utah, and was home to a Mormon temple. We contacted a realtor for advice on finding a rental house, and they just laughed. Our third realtor informed us that rentals came out biweekly and were normally taken before you got a chance to call. The list was coming out the next hour or so, and we could get a copy from her office, but it probably wouldn't help. We drove to her office and waited on the list. When the list came out, she gave us a copy and we left.

When we got in the car, Steve drove, and I called the houses. There were four houses on the list that fit where we were financially. I called the first one, and they said it was available. I asked them to hold it, and they said they would for half a day. In one hour's time, we set a time to meet and looked at it.

I called the next two houses, and they were already taken. So in my thinking, we had our house. We met the agent handling the house, and his name was Carl Goldberg. He represented a wealthy client who owned a lot of properties. We looked at the house and agreed to take it. We set up a meeting in Carl's office for the next morning. The rent was going to be $1,500 a month with some change.

Sharon and I had about $750 in the bank. So the next morning, Steve and I went to Carl's office. It became clear to me that he himself was the wealthy investor he represented, but I never discussed it with him. We sat down, and Carl asked what line of work I was in and what was bringing me to Mesa, Arizona. I shared with him that after a year in prayer about my family's next step, God led me to come to Mesa to start a church.

Carl looked at me in surprise and started laughing. He asked if I was serious, and if I expected him to believe God spoke to me, telling me to come start a church in Mesa.

I told him, "Absolutely."

He informed me that he was an atheist and asked if I had a comment on that.

I told him that him being an atheist Jewish man was as funny to me as me being told by God to come here was to him.

He asked what job I had and what verifiable income I could prove. I said I had about two-thirds of what I needed promised in support by friends and no job yet.

Carl laughed again and said, "You expect me to rent you a house with no job or verifiable income to show for your ability to pay?"

I told him I did. "Carl, God has promised me he would provide, and he will."

Carl looked at me and laughed and then said to us, "I will rent the house to you on one condition. You have to come into my office and let me laugh in your face on the first day you are late on your rent!"

I grabbed his hand and shook it. "Deal!" I said. He said he needed $1,200 security that same day in order to write the contract. I told him I needed to go to an ATM, and he said one was just outside his window and pointed to it.

Steve and I walked out to the ATM to get the money, and my card would not work. My plan was to get $750 out to give as cash and write him a check for the rest. I tried three times, and the machine would not give me any money.

Carl was watching from his window, and finally Steve said, "Try $300," and I did, and it worked. He got $300 from his card, and we went back in to Carl.

Steve and I sat down, and Carl then wanted a $1,200 check to hold for security and $750 cash for him to give me the keys. He said he needed three month's rent the day we moved in and that the third month would be for our last month we were in the house. Total, he wanted $4,500 in rent, $750 cash we had just given him for the keys, and a $1,200 security check that would be cashed when we moved in and held in the account until we moved out.

Steve had $150 in his pocket, and we added that to the $600 to give Carl his $750 cash. Then Steve did something that shocked me. He took out his checkbook and gave Carl the $1,200 security check. Carl told Steve he could not believe that Steve was dumb enough to write a check on a promise from God.

Steve told Carl that he was a retired lieutenant colonel and combat F16 fighter pilot in the war. He said if he felt sure about anything, it was a promise from God. Steve then said to Carl, "I am giving you this check with one condition."

Carl asked what it was, and Steve said that when we got it back that Carl would shake our hand and admit that God had kept his promise.

Carl took the check and said, "Deal!"

Both of those men became good friends to my family and I. Steve still is in touch, and he helped and prayed for our church the entire time we were in Arizona. Carl and I met at least once a month for lunch, and he never got to laugh in my face.

God is faithful. Many a time it was last minute, but God showed Carl something. Carl has not accepted Christ that I know of yet, but he visited our church two times and said he respected my Christianity. I have lost contact with him, but I still pray he and his family will be saved. He remains my very dear friend.

Buddy Don't Move; You are Probably Going to Die!

I traveled and preached as an evangelist during my years in Charlotte. Just a few weeks before we were to move to Arizona, I had my final meeting in a small farming community in Iowa called Knob. Randy Miller was the pastor there, and he and his family are great people. He scheduled me to come and preach a five-day revival. I was trying to raise the money needed to move and was on a tight budget, so I decided to drive to Randy's church, trying to save as much money as possible.

I left North Carolina and headed for Knob on a Tuesday. The revival meeting was scheduled for Wednesday through Sunday. I was driving our Ford Taurus and was heading through Nashville, Tennessee.

I was just getting into Nashville when a little yellow car in the lane on my right side swerved into my back fender, almost hitting it. I turned around to see what it was doing as he swerved back away from me. I was going between sixty-five and seventy miles an hour and was following the line of traffic. It only took a half of a second to glance over my shoulder and then back toward the road in front of me. I was coming over a little ridge at the same time, and as I turned back to face the front, the eighteen-wheeler in front of me had just locked down his trailer and was stopped. I rear-ended the truck at full speed. The car behind me hit me, glancing off, and spun down the medium.

I remember thinking in slow motion in the split-second before I hit the truck, *This is going to be bad.* I hit the back of the truck, going close to seventy miles an hour, and the motor came through the firewall and ended up in the backseat with me. The front was a mangled mess. I did not pass out or lose consciousness, but I was knocked stupid.

It happened on the interstate which had three lanes of traffic, and I was in the left lane next to the medium. I hit my head on the roof and windshield of the car, and the steering wheel and shaft were gone. I ended up in the backseat with the motor on my right side. One of my eyelids was bleeding from being cut after hitting the roof and windshield, and my pinky finger on my left hand was broken and pointing in an unnatural way to its side. My knee was hurting and the pain was incredibly intense.

As I was coming back from dummy land, I noticed that the doors were not going to open. I knew I needed to get out of the car somehow. I found my briefcase, my Bible, and my pistol. I grabbed my Bible and pistol and put them in my briefcase. I did not know if my face was cut up badly, so I leaned forward and was watching to see the amount of blood dripping on my shirt to get an idea of how bad it was.

Here is what happened. The eighteen-wheeler came over the little ridge to find a station wagon with a rope tied to a truck from its bumper stopped in the fast lane of the interstate. The two drivers were standing outside of their vehicles in the median talking. The truck came over the ridge at seventy miles an hour, saw them, and locked down the brakes. His trailer was loaded down, and the truck stopped just before he hit them. I glanced over and looked back just as he had locked it down, and I didn't have time to hit my brakes. *Bam!*

The two people got in their station wagon and truck and sped away. I was looking for a way out of the car when this old boy comes running up to the door and screamed, "Don't move, mister! You are probably going to die!" He stepped back and looked at the car and said, "Looks like they are going to have to cut you out of there with the jaws of death!"

I looked at the man and said, "Buddy, get away from my car!" I was almost able to focus by then, so I rolled into the back of the hatch of the Taurus and kicked it open with my working leg. It opened, probably because my car was clipped by the car behind me and the back driver's side was damaged. I crawled out and stood up beside my car. The only crippling pain was in my left knee. Evidently, the motor hit it as I was being pushed into the back from the crash.

I was always told that if you break your leg or knee, you will not be able to walk on it. So I picked a spot down the medium about thirty yards away and started walking toward it. There was a cup laying in a drain, so I went over and bent down, putting the pressure on my knee, and picked the cup up. I almost passed out, but I managed to pick the cup up.

I turned and started walking back toward the car, and an ambulance pulled past me in the median and stopped beside the car. I walked up to the ambulance, and two guys jumped out and began looking all around my car. I sat on their rear bumper and rubbed my knee. I asked the guys what they were doing, and one said they were trying to find the body. I started laughing (not in a funny way) and stated that I was the body.

The guys did not believe me. One of them replied, "Whoever was driving this car is dead or close to it." I showed him my finger's unnatural position and the bleeding over my eyebrow, and they jumped over to me. "Don't move!" they said, and they opened the door to the ambulance and helped me in and I sat on the bed.

There was this neck brace they kept trying to put on me. I do not have much of a neck and it would not fit. After several attempts, they put it on and taped it. They told me to lie down on this gurney, but I did not fit too well on it. One of them got my briefcase, and we started toward the hospital.

They rolled me into a room at the ER, and a doctor came in and started poking and checking. I told him I was okay, but my eye was cut and my finger was broken, but the main thing was my right knee was killing me. He took the stupid neck thing off and they took me in for X-rays. I had a broken finger and my kneecap was broken in half and separated. The doctor told me they were going to drain my knee from fluid and push it back together and put a cast on my leg.

In the mix up, the doctor thought someone had already given me something for pain. He was going to push my kneecap back together. I tried to tell them they hadn't given me any painkillers, but no one listened. He drained two big vials of fluid out my knee and started getting ready to push the bones back together. I pulled my finger straight at the same time they pushed my kneecap together, because I knew I would not feel both at the same time. It worked, I only felt the knee! I called the airport and got a flight to St. Louis, and then a little puddle jumper to the closest airport to Knob, Iowa. Randy agreed to pick me up from the airport.

The hospital put a leg cast from my ankle to my hip on my right leg. I was told to wear it for eight to ten weeks and then go to a specialist. The only pain medicine they gave me was Tylenol. I was hurting all over, and by the time I arrived in St. Louis, my body throbbed with pain and my stomach was messed up.

I reached the gate for the puddle jumper early and needed to go to the bathroom. My stomach was very upset, and I had to go. The bathroom closest to my gate was small and cramped, but no one was around. I have to have privacy when I did such things and was thankful for that at least. I went into the stall and tried sitting on the toilet with my leg cast. The stall was so small, I could not do it without the stall door staying open and some of my leg sticking out into the aisle. Again, I was thankful for nobody being around.

Just as I got situated and able to do my business, the door to the restroom opened and a line of men came past my stall. Evidently, a plane just landed, and this small restroom was the first one from their gate. I had just passed the point of no return when they came in, and as they passed my leg sticking out in the aisle, they had to turn my direction to fit between my foot and the sink. A short line formed for the urinals, and I had the pleasure of meeting eight or nine men as we did what people do in airport restrooms.

The little plane to Knob was too small for me to fit in a seat with a full leg cast. I was put in the back of this sixteen-seater in the attendant's seat with a seat belt on my waist and another across my cast laying in the other seat. I could not move.

The attendant made me a glass of water with ice and a straw and left me in the back. If you have flown on a small plane, you know how bouncy they get, and it's worse toward the back. At one point, we hit an air pocket, and the plane just dropped, and as it did, I was holding my cup, but the ice water was about ten inches above the cup in the air. The plane caught, and the water and ice came down on my lap.

When the attendants came back to help unstrap me, they looked nervously at my wet crotch, and I smiled and said, "Ice water." I had to walk downstairs from the plane and across the tarmac with wet streaks down both sides of my pants just like I had peed all over myself. It was a humbling day.

That was my last meeting as an evangelist. Even with all that, God blessed the meetings, and we saw him do some things in that little church. I remember thinking as I was lying in the ambulance, *Lord, I don't want to be stopped from going to Arizona.*

God said, "Then don't let it stop you."

It didn't, and God blessed despite the challenges.

Here We Go!

One week after the accident, we were scheduled to leave for Mesa. On the Friday before we were to leave, we had enough money for the moving truck, but nothing else. I had a full leg cast on my right leg and a promise from God he would provide. Our plan was to pull out Monday morning. Rusty had our Sunday school class and bus ministry friends come help us load the truck. By early afternoon on Saturday, we were loaded and ready for the 2,092-mile trip to Mesa, Arizona.

The only thing missing was the money for traveling and what was needed upon arrival. Sharon's parents were following our moving van with the kids in their car. On Saturday, I had less than $100. I put my work truck on the street with a for sale sign and sold it that afternoon for cash.

The next day, our church had our family say goodbye, and they prayed over us and took up a love offering to help. People we knew and loved came by and gave us money and hugs, and on Monday morning, we left Charlotte, North Carolina, for Mesa, Arizona.

The trip took three days of driving and, for the most part, was uneventful. We pulled into the driveway of our rental house/church building early afternoon Thursday. We paid the three months' rent and security deposit required by Carl, our Jewish landlord. We needed to have the utilities turned on and buy a refrigerator and a family car since I smashed our other one.

291

The utilities deposits cost a lot more than we figured, but by Friday morning, we had them paid and had a refrigerator. We were running low on money and still needed a car. Because of the way our support was set up, Sharon and I agreed to try and buy an older car for cash to avoid having payments. I remembered seeing an older but nice looking white station wagon in the used car section of a dealership we passed coming into town.

Sharon and I drove over to where it was, and it looked to be in good shape. I asked a salesman what their absolute bottom dollar cash price for the car was, and he came back with $1,500. It seemed way too low for a dealership, so I asked him what was the deal with the price. He told us that the car was in good shape with maintenance history and good tires. The only issue was that it did not have air-conditioning. Sharon and I had never been in Arizona during summer. It was the first of spring and eighty-five degrees that day.

Sharon and I looked at each other and said to the man, "Deal," and bought the car. A funny note, a few weeks later, the weather reached over 100 degrees one day. In that part of Arizona, when the spring weather goes over 100, it does not come back under 100 for six or more months. That first year we were there, Mesa broke a record for the most consecutive days that the temp was over 114 degrees. It was like 147 or close to that many days. We then understood the great deal on our car without air-conditioning.

I remember what I am about to share just like it was yesterday. After one year of secret prayer, several months of preparation, my family was in Mesa, Arizona, to begin a Baptist Church in a Mormon city. Everything was in place, and we had our refrigerator, non-air-conditioned car, and our utilities were on. I only had to return the U-Haul truck.

I wobbled out (in my cast) and sat on the back bumper of the truck. I had $128 to my name and now lived 2,092 miles away from anyone I knew. I had only promised income from a few supporters and no idea how much the cost of living was in Mesa. My wife and four young sons and I now lived in a foreign land with very little money.

The thing I remember about that time was the thought that struck me sitting on that bumper. "What have you done?" was screaming in my ears. Panic started taking my thoughts, but then I closed my eyes. I spoke to the devil out loud (any neighbors hearing would think I was crazy). I said to the devil, "God called me here and God will take care of me and my family here!"

Please don't think that I share this because I am some kind of super Christian of great faith. I am not. Please do know that I serve a super and great God who will do the same things for you.

100 Doors a Day

We got settled into our house, and I began the work of building our new church. I started by going to people's doors and asking them to come visit. The area where we located had a heavy Mormon population. In fact, we were a little less than a mile from a Mormon Temple.

The Mormon church is known for their evangelism, and so when I started knocking on doors, people were not as surprised as they would be in an area of another influence. I found out from visiting that we were in a population that was more heavily Mormon than Salt Lake City. I can't tell you how many people asked me, "When did the Baptists start visiting door-to-door?"

The first summer in Mesa was a totally new experience in several ways. One, I had never been anywhere that was 118 degrees outside. That summer broke a record for the most consecutive days with 114 and above degrees. The heat lasted close to 147 days in a row, and some days, they shut the airport down because it was too hot for the airplanes to take off.

There were no woods or trees like back home. The only grass and trees were brought in as landscaping, and apart from your subdivisions, the natural land was covered in desert, cactus, and giant rabbits. In the neighborhood where we were, the city blocks were one square mile blocks with subdivisions inside the square mile and commercial buildings on the bordering streets outside the houses.

Every major road was east to west and north to south in square mile squares. A few of the square mile sections had not yet been developed, and they were desert scrub trees and scrub bushes with hundreds of giant rabbits living in them. They were funny to play with.

My first step in planting the church was to get people coming to our Sunday and Wednesday meetings. So I made a goal of visiting 100 doors a day, leaving our literature, and inviting people. The city, at the time we moved there, was one of the fastest growing areas in our country. They were building six houses per acre. Many times, people would have more square feet inside their house than they had yard outside. It was a lot easier walking from house to house because of how crowded the neighborhoods were. It took me about an average of three and a half hours to five hours to visit 100 houses. The work was simple—x number of doors would produce x number of visitors; at least, that had been the case everywhere else I had ever lived and served.

My wife and four boys made up our church at first. A family who knew my wife's parents eventually started coming, and we began. I walked everywhere I visited and spent Monday through Friday and many Saturdays visiting door-to-door. I met a lot of people who did not mind talking and found people open about their beliefs.

Another difference was that most people (70-plus percent) were active Mormons or claimed to be, and the largest group after that was nonbelievers. There were a few others, but of all the people I visited, the clear majority was first, Mormon; second, non-believers; third ex-Mormon and not interested. I found it challenging and inspiring because so many people either were being deceived or not believing at all. The Gospel is truth and speaks for itself, so all I had to do was give these people the Gospel and let God do the work in their hearts.

I spent eight long hot and discouraging weeks, going door-to-door, meeting 500 to 600 houses times eight and did not get one single visitor to our church. I knew starting a church from scratch was not easy, but man, I felt like a farmer trying to plow granite. One day, I was just not able to go to one more house and told my wife to load up the boys into our station wagon without a/c, and we would go out in the 118-degree desert and have a picnic. I was as discouraged as I had ever been in my life.

We packed up the boys, drove the hour out into the desert, and pulled the car off the road to find a spot where a picnic was possible. I walked just over a little rise in the road, and all I saw was a giant desert landscape for as far as eyes could see with thousands of saguaro cacti staring at me.

It was hot. I felt so defeated as I stood there looking out at so many cacti. I told my wife, "Look, honey, every one of those cactuses are shooting me the bird." That was how I felt, so we packed up and explored till we found a friendlier place to hold our picnic.

It was a few weeks after that when we started getting visitors to come to our services. In my first few years, I found that it took about 3,000 doors to get a cold case visitor, and it took about five visitors to get one to join with the work in the church. It was like plowing granite.

Carl

My landlord for our house in Mesa was an atheist Jew. He was wealthy and very outspoken about his faith as an atheist. I was upfront with him about my reason for moving to Mesa and renting from him was to start a church. Not only start a church, but start it in the house I was renting from him. In fact, the only reason he agreed to rent to me was that I had to promise with a handshake that on the first day we were late on our rent, or as he put it, God failed to provide, I would come to his office so he could laugh in my face! I knew God had called me to start this church, and so even with very little promised support and no job, I shook hands and agreed with Carl. I knew God provides where he leads!

Carl and I became good friends, and I consider him a good friend even today, although I have lost contact with him. If he called today, I know I would be talking with a sincere friend. We started meeting every few weeks for lunch, and without fail, we would always talk about our differences in belief. He attended a conservative synagogue, and his wife believed in the God of the Old Testament, a real Jew in her faith. Carl went with his family to keep the peace, I gathered.

I gave Carl Christian books that I hoped would challenge his views and he read them. In return, I read his books on atheism, and we would go to lunch to discuss the things we had read. Carl used to always tell me two things that bothered him about me. The first was he would say, "You are the only Christian I know who is not using your Christianity to get money. In fact, your Christianity costs you money!"

He often would say that bothered him because every other believer he knew was all about money, and I was not. The second thing that bothered him was that he really wanted to like me as a friend (which I knew we were), but because I was a believer in Jesus and in biblical truth, he had a hard time with my ignorance.

One day, we were discussing the age of the earth and that I believed in the biblical account of history, not only in what it said, but also in the timing of history. I told him I believed that the historical timeline of Scripture is accurate and that man's history on earth is a little over 6,000 years. Carl would get so angry, saying I was deny-ing proven science, and was willingly ignorant. I told him that evo-lutionary science is only theory and I believed in creation as truth.

Carl decided one day to visit his Rabbi at his synagogue and get his argument on the age of the history of man on the earth. He met with him and told him his reason for meeting was to get arguments to convince me to see the truth. The Rabbi, being an orthodox Jewish Rabbi, told Carl that he thought I was right and asked Carl to compliment me for believing Scripture.

Carl and I went on and on like that, back and forth, for the entire almost six years of my time in Mesa! He and I became closer in our friendship, and Carl visited our church one special Sunday. It was a day when we did a Christmas dinner for everyone who came and gave a nice Bible to everyone who visited. We would not allow our visitors to give any money on that day, and we gave a clear simple explanation of the Gospel.

The event was held in a local hotel conference center, and the meal was catered by their chef. Our church spent over $5,000 dollars for everything on that Sunday. Carl and I sat together during the service, and we had 168 people on that day and our church at that time ran fifty-plus. After the service, Carl being a businessman could not wrap his head around why we spent that much money on people who did not attend our church.

I was able to share with him that the most important thing in Christianity was Jesus's death, burial, and resurrection. I said that if any one person visiting would open their heart to Christ, they would be saved for eternity, and that was worth more than any amount of money we as a church could spend!

I was, at that point, free to say to Carl that I was afraid for him and his family. Afraid that, they would die and spend eternity in hell. I asked him to please open his eyes to the truth of Jesus for his and his family's sake. Carl took the Bible we gave as a gift (it was a nice one) and he did not accept Jesus, but he did thank me for caring about his family and himself enough to ask him to accept Christ.

Carl called me a few days later to tell me that when I was sharing about Jesus taking our sin and dying in our place to pay for our forgiveness that he had never heard Christianity explained that way. I thanked him for attending the service, and to this day, pray that when I get to heaven, I will see Carl and his family there!

Paying the Bills

I spent one year praying about our next step after our attempt to work in Mexico failed. I was working with Dr. and Rusty Price in ministry, but not on the level of my commitment I made in Panama City. Rusty was praying privately about Cuba while I was praying about whatever God would have my family do.

At the same time, one year later, almost to the day we started praying, God answered with Rusty called to Cuba and me called to church planting. Fast-forward a few months, and there we were in Mesa, Arizona, starting a Baptist Church in a Mormon town. We had a little over $2,000 dollars of support coming in a month with over $3,000 dollars in bills going out each month.

Internally, I was struggling with how to pay the difference in our bills. If I worked full-time, then I would not be able to visit door to door, and therefore not be doing what the $2,000 dollars of support was paying me to do. If I did not do something, I would end up being late on my rent and would have to let Carl laugh in my face for God not meeting our needs.

Mesa is a city with a Mormon Temple and a very large amount of its people being Mormon. It would be hard enough starting a church working part-time and impossible to do working full-time. I struggled with the need in my heart to try to help God take care of my family's needs. I also suffered from a broken kneecap during the first few months we were there. It happened in a car wreck the week before we moved. The doctor at the emergency room had pushed it back together and put me in a leg cast from my ankle to my butt. I had to do everything in that cast. It was supposed to stay on for eight weeks, and then I was to follow up with the leg doctor in Mesa.

I was trying to come up with a way to make up the difference in our monthly needs. I decided to cut my cast off and find part-time work while doing full-time church planting.

I began scuba diving at golf courses for golf balls. There were several courses that I exclusively had the rights to dive the ponds and scoop up the golf balls. Our company had a contract to sell them back to the clubhouse, and I made five cents per ball. Normally, I could get 3,000 balls in four to six hours.

Working as long and hard as possible, I was making almost enough to pay the difference in my monthly needs. Deep down inside, I knew God had called me there to build his church, not dive for balls. I was torn inside, and finally, one day, I prayed and said to the Lord that I would trust him for our bills. I asked him to show me if that was what he wanted me to do. I knew it was, but I needed him to make it very clear!

The following day, I was diving at a nice course, southeast of Mesa, and was finishing up with one of the ponds that was full of balls. The bank was steep, and I was still limping badly from my broken knee. As I was stepping up the bank, I stepped on a wet smooth rock, and my foot slipped out from under me. I went straight to the ground, landing hard on my knee with all my weight and my tanks and belt. I momentarily blacked out from the pain, not knowing how long I was out.

When I came to, I felt like my knee was broken all over again. I could not move or get up. It dawned on me at that moment. God was making it *very clear* what he wanted me to do. I started laughing (and still crying) and laying on my back in scuba gear, not able to move much. I prayed to the Lord, promising from that day forward I would work full-time, building his church and trusting him to pay our bills!

The answers to prayer that followed the next five years were unbelievable. Every month, my children saw God send in enough money to pay our bills. Very seldom did we ever have extra, but we seemed to always have enough for the present need. My family has had the privilege of seeing God answer prayers on a level that makes it impossible to think Jesus and God the Father do not exist.

One story stands out, and I want to share it with you so you can understand what I am talking about. One day as we were taking our children to school, our family van broke down. I had it towed to the garage where I normally took our car. The mechanic said it was the transmission and that it would be between $2,000 to $3,000 to replace, depending on what all was needed. Sharon and I paid the last $80 to our name for the towing.

I told the mechanic that it would take some time to get the money, and he said okay. When we got home to our four sons, we all sat down in the living room. I told them that we needed the money to pay for our van to be repaired. We did not have any of the money, and they would have to stay home from school until we could get it fixed. As a family, we placed the estimate on the coffee table before the Lord and joined hands. Each one asked the Lord to provide all the money it would take to get our van fixed. We ended our prayer and decided not to let anybody know about our problem. We determined that we would trust God for this need.

A few hours after that, I received a call from a friend back in North Carolina who said that he was praying for us and that he felt led to call me. He asked how things were going. I told him that things were going well and that our church was slowly growing. I did not plan on saying anything about the van. My friend then stated he felt that something was up and that God told him he was supposed to find out what it was and to take care of it.

I told him about our van and that we had prayed that morning for God to provide. The friend said that was why God wanted him to call. God let him know something was up and that he needed to call. He took the mechanic's number, and by the next afternoon, our van was fixed, and the boys had a day vacation from school.

In the almost six years in Mesa, God showed himself to our church and family and repeatedly took care of our needs. Sharon and I spent many nights with our children sleeping, and we would be praying. God is faithful. That is why sometimes I get a little upset with people who insult Jesus and God. They say they do not believe in him, but they evidently believe enough to insult him. I hope for the day they allow God to show Jesus and himself to each of them!

People

God blessed our family with wonderful friendships made during our time in Mesa. We have one family in particular that is family to us now—Darrell and Terri Bryant. They are more than friends, like in the Bible where it speaks about friends that stick closer than a brother. I cannot say with words how much the Bryants mean to my family. Terri is my daughter's godmother, and all my boys call her aunt. We love her children, and again, I can't say enough about how much they mean to us.

Darrell and Terri are a couple that brought and helped develop leadership in our baby church. God used them as much as anyone in the development of our people. What a blessing working together with them those years was to our family!

One day, I was visiting door-to-door and came to a house in our neighborhood that had a sprint car (for racing) in the garage. I walked up and introduced myself to the man, and he said his name was Jerald Slinkard, but his friends called him "Slink." He was not a churchgoer and liked to drink, fight, and run around too much for churchy folk. We formed a friendship, and he ended up attending our church. He was a heavy equipment operator and had two boys who raced sprint cars in Phoenix on Saturday nights. Slink used to race but had slowed down from it because of his age. He really liked my boys, and we got to spend a lot of time together. His boys even came to church from time to time.

I began going with Slink to the races on Saturday nights and sometimes worked on the pit crew for his boys as they raced. I met all types of unchurched people and even had some of them come to church from time to time. Slink was always happy, and I hardly ever saw him down except when his kidney was acting up. He had a dead kidney that he refused to let the doctors remove. As a result, about every other month or so, he would be locked up in his house, passing kidney stones. It took a day or so, and then he would be back in good spirits.

Slink and his wife became regulars at church. I was always after him to read his Bible daily and spend time in prayer as Christians should. He would always make excuses, and one day, I realized why he was not doing it. I went with Slink to the parts house for several special order parts for his sons' race cars. When we got them, the man made Slink sign for them, and I noticed he signed with an X. Slink was a very smart man, but it dawned on me that he could not read or write.

I did not let on that I noticed Slink could not read. I now understood why he did not read his Bible. It was because he could not read anything. I went to Slink's house one day and gave him a Walkman and a copy of the Bible on CDs. I mentioned to Slink that I knew how busy he was, and I suggested he listen to scripture on the Walkman. He said he would and began doing it. Just a short time after that, Slink gave his heart anew to Christ. He became a follower of Jesus, and his friends could see the difference God was making in his life.

The mayor of our town was threatening the church. We had to stop meeting in our house or he would have me arrested. I called and set up a meeting with him to discuss the issue. Slink assured me he was a friend of the mayor and wanted to come along for the meeting to help. When we got to the mayor's office and sat down, I could tell that he was not happy to see either of us. The mayor informed us of a city ordinance against church plants meeting in houses. He continued that I would be arrested if we continued to meet.

I explained that I understood his position but that I was not in a position where we could quit meeting. I also understood he would do whatever he had to do to please the powers he answered to, mainly the local church leaders. We showed ourselves out, and as we were leaving, Slink informed me that he had been in the mayor's office the day before our meeting. He wanted to tell the mayor about our church. Slink said, "I told that man he had better treat you fair or there would be hell to pay from him." That explained why the mayor was a little tight during our visit.

One Sunday morning, I asked a local pastor to speak for our church. I was hoping to kindle the friendship thing that was, for the most part, nonexistent between the Bible churches in Mesa. The pastor had started his church long ago and began telling our church some of the stories. This pastor was a very legalistic type preacher and said when our church was this church's age, we used to have people coming who cursed. As he said that, Slink stood up and said, "Well, hell, Preacher, we still do!" It was never a dull moment.

Just up the street from us was a man who lived by himself named Mr. Crow. He was a retired navy man and was bad to curse. I met him one day, and we became friends. He would see my family from time to time when we were on walks, and he really liked my wife and my boys. We would invite him to dinner from time to time, and he would come. His cussing was extreme and he did not even realize it.

He lived alone and it was a lifelong habit. He did not think anything of it; after all, he was a sailor. We would tell our boys when Mr. Crow was coming over not to repeat what they heard him say. I witnessed to Mr. Crow many times along with my wife over several years. He always used the same excuse. "What kind of man would I be to live my life so long without Jesus, only to ask him to save me now that I am old and ready to die?"

I would always tell him that Jesus wanted to save him if he would just ask him to!

One of our supporters was a retired navy pilot who flew for US Airways. He was a lieutenant colonel in the Navy. He came out from time to time and would help try to get Mr. Crow to come to Christ. They became close friends, but Mr. Crow never accepted Jesus. We left Mesa with Mr. Crow having never accepted Jesus. I prayed for him often, and a funny thing happened. Several years after we moved away from Mesa, a group of businessmen contacted me. They flew me out to Mesa to discuss the possibility of starting another church. I met with them for four days, and they were all good men, but by the end, we could not come to a working agreement, so I was to fly back home.

On the morning of my flight, I decided to go by Mr. Crow's house to see if he was okay. When I walked up to his door and knocked, the lady from next door answered. She told me that Mr. Crow was deathly ill with liver cancer and would die any day. He had not been out of bed in weeks, and she came over from time to time to check on him. She went and told him I was at the door.

He got out of bed and met me in his living room. He was very weak and told me that he had tried to contact me when he was diagnosed with cancer and could not. He knew he was not going to live much longer and he tried praying. He prayed and asked God if he could speak with me again, and here I was.

I sat beside Mr. Crow and told him again how Jesus loved him enough to take his sins to Calvary. I shared how God the Father also loved him enough to have Jesus die in his place. I continued that if he did not take Jesus into his heart, Jesus would love him anyway, even if he died and went to hell.

Mr. Crow said again, "What kind of man would I be to get saved now when I am almost dead?"

I shared with him that I did not know he was sick and that God used four businessmen to fly me back to Mesa so I could come see him. I reached out and took Mr. Crow's hand and prayed and asked the Holy Spirit to bring conviction and give repentance to Mr. Crow. I looked at him and asked again, "Mr. Crow, will you ask Jesus to forgive your sins and come into your heart and save you?"

Mr. Crow said yes and bowed his head and, on his own accord, prayed and asked Jesus into his life. When we were through praying, he said, "Well, I reckon you and I will not be seeing each other again."

I agreed and said we would in heaven. He asked me if I would let the Colonel know he asked Jesus to save him. I promised him I would, and I did.

Mesa was some hard wonderful years, and we made wonderful friends and saw many people come to Jesus. If Mr. Crow and Slink were the only two to ask Jesus to save them, it would be well worth the blood, sweat, and tears!

Opposition

The mayor of Mesa was threatening us to stop meeting in the house, but we did not have anywhere else we could go. In Mesa, a new church plant could not rent any place without providing approved building plans, a starting construction date, and a projected finish date. It was pretty much impossible to start a church there legally without deep pockets or backing from someone who had them.

We had a retired military man in our subdivision that took it upon himself to be the neighborhood police patrol. He often walked through the neighborhood with a measuring stick, taking notes of anyone who had grass or weeds above the neighborhood watch standards, and would report them. One year, he called the police 300 times. Everybody, even the police, were tired of this guy. He was especially hard on Slink and, when he found out we were having church in our house, on us as well.

He would call the police on us every Sunday and Wednesday nights. He would measure Slink's distance between his tires and the curb and call if he was too far out. We were getting constantly harassed by the city and the police and this guy.

I finally went to the mayor (without Slink) and informed him that it was not possible for our church to meet anywhere else at this time. He was forcing me into a position where I had to either obey him or God. I reminded him about how the Mormon Church had settled the west. It is common knowledge that what they did was much worse than what I was doing.

I then shared with the mayor how I would help him in any way I could, other than our church meeting in our home. I committed to him that with any other issue I would be on his team. I acknowledged knowing of the pressure that was being put on him to stop us. I said that if or when the day came that he chose to arrest me, I would not allow him to put me in jail in the middle of the day in plain sight of the powers he was trying to please and then release me at midnight with no one around. If he arrested me, I would stay in jail until the media got involved, and then we would see how the laws in their town against church startups would hold up in court. We were able to come to an understanding of sorts, and I left his office.

We still had the neighborhood Barney patrol calling the police on us and on Slink, and with time, he seemed to be getting worse. One Saturday night, I was working with Slink in the pit for his sons' sprint car racing team. I was introduced to this guy who knew Slink. He was a big rough-looking man named John.

John was fascinated by my working on the pit crew and being a preacher. The next week, John came pulling up to the church service on a Harley with a woman on the back. They were wearing biker colors and were covered with tattoos. He was a member of a nationally known motorcycle gang. I did not know much about that nor was it a problem. I was pumped about having them both in the service. We had a good day, and afterward, John came up to me and said he really enjoyed the message. I found out that he had been raised in church as a deacon's son. He said he enjoyed the service so much that the next week, he was going to bring his wife and kids. John began to attend church with us, almost weekly for a while, and the next visit, he did bring his family.

Slink ended up getting into an altercation with our neighborhood nutcase when Slink caught him measuring his grass. Slink ran him all the way back to his house, threatening to whip him, and the man called the police on Slink. It ended up with a warning and "don't do it again" type thing, and the police left.

John just happened to pull up during the last part of it, and Slink told John all about the problem. Slink shared with John all about this old boy and how much he was harassing our church, my family, and himself. A few days later, Slink drove up into my driveway and said John asked if I would come to his work and meet with him about something. Slink then shared with me some stuff I did not know.

John was not just a biker, he was high up in the biker club and held a lot of power. John owned several car body shops all over Phoenix, and the one in Mesa was where we agreed to meet. Slink said that I was to go alone and be careful when I drove up to the place.

The next day at ten (our scheduled time), I drove to the shop John owned. I pulled to the side gate, and a guy stopped me and looked in my car and then told me where to park. I pulled in, and two guys came up and asked if I was Frank. I told them I was, and they walked me through the car bays. No one had worked on the cars in the bays in a while as each one was covered in dust.

They led me to the back door of the shop, leading inside the office, where two more guys were standing, and one of them told me to follow him. He walked me down a connecting hallway toward a door at the end where two more men were standing. The largest man told me to spread my arms and he searched me. He then opened the door, and sitting behind a desk was John with another big dude sitting in the corner.

John was surrounded by a small army. John excused the big guy and asked me if I wanted anything to drink, and I said no. I asked him what was on his mind, and that's when he told me he had been raised in a really religious home. He said he enjoyed our church because we were not afraid to tell the truth but did not judge people. I thanked him. Then he said that Slink had told him about how much the neighbor had been harassing Slink and our church and my family.

John then said he was going to trust me not to mention (until now) this next part of our conversation with anyone. He started by saying, "I normally get big money for this, but I was thinking, since it was for the church, I could make the neighbor guy disappear." It would cost fifty bucks for beer for his guys and that I would get a ring finger in return. He was not joking.

I started laughing and told John I was thankful for him caring enough about our church to help us like that. I said to John, "As tempting as your offer is, Jesus would never let me ask you to do that."

John said he thought I was going to say that, but he wanted to give me the chance in case. I thanked him and told him that I was praying about it and that God would take care of the problem.

In our neighborhood, every house had to have a concrete block fenced backyard, eight feet high. No exceptions. So, every yard had a private block fence eight feet high enclosed by a gate. Well, shortly after my visit with John, I went by our neighbor's house, and there was a for sale sign up and the man was moving. He actually moved before the house sold. I was wondering what was up. He put the for sale sign up and moved on the same day.

A few days later, Slink came by and said he had found out what the deal was with the neighbor guy. Evidently, somebody threw a bag full of large rattlesnakes in a potato sack over his wall into his backyard and they were slithering all over. Tied to the sack was a card that read "*Move*" on it, and the old man did. I have often wondered how that happened. Also, it is funny how God answers prayer sometimes (for everyone but the snakes).

Chaplain

One of the most intense and productive ministries I had in Mesa was at the local hospital. I was there praying with someone one day and just happened to meet the hospital chaplain. He invited me to have coffee with him, and I did. He started by saying that he was responsible for all the chaplain activities at the hospital and they needed non-Mormon volunteers.

I asked what that was, and he said that the Mormons took care of their own sick and had their own hospital people which was 85 percent of their needs. What he needed were chaplain volunteers who would be on call to visit any other patients. His biggest need was in the emergency room and ICU units and for people who could be called at any hour. He also needed people who could manage deathbed and unexpected death situations.

I explained I would be more than happy to be on call, day and night, if I could help. I gave him one condition that he had to agree to. When someone wanted to speak with me, I would only tell the person what I knew to be biblical truth. I was not going to be whatever people wanted to hear or what their faith claimed. I would only do it if I could share Jesus with them and their need for salvation through biblical repentance and faith.

He agreed as long as I introduced myself as a Bible chaplain, and we both agreed. I ended up over the next three years being able to share Jesus with a large amount of people as they were dying and with families of those who did. I will share a few of the most memorable ones.

One night, about 2:30, I received a call from the night nurse in ICU. They had a Catholic lady who was dying and was panicking. They called for a priest to come, but for whatever reason, no one would come before morning. They were not sure she was going to be alive the next morning. The nurse told her they had someone who was a Bible chaplain that would come if she wanted. She said yes, and they called, and I was there about 3:00 a.m.

When I got to her bed, she asked, "Bless me, Father?" and she said she had forgotten and needed the words to the prayer for peace.

I shared with her I was not a Father but that I was a pastor and I could show her from the Bible the prayer for peace. She agreed, and I showed her from Romans the verses that told how to be saved and have eternal life. I then showed her how Jesus would be with her when she was dying.

She listened, and when I was through, I asked her if she would admit she was sinful and confess her sin to Jesus (not me) and ask Jesus for eternal life. She agreed and took my hand, and a little after four in the morning, the sweet dying lady accepted Jesus. When she was finished, she said, "You really are not a Father, are you?"

I said, "No, but now I am a brother."

She shared that she had two daughters up north that were praying for years that she would be born again. She asked if that was what she had just done, and I told her it was and that she could trust Jesus to be with her through her death. I showed her the scripture where it says Jesus is the prince of peace. I sat there with her while she called both of her daughters and told them she had prayed and trusted Jesus. They were so thankful, and the dear lady went home to heaven the next day.

I was called one evening around 6:30 and asked to come to the ICU unit. When I got there, the nurse told me that a Kathy Reed was in her room with her husband who was named Ralf. They told me that both were in their late eighties and that Mrs. Reed was short for this world. They wanted me to sit with them as Mrs. Reed died, because they were afraid her husband would die from the stress of her death as they were extremely close. I opened the door and went in and sat down by Ralf's bed.

Kathy was on the other side of Ralf and was starting to have the labored breathing that comes with dying. I introduced myself to Ralf and asked if I could stay awhile, and he said yes.

I asked Ralf if he was a Christian, and he said he was and had been most of his life, except his four years in WWII. He feared God could not forgive him for those years. He shared how he met Kathy and that she was an actor when she was younger. She left acting as she got older because she thought it was not a good life for a Christian.

I asked Ralf what movies she was in, and Ralf told me she was Darla in *The Little Rascals*. I looked and could see the resemblance. As we talked, Ralf would often get up and go over and kiss Darla (Kathy) and rub her feet and pat her hand. I asked him if they had ever been apart and understood him to say they had been together since their early twenties.

I sat with them until late that night and finally went home and caught a few hours' sleep. The next day, before noon, I went back and sat with Ralf until Kathy passed that evening. During the time we were together, I was able to explain to Ralf that Jesus could and had promised he would forgive any sin Ralf confessed. I prayed with Ralf, and he gave his combat years to Christ and asked God for forgiveness. I asked him if he and Kathy had ever talked about their deaths, and he said they had.

Ralf said that Kathy had always said that she needed to go first because Ralf was the stronger one, and she could not handle being last. I shared with Ralf as Kathy's signs of death were increasing, and it was clear time was short, that he had something he could be thankful for.

"What is that?" he asked.

I told him that he sure beat old Alfalfa out by getting Darla. He looked at me and laughed and said, "I did, didn't I?"

As Kathy's time came, we held hands and prayed for God to be with them both. Soon after that, Darla of *The Little Rascals* went to be with Jesus with Ralf standing at her side, holding her hand. Ralf lived a few short weeks after Kathy's death, and now they are together again in heaven.

I received a call one afternoon, and they asked if I could assist a doctor who had to tell a patient who unexpectedly only had a few weeks to live. When I got to the hospital, the doctor met with me and explained that this was a typical Western man in his late thirties with a wife and two girls. He had always been in good health and was a cowboy through and through. He had a stomach bug and could not shake it, so he came to the hospital because he did not have a doctor. He had never been sick.

The doctor said he had an aggressive type of stomach cancer in its final stages and would not live longer than a couple weeks at most. At this point, all they could do was treat his pain. He and his family had no clue this was the case, and we were going in to tell them.

We walked into the room, and it looked like the scene from a movie. The man was a strong young handsome cowboy with a gorgeous wife with two beautiful girls from ten to thirteen (I guessed). The doctor walked in first, and I followed.

The man asked the doctor who I was, and the doctor told him I was the chaplain. The guy asked why he needed a chaplain, and the doctor looked him in the eyes and said, "Because I am having to share some very bad news with you. Do you want to have your family leave while I tell you? Or do you prefer them to stay?"

The wife and husband grabbed hands and drew the girls close. The doctor told the man that he would not be leaving the room. The man said he did not understand, and the doctor said to him, "I am sorry to tell you, but you have an advanced case of cancer and will not live more than one, at the most two weeks."

The world stopped, and when the doctor's words struck home, the man just started cursing and screaming out at God. He told every-body to get out of the room, and we left. I stayed just outside for a few minutes and then walked back in the room. It was just him and I, and he asked, "What are you going to do? Start trying to tell me everything is going to be all right?" He was very bitter and sarcastic and angry at God and, in that case, at me also.

I told him that I did not think everything was going to be all right and that he was going to die soon. I also said I was not interested in saying things that were not true. I shared with him that I was an atheist before I became a preacher and understood what he was feel-ing. I mentioned that there were some things he needed to consider, no matter if he believed in God or not.

He looked at me, and I asked him if he wanted me to stay and talk or leave. He asked me to stay. I stepped into the hall and asked his wife and daughters to give me a few minutes alone with him, and they agreed. The man told me he was not a Christian, but his wife and daughters were. He said he never had time for God and now did not know what he thought.

I said that he needed to not be selfish and that he should think about a few things. I mentioned that I was usually asked to come to the emergency room after someone died to tell the family. I continued that if he had been in a wreck or an accident, he would be dead now and not have the next week or maybe two to spend with his wife and daughters. I told him that I understood he did not know God, but that God knew him and God loved him and his family. I explained that God saw fit to give him some time to say what he thought was needed to his girls and to his wife. God was giving him a chance to die, leaving nothing unsaid.

I shared how scripture says that God knows how many days we all have and that no one is promised old age. God's son died at thirty-three, and God used his death to save everyone who calls on his name. I knew he would need time by himself to process this death thing, but now he had a wife and two daughters that I could tell he loved and who very much needed him to be strong for them.

He thought about it a few minutes, and I added that he should make it his goal to spend his last hours preparing his girls and his wife for his death and that he should also not let them leave anything unsaid. I then asked him to realize the gift God was giving him with this terrible news.

I visited them every day for the next few weeks, and he did live almost fourteen days. He spent his time telling his family how much he loved them and how proud he was of them and that he knew they would be okay. He also accepted Christ a few days before he died. The last day I was with them, we all held hands and prayed and asked God to be with them all as he passed. He said to me after the prayer time that he probably would have never received Jesus if he had not come down with cancer. He and his family said as hard as his death was for them that his getting saved was the most important thing. They were right. When he died, he had said everything he needed to say to each of his family and they to him.

One night, close to midnight, I was called in for a man in ICU who was not expected to live into the next day. The man was Jewish

319

and had asked for a rabbi, but again, for whatever reason, the rabbi could not come till morning, so they told him about me. He asked if they would call me, and they did, and I got to his bedside a little past midnight.

The man was a huge man, older, but looked like he could fight a bear and win. I walked in and asked him what it was he wanted to talk about.

He said, "Aw, you know, death and things!"

I asked about his beliefs, and he said he was raised Jewish and believed in God, but he was not real sure about the Jesus thing. He said he was not against it, if it was true; he was just not sure.

I told him the short version of how I had come to Jesus from having been an atheist, and he listened. He did not seem to be upset or worried, and I asked him if he was upset or worried this close to death. He said dying did not bother him and he was ready; he just wanted to make sure he was where he needed to be with God when it happened. He was very intelligent and alert to be so close to death.

He shared with me that he had tried praying to Jesus once. I said, "Oh yeah, when was that?"

He then began telling me an amazing story of a time in his earlier days. He was at Bastogne. He was with Easy Company in World War II and had been rushed to Bastogne to try to stop the German advancement. He said that they were surrounded and took beatings, day in and day out, for a long time. I had read everything I could get my hands on about this battle, and here I was sitting with a man who experienced the entire thing.

He started by saying that the winter was brutally cold and supplies were always low. The Germans were always testing their lines, and many times, they were down to their last few rounds of ammunition. He was dug in with five guys, and there were not many other guys close enough for support. On the day he was talking about trying prayer, it started with an all-out assault with the Germans coming straight at them, trying to break through the lines. They were taking heavy fire and were running out of ammo. It came down to the place where he was the only one alive in his foxhole and was just about out of bullets.

He knew he was dead because bullets were hitting all around him, and no one else near him was alive. He closed his eyes and prayed, "Jesus, if you are real and you get me out of this, I will believe in you!"

He said the next thing that happened was crazy. From behind him, the trees just exploded, and tanks came running through the lines toward the Germans. He said one tank ran over his foxhole, and he had to dive down in it to keep from being run over. When he looked up, the Germans were turned around and running away.

This man, who turned out to be Patton, was screaming loud enough to hear, "Hurry up, you bastards, they are getting away!"

He said he jumped out of his hole and yanked a guy off the back of the tank and hugged him.

I asked him if he ever did give himself to Christ, and he said he had not. I asked him why, and he said it was a foxhole conversion. He said, "I should have died then, and only God kept me alive." He was not worried about dying now. He believed in God but wanted to do the right thing with Jesus. He wanted to keep his promise from Bastogne.

I shared with him what scripture says about accepting Jesus, and he was willing and ready. That night about 2:30 a.m., my Jewish friend became my brother in Christ. Sure enough, he went to heaven the next day before noon.

Give Me the Answer to Life in One Easy Sentence

I was called to the emergency room for a kid who had smoked some bad dope and had therefore destroyed his lungs. When I got there, the doctor grabbed me and had me lay over this boy to try to control him while the doctor was treating him. The boy threw up blood all over both of us, the ceiling, the walls, and the floor. He died with us not being able to do anything but hold him down.

We went back into a room just for doctors, and the nurses were getting us some scrubs to put on because we were both soaked in this boys' blood. I sat there with the doctor as he talked about trying to save people like that boy and his frustrations with the social issues that were killing our kids. He mentioned how often his hands were tied from speaking the truth because of the politics and policies dealing with teenage sexuality and drugs.

I shared with him that I too struggled with the same type of thing in my business of trying to save souls. He was not a believer and found religion as a problem rather than a help, but we became friends and had coffee from time to time when we could.

One day, I was walking through the emergency room, and the doctor shouted, "Frank, tell us the meaning of life in one easy sentence."

I looked at him and said, "Life is a struggle, then we die!" I then said if he ever was serious with that question, the coffee would be on me.

About a month and a half later, Doc, as I called him, called my phone and said he was ready for the coffee. We set a time and agreed to meet. When we did meet, he told me he was dealing with his existence. He was hard-pressed, seeing if there was any purpose in it. It was one of the few times we both had time to talk.

I shared with him how I had come to know Jesus, and that before coming to Christ, I was troubled with myself, asking those same questions. I continued telling him God created us in his image, and that makes a human life valuable. I continued that we are eternal beings in need of a savior, which adds reason and purpose for living.

After a few more coffees, Doc received Christ into his heart just a few days after that conversation. He soon became an active Christian. I introduced him to a Christian nurse at the same hospital, and they eventually got married.

A few months later, in the middle of the night, I was called to the bedside of a lady in the ICU who was dying. It so happened the nurse that married my doctor friend was on duty. When I got to the room, the nurse told me that the woman was already in her final stages of life.

I went in and took the woman's hand, asking if I could pray with her. She nodded her head yes, and I prayed, holding her hand. It was clear by the spirit in the room that this woman knew the Lord. While standing there with her, as I had with many people before, a strange thing happened. The Lord spoke to me and asked me to step outside. He let me know that he was coming for her spirit and that it was a personal and private thing between the two of them. There was no audible sound, but it was God speaking, making it very clear to me that I was to leave.

I walked outside of the room and asked my nurse friend for a cup of coffee. She said that I should go back inside because the lady would be passing soon. I told her God told me to leave so he could take her home now. The nurse said, "Yeah right." She looked straight at the woman's door when her monitor went straight lines. The woman was gone.

God took her as soon as I left. That lady had a special walk with God, and it was obvious at her passing. The Bible says, "Precious in the sight of the Lord is the death of his saints" (Ps. 116:15, KJV).

Can't Meet in Your House Anymore!

We were getting more and more pressure from the city to stop meeting for church in our home. We were also full and needing more room to grow. Our church decided to take a six-week period to pray and fast, asking God to open a door and give us a new place to meet. We scheduled people on each of the days to fast and pray, and several people did extended fasts. We had at least one person each day for six weeks praying and fasting, asking God to open a door for our church. Many of the days, multiple people were praying, and people from all over who knew our ministry joined in the prayers!

During that six-week time, one of our members, Debbie Good, contacted me about a house on a couple of acers that would be suitable for conversion into a church building. I met her at the property and saw that it would work. They listed the property at $250,000, but we did not even have $250 in the bank.

I told Debbie that it looked like a good opportunity, but I did not see any way we could get the money or financing to buy the place. My faith was not as strong as Debbie's. I left, putting it out of my mind. I drove by the place from time to time, thinking it was a good place for a church.

We finished the six weeks of prayer and fasting, thanking God for his provision and promises. We committed to trusting and waiting on him to open the door. Our church pledged to practice thanking him for what we did have and focus on God's blessings more than our needs. I soon received great peace that God was in total control of our needs and that he would move mountains for our little church when he was ready!

Debbie called a few days after that and asked if I would meet with the owners at the property. I reminded her we did not have anything to bring as an offer and would just be wasting their time. Debbie is an awesome Christian, and I love her faith. She was a determined woman, and I reluctantly agreed to meet with them that afternoon.

We arrived, and she opened the door, and we walked through the house. It was very suitable for a church and had potential for expansion and growth. It would take very little to convert into a church, and it would allow room for growth. I was trying not to get excited.

The realtor expressed that the owner was open to selling to a Baptist church. In that Mormon area, their willingness was a hurdle in and of itself! A small mountain to be sure! The agent asked if we were interested in the property. I said that we were not in the best position to get financing for a mortgage yet, but I did like the property. I told her we would be willing to make an offer if they would be willing to come off the price some.

We left with an understanding that we were interested. It was understood mountains would have to move for us to go any further with an attempt to purchase. A few days later, the agent called Debbie and shared that the owner was willing to come down to $210,000 for the property. Another mountain! That was a God price (and good price too), and we agreed to meet with the agent again.

By the end of the next meeting, we all decided to make the offer of $210,000 for the property with a six-week window to raise the money for a down payment and acquire financing. After looking around, we settled with the local bank we already did business with. They agreed if we could put 10 percent down with the value of the property, they would finance the deal. Another mountain. Our church decided to ask God to help us raise $25,000 as a down payment in four weeks.

I sent a letter to all our supporters and prayer partners, sharing with them our opportunity and the need for $25,000 in four weeks! The first response was from a missionary couple in Japan, Chuck and Lynda Truitt. They are and have been missionary friends of ours since college. They served with faithfulness and in hard places for many years, and are, on God's standard, successful. I know for a fact that they did not have enough monthly support and lived on a very tight budget.

They sent us a love offering of $1,000. When I saw the amount of the gift and who sent it, I realized God was obviously doing something! Within four weeks, our church family, our personal family, and our supporters gave over $25,000! The extra allowed money for renovations. Last mountain (so I thought)!

Before I tell you the rest of this story, let me share something from my life's experience. I have lived as an atheist and a Christian and found some things to be true. If a person hates, they look for targets to hate. If a person loves, they look for targets to love. Prejudice and hate and love exist in both worlds. I know Christians who hate and atheists who love. The problem is not with the title the person carries, it's with the heart a person carries. Also, if you sit long enough in a garage, you still will not be a Volkswagen.

Christ does not produce hate. Professing Christians are not given permission to be mean. Scripture says, "We will know them (Christians) by their love." I do know for a fact that religious people can be mean and will even crucify you if you make them mad.

We began the loan process and thought everything was settled and good to go. We were just waiting for the loan to finalize. One day, I received a return to sender letter from another state address in our mailbox. It had my address as sender on it. I opened the letter, and it was a two-page typed letter insulting and debasing the Mormon church. It contained my signature. It was a letter I did not write with my forged signature on it.

I soon found out it was sent to hundreds of people all over the western and Midwestern states. It was mailed to people who happened to be influential Mormon business people. I do not agree with the teachings of the Mormon church and am sure they would not agree with my doctrine. I in no way would nor did I use the wording and tone that the letter reflected. The letter saturated our local area, focusing on civil and government and banking leaders. It was insane.

I tried to get the post office to investigate and find the one(s) responsible. Without a lawyer, I could not get them to do anything other than admit it had happened. I received several more return to sender letters from several states, so I knew the list of addresses used was not up to date. The postmaster told me it was not worth their time to worry with it.

The following week, I was informed by the bank that our loan application had been denied; no explanation other than they felt it was not in the bank's best interest to award the loan. I thought to myself, *This stuff is like a science fiction movie!* I could not believe it had really happened and that we had lost our financing.

Our church prayed to God who knew the full circumstances of the letter and the loan denial and asked him for *help!* We could not get a single local lender to talk to us about financing after that, and the mayor was now bearing down hard on our church. We had enemies that we did not even know and with some of the Mormons I did know.

We asked the Lord if we should send the money back to the givers or go forward with finding financing. I called our sending church's pastor, Dr. Bradley Price, and asked his advice. He advised we stand still and wait and watch; God would work for our church.

The next day, a businessman from our sending church named Mr. Richard called me. He was a very wealthy man and owned businesses all over the world and was a financier. We were on a first name basis, and he attended our church whenever he was in Phoenix on business. Mr. Richard had talked with Dr. Price and heard about the church's situation. He was willing to finance our church fully for 15 percent interest until a lender bought the loan.

I told him it was a very generous offer and I would pray about it. As I prayed, I could not get peace about Mr. Richard's offer. I called and told him so. Mr. Richard asked why I couldn't, and I told him truthfully that I did not feel I could trust his motive for helping. I did not know why I felt that way, but in my spirit, I knew something about it was wrong. I expressed that if he knew God wanted him to help, he would help with a less than 15 percent interest. I had no problem with interest in a business deal, but the bank was talking 7 percent before the letter.

We left the conversation with me not feeling that I could trust why he was helping. I knew him and trusted his character as far as his word and honesty. I just did not trust his motive but did not know why.

The following week, Mr. Richard called me from overseas and said that he had been thinking about our church and wanted to help. He told me he wanted to do it because the Lord wanted him to do so! He then asked that I call his office and give them our bank information and he would wire the $150,000 needed (we had the other $60,000 by then). He continued that we would do the paperwork when he came to Phoenix. He asked me to name whatever interest amount, and he would take it. The final mountain!

I thanked Mr. Richard and told him the 7 percent the bank had offered seemed right to me. He told me that whatever I decided was fine. He wired the money that afternoon, and we had cash to pay in full for the property.

We closed the sale of the house two weeks later with cash (still not having done paperwork with Mr. Richard). We soon finished the first stages of renovations on the building and could meet in it. We had the final Sunday morning meeting in our house with the next church meeting moving to our new property. God answered our prayer.

The following Monday, my wife answered the phone, and it was the mayor's office. They informed us that they planned to arrest me if we met one more time in our house and that the city officials had enough of our ignoring their warnings. Every week, we placed a sign out on the road beside our house stating our church and its times. The mayor's office was constantly threatening my wife over the phone about the violations that sign was causing and the wrath that was coming. My wife was able to inform the city officials and the mayor that we were finished meeting in our house and now owned property and would be meeting in it. God made a way and no more sign in front of our house!

Death of a Vision

There is a verse in Proverbs 20:24 that says, "Man's goings are of the Lord; how can a man understand his own way?" (KJV) Life throws things at you sometimes that just does not make sense. This is one of those times. Sharon and I gave a lot of ourselves. It was like we were plowing granite in Mesa for more than five years. I assumed all along God was going to keep us there to pastor the church he used us to birth.

I received a phone call one day from an older (early eighties maybe) evangelist that I had heard of but never met. His name was Dr. Grant, and he was a church planter who had started churches and coached church planters much of his ministry. He heard about our church and was interested in getting to know our people and Sharon and myself. I asked if he would speak for us when he was in town, and he agreed.

He spoke for us on one Sunday soon after that call. We spent the following Monday together, mainly me listening to his stories of church plants over the span of his life. I had the blessing of asking his advice as not just a pastor, but as someone who had fought the same battles that I faced everyday as a cash-strapped church planter. We became instant friends, and our hearts were knit together.

When Dr. Grant was leaving, he told me that he needed to tell me something that I did not want to hear. I had no idea but chuckled and said, "Go ahead." He said that I needed to realize that just because God had me plant our church, that did not mean God would have me pastor it.

I was cut to the heart and strongly argued that God did not move me there to plant a church from nothing and to work five-plus long hard years to leave it when it finally got going. Dr. Grant told me to listen to an old man who had spent his life church planting. "The local church belongs to God, not the pastor or the people. He (God) will put a pastor in his church. Do not assume you are that man, just because it feels like your baby!" He left, and I just thought he was just talking, not wanting to entertain the idea of not staying at my church.

A few weeks later, I went to our new building and started to set up what was going to be my office as senior pastor. As I was trying to lay out where my desk and bookshelves and seating would be, I was feeling uneasy and even a little bit like I was doing something wrong. I worked around the church a while and started to go back to the task at hand, and the Lord spoke to my heart. "This is not going to be your office. Don't fix up someone else's office."

I did not want that word and was kind of put off at how forcefully God gave it to me. I filed it in the back of my mind as a memo to visit later. A few weeks after that, God woke me up one night and told me he was going to move me from the church. I had not shared with anyone what God had said to me in the office and through Dr. Grant, but this time was different. I could tell God was not only telling me but was waiting for a response from me. I remember the exact event as I type this. I rolled out of bed and knelt and told the Lord that I did not understand it, but I was his and would do whatever he willed. The next day, I told my wife that God had said he was going to move us.

To be fair, I need to explain that I had worked and sacrificed and pushed and driven hard against the powers of that valley and against hell itself. Now after five-plus years, I was completely spent, dead inside, and empty in every way. I was asking God for fresh oil in my walk, but I was struggling.

However, that was not what God used in moving me. It was, number one, his telling me he was going to do so, and secondly, our sending church went through a battle that leaked over into our church, and thirdly, the men of our church gave me no other option that I could live with.

I already explained the first reason, so here is the second. I am not going into much detail because it was their local church issue and no one else's business. But because of its effect on our church, I will share that part of their business.

A man in the church back home called during the time God was saying he was going to move me and informed me that he and some of the men of the church were going to have the pastor removed from the pastorate. He stated that he wished that I would not get involved because of the relationship I had with the church as one of its missionaries. They commissioned and sent our family to start the church we started, and in fact, they were our mother church.

I was asked/told by the man, named Mr. Richard, not to get involved or intervene in the process. Dr. Price was my pastor, and I knew he was not guilty of anything that gave reason for his being dismissed as pastor. I suddenly understood why Mr. Richard was so pushy with financing our church. He was telling me to stay out of their unjust attack on my pastor because they controlled our church mortgage.

They called their meeting to try to remove Pastor Price. I flew to North Carolina from Arizona and went into their meeting, unannounced. I addressed Mr. Richard and the deacons that were deciding Dr. Price and the church's fate. I told the truth and called Mr. Richard out on his leadership in this move to force out our pastor.

I asked them what they felt they needed more—God's man or Mr. Richard's money?

As in so many churches today, they chose the money. Mr. Richard approached me after the lynching of Dr. Price and said that he did not want it to affect the church in Mesa in any way. He said he knew he was responsible for leading the attack on Dr. Price but thought it best for the church that the men with the money stayed and Dr. Price left. Mr. Richard even admitted that he knew he would have to face God one day and give an account for doing it.

I told him that I no longer respected him as a man and that I could not continue business with him as a church because he was not, in my opinion, honest. I asked that he repent and confess before the church the part he played in creating and festering the charges against Dr. Price and that he ask Dr. Price for forgiveness in a face-to-face meeting.

He refused, and I promised him my fellowship and any dealings with him were over. After that, Mr. Richard called the men of our church and made the mortgage deal we had sweet enough that they would not follow my leadership on breaking with his company.

The third thing that sealed my leaving the church was that the men lost their willingness to follow my leadership. I need you to know that the men were all, and still are, good Christian men. What I am sharing now is not right versus wrong; it is leadership styles. After we moved into our building, I noticed that the more decisions I made and the more actions I took, the more my decisions were being questioned by the men I had put into leadership. It was obvious to me that the men did not want me to hold the authority of leading the church any longer. They trusted their own decisions more than mine.

It was getting to a place where I was questioned about almost everything I did and they wanted me to ask their permission. It came to a head after I returned from the meeting at our home church in Charlotte and the firing of Dr. Price. Mr. Richard called the men of our church without me knowing and convinced them it was in their best interest to keep the mortgage with him.

When I returned, I called a business meeting and told the men what had happened and what I had said to Mr. Richard and why. Without knowing he was talking with them, I shared that we needed to refinance the loan and do business elsewhere. I made it clear to them that this was not going to be a vote and that I had already assured Mr. Richard we were going to do this.

The men called a meeting that I was told not to attend, and they decided to take the business decisions over. They informed me by letter that upon their decision, and from that time on, they would be making all the decisions concerning the business and operations of the church. I would just be responsible for preaching with no vote or say in other matters.

When I received the letter from the men and met with them, I knew my time was over! I went home and typed out my resignation effective as of that morning. I could not pastor a church where I had no authority to obey God when he spoke and told us to do something. The men had come to a place where they did not want that to happen without them getting the final word.

To be fair, they were not trying to control me. They had lost their trust in my leadership, and I could no longer lead them as their spiritual authority. So I had to go. I still love those men dearly!

I never in my life hurt as much or as deeply as I did leaving that church. I had given everything I had birthing that work. I was spent, empty, and broken. It was as if "my baby had died." It was the death of my vision!

I moved back to North Carolina and spent eighteen months working and trying to pay off debt. I needed to get back on my feet and take care of my family. That time was and remains a very dark time, and I have never really gotten over it. A part of me has been dead ever since that time.

My family spent ourselves and $64,000 dollars that I know of from our family's money over a five-plus year time building that church. God only knows the late-night prayer times and days of fasting and hardship that went into that church. Our family did that for God and not for any other reason, and I am thankful we did!

God did build that church, and Dr. Grant was smarter that I gave him credit for. "Just because God used you to start it does not mean he wants you to pastor it!" It was a great church and we had great people who I deeply love to this day. It was also the death of a vision and almost my life!

About to Lose Both Your Girls!

Terri Bryant was and remains to be one of our closest friends. She prayed for Sharon to have a girl and sure enough, soon after leaving Arizona, Sharon became pregnant eight years after our youngest of four sons was born. I worked long hours during these eighteen months, and Sharon took care of the boys. We decided to find a midwife to help deliver our little girl. We did not have insurance, so Sharon and I looked around until we found a few midwives to go meet and decide on. Our plan was to use a hospital and a midwife so that if something went wrong, we would be close to a doctor.

We found a place in Salisbury, North Carolina. It was a birthing center, and we drove there to meet with them about having Heather. They had birthing rooms, a doctor in-house, and seemed to be just what we were looking for. When we got there, the place was a huge two-story building with the birthing center as the top floor. If you drove around the building, there was another entrance in the back for the bottom floor. We went into the office of the head midwife which was located on the top floor and were told we would have to wait as she was attending a birthing that needed her help.

As we sat there, I was impressed by how clean the place was kept. As the time passed, I began to feel less and less comfortable, so I told Sharon I was going to walk down the halls. When I started walking down toward the end of the hall, I could feel this oppressive spirit starting to bother me. I could not put my finger on it, but something in this building was wrong.

I walked around a little more, and finally, I stopped one of the nurses who was passing me in the hall. I asked her if they performed abortions in the building, and she informed me that the ground floor was for abortions and the upper floor (where Sharon and I were) was for birthing. That was what I was feeling—they were killing babies underneath us, and I could sense that in my spirit.

I walked back to the office where Sharon was waiting and told her we were leaving. As soon as she found out they did abortions, she was as ready as I was to leave.

The receptionist asked why we were leaving, and I told her because of the abortions. The main midwife called us later that day and questioned our motives for leaving. She felt that the abortions that they performed should not in any way affect their treatment of my family. I told her we had two reasons why we would not use them. First, we feel strongly that abortion is murder and we are not going to knowingly give our business to support anything that profits from murdering babies. Secondly, I said that if my wife had complications (oddly enough she did), I would not be able to trust a doctor who had just committed multiple murders of newborn babies to do his best to save ours. We did not choose them.

We ended up deciding on a doctor in that same town and set up payments with him and the hospital. When Sharon's due date came, the baby was taking her time (typical female), and Sharon went to the doctor to discuss the possibility of inducing labor. It was a Friday morning, and Sharon had woken up, not feeling well. She was plain sick by the time we reached the doctor's office, and they took her back right away.

It so happened that Sharon's sickness was related to the baby. It seemed that Heather's water sack was leaking and she (Heather) was sick also. The doctor had Sharon admitted into a room and he was going to induce labor, but Sharon started labor on her own. When she was a few hours into her labor, Heather was born.

During Heather's birth, things in the delivery room went crazy. Heather had a very high fever (over 104), and Sharon had ruptured an artery and was bleeding uncontrollably. Alarms went off and the room was suddenly filled with several doctors and three times as many nurses. I was pushed against the wall and out of the way as each doctor was screaming orders to the nurses and everyone was working different jobs at the same time. It all looked very confusing to me, but they were trying to save both my girls' lives.

One nurse came over to me and said I needed to leave the room, and I told her I wanted to stay. She took hold of my arm and started walking me toward the door. She said, "Mr. Penley, you are about to lose both of your girls, and we are trying to save their lives. You need to go outside!"

When I got outside, I watched for what was just ten to fifteen minutes but seemed like forever. People were running in and out of the room, and the doctors were still screaming out orders as they were fighting to save both my girls! I thought about what I had said to the abortion clinic about complications and thanked God we were not there.

The door opened, and a doctor with several nurses were taking Heather away to another part of the hospital. I had not yet even seen her. The door was left partially open, and the doctor was screaming for more blood. They were catching Sharon's blood in what looked like a garbage can. They shut the door, and I just sat down and started praying.

It took twenty minutes and two blood transfusions for Sharon to stop bleeding. They put her in a room and told me they were going to have to keep her for a few days longer because she had lost a serious amount of blood. Heather was somewhere, and we were told that we would be able to see her when they got her stable.

We called everyone we knew and asked them to start praying. After the rest of that day and that night, we still had not seen Heather. The next day, about 10:00 a.m., it had been eighteen hours since Heather's birth, and we could still not see her. We did not know what was going on. The doctor for Heather came into the room and told us that she still had an extremely high temperature and they were treating it. They continued that she had developed an infection from the leaking sack and they were trying to fight off the infection as well. The doctor told Sharon to rest and said he would have Heather brought to us as soon as he could. He looked at me and asked if I would step outside into the hall with him for a second, and I did.

Once in the hall, the doctor looked at me seriously and said he did not want to tell my wife because they did not know what they were dealing with yet. He said that they had run every test that would be good news so far, and none of them seemed to be the problem. He said, "What I am saying to you is that the only tests left to run will be bad news. Terminally bad." He said it would be hours before they knew and that I should go home and catch a few hours' sleep and come back so I could be with Sharon when they broke the news to her.

I drove home and called a few of our closest friends and asked them to pray. Then I passed out for a few hours. I woke up, cleaned up, and as I drove to the hospital, I called people and asked them to pray. I got to the room, and Sharon was still weak but awake. I told her that the doctors were running serious tests on Heather and we should find out something soon.

A few hours later, to my surprise, the nurse rolled Heather into our room for Sharon to hold and feed. No doctors, no fever, no explanation—just Heather, and it seemed all was well. The doctor walked in a short time later and spoke to Sharon about the fever and the infection. He said Heather seemed okay now and walked out of the room.

I followed him and asked him what the deal was. He said that it was the darnedest thing he had ever seen. He told me that while they were testing her for different types of cancers, her temperature left her and her symptoms disappeared. She was normal within a relatively short time. "We have double-checked her, and everything is normal." He continued sharing he was not a religious man but that Heather's situation was what most would call a miracle.

I just walked to the end of the hall and leaned into the corner of the building. I just breathed a prayer of thanks to God in heaven for answering Sharon's and my and many others' prayers and for touching my baby girl and saving both of my girls!

I would like to say to those who read this story and did not get the answer that changes everything and saves your loved ones, I have been there too; and please don't assume that God loves you any less. I promise you God loves you just as much as he loves everyone else. This world that is full of death and violence and brokenness is something that God will fix someday soon. If you have been hurt deeply, don't reject God. He will help you and comfort you if you let him. Call out to Jesus and tell him all your pain and sorrows. Jesus will walk with you through it, and God will do his work in your heart! I promise! I am thankful for when he did answer and save my little girl, and I also felt his comfort during each death of my loved ones.

Let's Go and See!

I moved my family to the metro Atlanta area and began serving in a local church as an assistant pastor with a friend of mine. It was a place for me to serve until God opened the next door for our family. It was a good church with great people, and God was working in people's lives. My place there was just a service position where I did the stuff no one else wanted to do. I cut the grass, cleaned things, and I was able to teach the children's church on Sundays, which gave me a chance to help people come to Christ and grow.

I was speaking for churches who needed pastors, but I would not fit with the ones I visited. Too many churches spent their money on themselves and saved people. Their burden was to make themselves comfortable and not on the great commission. I could not survive in that type of church nor could the church survive me. I would have to ask committees for permission to lead or, God forbid, he speak to my heart to do something crazy!

My friendship with Rusty had remained strong, and one day, he called me with a burden on his heart. Rusty had, during the eight years that passed, started a Hispanic church in Charlotte as well as a medical missions group that was sending more medical aid to Cuba than Europe and the rest of the world for a time. God had opened the door for him through connections with suppliers, medical people, and US senators to allow and carry medical supplies and training into Cuba legally, which was worth millions. He had tried to move to Cuba time and time again, with no success, and was now working in Cuba from Charlotte, North Carolina.

In eight years, his ministry grew to where they sent tons of medical supplies to Cuba several times a year. He took specialists who visited and trained the Cuban doctors in their fields while supplying the most up-to-date equipment. It was amazing what God was doing for these people medically through Rusty's vision and efforts.

One day, I got this call from Rusty that was to rock our world. Rusty shared that he was heartbroken for Cuba! He was one of, if not the largest, medical donors to Cuba. But he had not been able to share the Gospel with the people. His burden was to share the life-changing message of Christ with them.

For eight years, they had shared much needed aid to the island but had not been able to share the most important thing with them—salvation. As Rusty was telling me this, I was beginning to understand where he was going with it. His next words would be words that have forever changed my life, his life, and hundreds (if not thousands) of Cuban lives.

Rusty said to me, "I want to go to Cuba, just you and me, and preach all over the island. I want to preach to every place we can and do it until they either put us in jail or kick us out or do whatever to us! I want to test the waters and see what will happen!"

It was and is illegal to hold open meetings in Cuba. They are communists. Also, there is no due process in Cuba and it had no Embassy for Americans. In Cuba, the government does whatever they want to you, and you have no rights, no say, and they can put you in jail or even kill you without a trial. No justice or rights, just oppression.

The reason Rusty wanted just the two of us to go was because we had no idea what would happen. It was something that he was willing to do, and he knew I was ready to do it as well. However, he was not wanting to risk others.

He had a church connection in Havana that was a church before the communists took the country over in the '60s. One of the deacons of the church, a man named Pablo, became the pastor and had pastored it ever since. He had spent eight years in prison for pastoring and was older and was assisted by his son, Amittay.

Amittay was a medical doctor and assistant pastor to the church in Havana. He and Rusty had become good friends over the years, and Amittay had helped distribute the medical aid throughout the island of Cuba. Rusty, with the help of Senator Jesse Helms and Senator Max Burton, made it possible to get aid past the embargo and for US citizens to be able to fly into Cuba, which was illegal to do without permission.

The plan was simple. Rusty and I would fly into Cuba and visit Amittay and the church in Havana. I would be the speaker, and Rusty would be the translator. Once we spoke at the church in Havana, Amittay would send the word ahead that we were coming, and the three of us would travel and preach until we were stopped. The obstacles where that it was illegal for a Cuban to travel anywhere in Cuba without signed permission from the government. It was illegal for Amittay as a Cuban citizen to be in a car with Americans. Cubans could not rent cars or buy in stores or use hotels. Basically, everything about the trip was illegal. Not to mention preaching Jesus in illegal meetings as many times as possible.

Amittay was well-known as a brilliant doctor and as a pastor throughout the island. He had the connections to open doors for meetings, and finding the places was not going to be an issue. The main issue was that we were about to enter a communist country and travel the entire 900 miles and speak to as many people in as many areas as we could fit into sixteen days.

I mentioned a few of the minor obstacles, but also in Cuba, everyone around must be treated as an informant for the government. If you are in a group of four or more people, the rule of thumb is that one out of those four is an informant for the government. Everywhere you go in Cuba, you are followed, observed, and monitored. If we visited homes, government observers were supposed to be present to listen to our conversations. Every meeting we would be speaking in would have government informants.

So to sum it up, basically Rusty was so burdened for the people of Cuba to hear the Gospel, he was willing to risk whatever Cuba would throw our way to try and get it to them. Amittay and I were both in.

The other side of the coin that I have not mentioned was that we would possibly be preaching to some people who had never heard the name of Jesus or of the Bible. Certainly not having heard that, they could be forgiven and eternally saved by repenting and receiving Christ. Who would not risk anything to be able to have such a chance? I was humbled and so thankful to be invited and to be able to serve God in such a way with two of the men I respect most until this day. I was all in, and we set the dates to go!

Sixteen Days

I have traveled to communist countries before and am always affected by the oppression some people live under. When I visited Albania and was leaving the plane, we were welcomed by a soldier with a machine-gun pointing his barrel in the direction we were to walk. In Venezuela, we were out of the cities for the most part, but the socialistic attitude in Caracas was very evident.

Haiti is not communist, but it is oppressive. When traveling as an American, especially to countries of limited freedoms, I am reminded constantly of the freedoms that often can be taken for granted—the freedom to work where you choose and to change jobs as you wish, the freedom to own property, the freedom to travel across town without having to ask permission, the freedom to think on your own, harbor opinions, then to speak your opinion without fear. These things most Americans hold true are not the norm for many peoples worldwide.

When we arrived in Cuba, I was ready for a third-world type of living standard. I had seen it enough times and welcomed it. I knew we were walking into a communist government and without an American embassy. Rusty had been there many times, and I knew we would be fine. I was not ready for the step off the plane and into a world of government control, but I was visiting them.

We flew into Havana and walked off the plane and down the landing steps onto the tarmac. The guards were not holding machine-guns on us, and we walked into the border control and customs. Rusty and I appeared to be the only Americans, but a lot of European tourists were there. We had no problems with the customs agents, and they searched through every part of our luggage.

As we walked out into the front of the airport, Rusty and I met Amittay who was waiting there for us. He had a '53 Ford with a Russian diesel engine in it. In Cuba, you could not own a car unless given permission. Then you could only if the car was older than the date Castro took over (1960). All over Cuba, 1959 and earlier model cars are everywhere.

Amittay lived in a very modest home over the top of his medical clinic in a little town of Chico. Chico is a metro area of Havana. He was the doctor responsible for that area, which just happened to be the home of the national Cuban boxing team.

Our first meeting was held in Amittay's father's church in Havana. Rusty had helped the people build the church on the top floor of the house of Pastor Pablo. It was a large open room with small rooms to the side for small groups to meet in. It had seating for 100 or so but could be packed to many more. There was an open porch area out the back with standing room for others who could look in through the open windows.

Rusty wanted me to speak, and he would interpret. The plan was that I would share my personal story of how I had come to Christ and some of the things God did for me after accepting him. Rusty would interpret, and then we would open the altars for anyone who wanted to come to Christ or just come and pray.

We started with a full house, and I was not used to speaking with an interpreter. I also had been in the shower at Pablo's house and was soaped down when the water was cut off. I had to dry off and put on my suit without showering the soap off. The church was packed to overflowing and the night was hot.

There were 180 plus people in a room built for eighty to a hundred with another forty to fifty looking through from the porch. They had a few small fans, but not many, and it was hot. The people were in great spirits, and they sang, and then Rusty and I began our message. I spoke for probably an hour. At one point in the middle of the message, foam began coming out of my shirt collar because of the heat and sweat and the soap that was still on my body. It was quite funny, and I saw and soon began to understand why the Cuban people lived and rolled with the punches.

I explained about having lathered up and the water being cut off, and they just laughed, and we went on with the service, foam and all. It was in that first speaking event that I was so touched at how hungry the Cuban people were to hear the Bible and truth. I speak all the time and often see people on their phones, sleeping, or unplugged and not hungry for the Word. In Cuba, where scripture was taken from them and unavailable for years, these people were hungry for the teaching of the Bible and the message of Christ.

We set out from Havana toward the other end of the island and were then going to work our way back. The plan was that over the next fourteen days, we would speak wherever the door opened and as often as possible. It is 900 miles from one end of Cuba to the other. My memory does not recall every time we held a service, but we ended up speaking five to six times each day and well into the night. I have never experienced a place where so many people were willing to walk, wait for hours, and stay up late to hear the message of Christ, little children to the elderly, and many of them walking miles to attend the meetings.

The meetings were technically illegal, so often we would not know where we were going. We would drive to the next city or village where word of our coming had them ready. Someone would be waiting by a stop sign or something of the sort, and we would follow them to the meeting place. I noticed they would wind us through the area so we would not be able to describe our location if asked by anyone.

I remember that we would be scheduled to be at a place at 7:00 p.m., and we would roll in after midnight. The person would be waiting at the meeting place and take us to the location of the service. We would walk in, and the place would be packed with people who had been there since 5:00 that afternoon, waiting. Children, babies, teens, adults—all dressed in their best, waiting to hear the message.

We would preach late into the night, and the people would have two to three or more miles to walk home, and yet, they still sat till it was over. They would then walk home in time to go to work or do whatever their day held. I was so humbled to witness such true hunger for spiritual guidance. I have three services that stick out on this first trip that I will share.

The first of the three was in a very poor small fishing village on the other end of the island from Havana. Niquero is the name, and this village was on the seashore and very poor by even Cuban standards. There was a pastor and his family there who had a church we were to speak at—Rafael and his wife, Tami. They had two boys around ten to twelve named Isaac and Elon. I fell in love with their family and became very close with the boys.

They called me Tio Sapo (a name that has stuck with me over the years) which means "Uncle Toad Frog." They said I looked like a large white toad. They were fascinated by my big white belly. They had not seen many white men before, and I struck them as funny. I fell in love with this family. Many of the pastors and their families were poor, but Rafael and Tami more than most. They lived on a very limited income.

At one point, Tami was cooking tomatoes with rags so the cloth fiber would help the tomatoes stay in their system long enough to give them nutrients. Tami had gone almost completely blind from malnutrition. Her eyes had just given out. When she realized she was going blind, she prayed to God, asking that he would let her see every morning so she could maintain her Bible reading. Sure enough, God answered her prayer, and in the mornings, God gave her a time where she could see to read her Bible, and after that, her eyes stopped working.

Rafael and Tami took care of many people in their village. They took us to see some of them, and one lady is worth mentioning. She had a bedridden child that was like sixteen years old. The child was grossly contorted and had problems that made her scream out in pain if she was touched. The child was skin and bones and was twisted and contorted, living in constant pain from birth. The mother had spent her every hour taking care of this child. I can still see her and the love that lady had for that poor child.

Rafael's church meets in a horse barn. It had mud floors and a large open space with stables to the left as you entered the double doors. It was a working barn and church, and he had a growing congregation. The barn was packed with people with more standing outside listening through the windows. I was again touched at how everyone was hanging onto the message and open and hungry for the truth.

We had great results, and many people made decisions for Christ. In Cuba, it was not the normal thing for people to make open professions of faith. With so many informants all around, it was not wise to show your profession for Jesus publicly. The people who decided to accept Christ more often would do it in their heart and then come tell the pastor in a private setting. That is why when people were baptized, they were making a huge statement.

To be publicly baptized often cost them something. They could lose their food rations or job or relationships. In our country, we take baptism for granted because we are presently free of persecution. In a communist country, when a person gets baptized, it often costs them something to be identified with Jesus. I thank God for everyone who trusted Christ in the little town of Niquero. I love Rafael and his family.

As I said at the beginning of this chapter, we had no idea what was going to happen when we started preaching openly in Cuba. Well, we ended up traveling from one meeting to the next, preaching five to six times a day and averaging three hours sleep a night, if that. We did that for fifteen days.

The second meeting I want to mention stood out because of the lateness of the hour and the response from the people. We were supposed to get to this meeting around seven in the evening. But we ended up not getting into the city (I have no idea of the name) until after 1:00 a.m. We were not even sure anyone would still be there. We found the person who was to take us to the meeting where he was supposed to be. He led us in a crisscrossing pattern throughout the streets to the location.

When we walked into the small meeting room, it was completely packed. It was hot with no breeze and way past full capacity. It looked like 200 people in a room made for sixty. The people had been arriving all afternoon and walked from miles away to be there, small babies to the very old. They had sat in this hot, unventilated, overcrowded room from midafternoon to after one in the morning, and according to the pastor, no one left. They just waited.

After a few minutes, I was soaking wet from sweat and the heat in the room. We had the service, and many people responded for Christ. We left after three in the morning, heading toward the next town. We could see the people walking back to their homes, many of them not going to get there before daylight. I thought about how Americans would react to a service in an overcrowded room with no climate control, having to wait eight hours before it started, and then going over two hours long. These people were so thankful that they could hear the message. What a difference between people who are blessed with prosperity and those who are persecuted and starving and not able to hear the Bible.

The third meeting was the one that God used in the biggest way to change my life. I saved it for last because of what came out of the meeting. Again, these meetings were happening in all types of places and group sizes—inside barns, houses, old buildings, and outside in open air and in not so public areas. It is illegal to have meetings in Cuba, and each one was an iffy thing for all involved.

This meeting was to be a two-day meeting in a town named Bayamo, a beautiful little historic town. The pastor in that town was Ramon, and his wife's name was Naomi. They had two children and were a very lovely family. Bayamo was a much nicer town and not as poor as Niquero. We stayed with the pastor's family and got to know them very well.

Ramon had the church folk talk up the meeting and get as many people to come as they could. When we arrived, I was surprised to see that it was being held in the backyard of a house not too far outside of town. The yard was an average-sized yard, maybe a quarter acre with chickens and pigs and a small garden. The yard was packed out with people everywhere. Some on the roof of the house and on both roofs of the houses on each side of that one. People filled both yards on each side of the house as well as the yard of the house we met in. Many of the people stood where we could not see them, but they could hear what was going on.

Behind the fences, along the backs of each yard, were people gathered as well. It was many people spread out all over and not possible to get a count. I was standing in the backyard of the house by the barn during the worship. I accidently stepped on a little pig during the song. Nobody seemed to mind, and they kept singing (except the pig), and I thought to myself, *That is the first time I've stepped on a pig in a worship service before.*

We gave our message, and I could sense the Spirit moving in a strong way. I finished and gave the invitation over to Rusty and returned to my spot near the pigs. Rusty did something that shocked me and everyone else. He asked the ones who were ready to put their faith in Jesus to make a public show of it by raising their hands. You could feel the tension, but people all over the crowd started raising their hands. On top of the roofs, arms were sticking over the edges, and over the side yard fences, hands were coming up, and people behind the barn and yards were saying they were ready. I had not witnessed an outpouring that strong of people openly taking Jesus the entire time on that trip. It seemed that four out of ten where saying yes to Jesus openly on that day.

After so many people responded, we advised them to each come to Pastor Ramon and let him know so he could help them with their next steps. An old lady who was a member of Ramon's church asked if she could say something. She stood up and told the people that God had showed her in a dream that he was going to give their church a building. She said God told her that men would come from far away and help them get the building.

While she was saying this, God spoke to me that I was the one who was supposed to help. I did not have enough money to pay attention, much less pay to build a church building. But God spoke to my heart, right there by the pig pen, and told me I was the man in the dream the woman was talking about.

I did not tell anyone about this at first, but I knew God had spoken to me. The next day, the meeting was called off because of the weather. We were sitting at Ramon's house, and Ramon said that God had opened a door for the church that did not happen in Cuba. He shared that a lady who owned a property in town had the same last name as Ramon. She was a member of his church and had asked the communist leader of their neighborhood if her son, Ramon, could build a garage in her backyard. The garage was a way for them to build a church with the government's approval.

The communist leader told Ramon that he had permission to build a garage that could be two stories high with classrooms on the second floor and with room enough to seat 200 on the first floor. Ramon said that the money was not the biggest issue. The issue was that in his time as a pastor in Cuba, it was unheard of to be given permission to build a 200-seat garage with Sunday school space upstairs.

Amittay verified that was the case, and the God-sized thing about it was that it could be done! God had opened a door for the church to be able to build a building with brick and concrete, electricity, and chairs, and a sound system.

I asked Ramon about the old lady who had shared her dream, and he told me that she was a Godly woman who had prayed for their church to start and had been a prayer warrior from the beginning.

We asked him what it would cost to build such a garage, and Ramon said it would cost $15,000 total. I shared with Rusty, Amittay, and Ramon what God had said to me about the old lady's dream. I told them that God had told me to help them build the church. As Ramon shared the opportunity that the communist powers in his neighborhood gave the church the go ahead to build, it was obvious that God had been working things out before we got there. In a two-day time, the door opened to put it all together. We all joined in prayer and asked God to raise the $15,000 needed for the building and for God to help us do it quickly before the door could close.

We traveled fifteen days all over Cuba, preaching as much and to as many people as we could possibly do. We averaged two to three hours of sleep a night, and I have no idea how many people we ministered to. We were in cities and in one tribal village and several small towns. The one thing in common was that the Cuban people were open and hungry for the Gospel of Christ.

We had traveled the island and saw hundreds of people claim Jesus in their lives. The heart of the Cuban people walking miles in the heat and sitting uncomfortably for hours, waiting just to hear the message. Then to see that many people receive Christ was something I have read about in the book of Acts and in old revival accounts of days gone by but have never experienced.

We did not go to jail or get arrested or get thrown out of the country. We know the government heard from their informants on every meeting we held, but they did not stop us. I was sure God spoke to me to get the money for the church in Bayamo. I also knew something in my soul was stirring from having seen God do in sixteen days what I had always wanted to see him do in our country. The only thing missing in our churches was the heart of the Cuban people—a heart that wants Christ!

Cigars

The lady who handled the medical aid that Rusty's group brought into the country was a sweetheart. She was a professional government official and loved her people and her country. She was so thankful for the millions of dollars of medical supplies that Rusty's ministry brought into her country. She knew Rusty long enough to understand his goals were faith-based, not political. She is a friend to the work and a friend to Rusty, Amittay, and myself as well.

We worked it out to go to Pinar Del Rio where her mom and dad lived. Cubans are not free to travel and visit, and it had been sometime since she had seen her parents. We planned a day trip to go check on a clinic there and visit with her family. Her dad was an older gentleman who had farmed all his life, a very hardworking man and someone I have great love and respect for from the times we have had the pleasure of spending in his home.

Her parents killed and cooked a pig for our visit, and we had a day-long meal with fellowship. He and his wife had been cattle farmers and had run a meat processing and delivery business before the revolution. He shared with us the hardships of losing his business, his wealth, and his farm. He was given a farm to work and maintain outside his city, and he drove his bike back and forth twelve-plus miles one way every day. He had to keep records of his livestock and produce because it belonged to the government.

He was a very strong-spirited man and was embittered by the oppression he was forced under as a farmer. He shared that every time he would get to a place where he was able to accumulate extra money, the government would come and kill and take some of his cows. He would have to pay them for every cow they lost. No matter how hard he tried, he had not been able to do more than scratch out a living for his wife and himself. Still, he was a friendly, humble, fun-spirited man.

As he finished sharing his story with us throughout the course of the meal and while sitting around afterward visiting, I shared my story with them. There was a communist representative there because we were not allowed to visit with them without a government representative listening to the conversation. The person was very polite, and it was not a problem, because that is how things are in Cuba.

I shared my life story about the death of my brother and the effect it had on our family. I continued to the point in my life where I put my faith in Jesus. I shared with them what God was doing in my life through Christ. At the end of the story, both the father and mother asked to pray and receive Jesus. Rusty led them in prayer as they both accepted Christ in that little living room in Pinar Del Rio. After the prayer, the lady who was the communist representative asked if she too could become a Christian. She also prayed with Rusty and accepted Christ as her savior.

The father said he wanted to celebrate their getting saved, so he went to his closet and brought out a bottle of rum. He asked if he could pour me a glass as a gift and to celebrate their conversion. At the time, I did not drink, so I asked him to pour a glass for he and his wife, and I would accept the thoughtfulness of the gift but let them share the rum. He said it was too expensive for them to drink and that he had it for special occasions only. He then said that he had some hand-rolled cigars that he grew and rolled himself, and he asked if Rusty, Amittay, and I would have one with him. I used to love cigars before I became a Christian, and had not had one in over twenty years. We gladly accepted and all sat on the back porch and shared a Cuban hand-rolled cigar together, celebrating the family's conversion to Christ.

Only in Cuba can three preachers and three new converts have cigars in celebration of their conversion. That is the kind of thing that could only happen in Cuba! I need to also say that Pinar Del Rio is the location in Cuba where the best cigar tobacco in the world is grown. If you are reading this and believe as I once did that believers should not smoke cigars, then disregard this chapter and please don't tell anyone my secret. I am forever thankful for being able to join Rusty and Amittay and see this awesome family come to Christ. I have also been a fan of Cuban seed cigars ever since that day.

The Well

On the last day we were in Cuba, Rusty met with the lady who processed his medical donations at the Hotel National. We sat on the rotunda at a table, drinking Cuban coffee. I was not involved with their conversation (Spanish) and was sitting there reading my Bible. A man I had met who was a neighbor of Amittay had given me a very rare Cuban cigar. It was the cigar that the government gives as a gift to dignitaries. It had a red ribbon for a band with no name.

I was sitting with Rusty and this lady, reading scripture, sipping Cuban coffee, smoking this cigar. I was reading Genesis 26, and when I got to verse 22, God spoke to my heart. He said I was to start another church! The verse talks of Isaac digging wells and fighting with the people around his camp over the rights to the wells he dug. In verse 22, they had moved camps again and dug another well, and no one fought with them for that water. He named the well Rehoboth. It means, "God has made a place for us at last!"

When I read that verse, I was not thinking anything but how good the Cuban coffee was and that the cigar was unbelievable also. I especially was not thinking of starting another church. I had already done that and was not up for that kind of battle again.

Rusty was in a very important discussion, and while I was sitting with them, I was really alone. I know as sure as I am sitting here that God spoke to me! The issue was that I had prayed and asked God to shake me in the sugarcane field (next chapter). I was still very dead inside from all of me that I left in Mesa, Arizona. I do not see myself as a very good pastor and tend to see things differently than most churches.

I do not think a church is to be run as a business or supposed to hoard money or ignore the lost. I believe churches are supposed to preach the Gospel all over, baptize people who are converted, and then train (disciple) every person they reach. I believe every penny that God gives the church should be spent doing the above. I believe the authority of the church is the same as the Christian, and that is scripture. I believe no matter how you set up your leadership structure, the church needs to be followers of Christ!

I did not want the battles that came with starting another church. I also did not have the strength to endure the spiritual war that birthing a church required. I was tired of always being broke and needing something from God. I wanted to drive cars that cranked when the key was turned. I was not feeling starting a church again. I did not tell anyone about that conversation with God that morning.

I did write it down in my Bible next to the verse. I knew God did not need my permission to call me, and I had just spent hours in a sugarcane field asking him to move on my behalf. I was just not expecting pastoring.

People bitch, complain, and don't listen. They are hard to love, selfish, and take you and your family for granted. I did not want to pastor again! God reminded me that everything I just said about people was true, but it was also true that I did the same to him and was the same way with him. He is right, and I wrote it down in my Bible, but I did not tell anyone about it. I just finished my cigar and coffee.

Sugarcane Field

On the eleven to twelve-hour drive back to Havana, we were driving through the middle of the island late at night, and I was the only one awake—nothing for miles but the moon, and stars, and sugarcane on both sides of the highway. It was about 3:00 a.m., and I was moved by the Spirit of God and what he had done throughout the entire island of Cuba. God, through Rusty's heart, had opened an opportunity for us to preach Jesus to thousands.

Some of the people, no doubt, had never before heard of his name. It was a God thing, and he made it so I could be part of this awesome thing. My heart was also stirred about having to go back to our church in America where we had turned church into a business. We competed with other churches by offering the newest or best so as to entertain and satisfy and mainly keep our members. We judge our success on attendance and offerings while our children and teens are leaving our churches by the handfuls.

I had spent sixteen days seeing life, excitement, salvations by the hundreds, and areas changed by the power of the Word of God. I was going back to a place where the Word of God was old news, half-believed, and not important enough to empower a spirit-filled life in many of our church members.

As I was driving, I was emotionally affected by the huge amount of people who had just turned to Christ. I was facing going back to a dead, powerless, broken church culture offering self-centered

Christianity that does not work. I pulled over and got out of the car and started walking through this sugarcane field. My eyes were filled with tears and I was praying out loud to God. I could not go back and be part of what we, in our country, have turned our churches into.

I fell to my knees, and in the Caribbean moonlight in the middle of Cuba, in the first few rows of a sugarcane field, I prayed. I told the Lord that I did not want to stay the same way that I was before this trip. I asked God to do a work in me that would allow his Spirit to work in people's hearts no matter where we were. I committed my heart to him again and promised to do whatever he led me to do.

When we got back to the states, I knew I was supposed to raise the $15,000 for the church in Bayamo. At the time, I was working with a pastor friend of mine as his assistant, and it was a good church. I had a friend that my heart was knit with named Charles Rawls. He has since become one of my closest friends, even closer than a brother.

I met with Charles for lunch and shared with him the best that words could convey of what God had done. I told him that during the service in Bayamo, God spoke to me, telling me to raise the money for the garage in Bayamo that would seat 200 people. I also told Charles that not only was I supposed to do that, I shared with him that he was supposed to help me raise it and that he was to go back with me to deliver the money! The funny thing was that God had spoken to my heart about that very thing. I felt compelled to get Charles to Cuba with me and to get his help with the money.

I was also wondering what God was going to do to shake my world to get me to the place we had talked about in the sugarcane field and at the table with the "start a church" thing. Over the next few days, God began working out the beginnings for all those things. In my life, God often begins moving in a good way but with seemingly bad circumstances, and this time was no different.

I started mentioning to people who I knew had a heart for the Gospel that we needed to raise the money for a church to be built in Cuba. The pastor that I was working for at the time asked to see me. We met, and I shared with him about Cuba a little, but he was not really interested. He shared that he understood I had mentioned to some people that I was raising money for building a church in Cuba and was planning on going back. I told him absolutely and that I expected him to give me a chance to get the church involved. I will never forget his answer.

He told me that he not only would not let me mention it to the church; he said if I mentioned it to anyone in the church and in fact raised any money from anyone in the church, I was fired. He continued that he was raising money for the church to put a new sign out front and that I had better not mention Cuba to anyone.

The pastor of that church is not a bad preacher. He is what many pastors are today—builders of their own kingdoms—more worried about his member's money getting outside of his control and church. I told him that he did not have to worry about firing me. I quit. If we are more worried about a new church sign for our church than a church in a city without churches and in a place where Christ had not been preached in over sixty years, I had to go. I wanted to throw up. I still think about it. Narcissism is choking our churches!

I was also working for an electrician who had hired me for a friend in the church where I had just resigned. When I quit the church, I also would soon be asked to leave him. God was shaking my nest a little and answering my prayers as well. I had my family (seven) and my two in-laws living with us and had just lost half my income with soon-to-be full income. We had one month's bills ($3,000) in the bank. I was worried about how I was going to take care of my family, but God has always taken care of us. My main burden was the church in Bayamo.

My family sat down together and prayed. We committed everything to God and asked for his guidance. My wife and I had money in savings. My mother and father-in-law had some (very little), and he had just been diagnosed with cancer. My two oldest boys both had savings accounts for their college.

As we prayed and asked God to help us raise the $15,000 for the church, we each asked God how much he wanted us to give. My wife and I felt that we should give half of our savings ($1,500), my in-laws felt led to give as much, and both of my sons felt led to give all their savings for the church. We had over $6,000 of the $15,000 in one prayer meeting with just our family. It was obvious that God was doing something. What an honor to be invited to be part of this opportunity for a church/garage to be built in a communist country where very few, if any, Gospel churches exist!

Also, let me say when God spoke to me about raising the money, I was the only one who knew for sure God spoke to me. Others knew I thought he did, but I lost my job (soon-to-be both jobs). However, my family gave their college funds, and my father-in-law who just found out he had terminal cancer gave a large part of his little bit of savings. Let's be clear, what Christian would not give as much or more for a Gospel-preaching church to be established in a part of the world where there was not a witness for Christ? Every true Christian would give half what they own to do that!

I could see God's validation from how he moved our family to give. Next, I pressed my buddy Charles again that God had told me he was supposed to go with me to Cuba.

Let me explain a little about Charles. He and his wife, Celena, are two very special people. They have given of themselves time and time again because of their faith in Jesus. Charles is a businessman, and Celena a very gifted educator. Charles' idea of a Christian businessman was to make as much money as possible and give it to the pastor when he needed it. Giving to a church sign was as important to him as giving to a new church plant in a non-reached area of the world if his preacher thought so. His service seemed mechanical and superficial.

I was getting to know Charles and his wife, and they had a real love for Christ. I was burdened that God wanted more from Charles than he had been taught to be from his church experiences. I was sure that was why God was impressing me to have him come to Cuba. I wanted Charles to see and experience what real Christianity looked like.

We met again, and I convinced him to pray about going back with me. Once he agreed to pray about it, I knew he was in. Charles also agreed to give and help raise the remaining amount of money needed for the church building as well as for our expenses to go back.

In six weeks, God touched the lives of Christian people to start this great opportunity for the Gospel. We had widows, children, dying, poor, wealthy, and everyone in between give to the church in Bayamo. I am thankful that every person who sacrificed to see this work happen will take their sacrifice in the amount of their giving with them to heaven. What I mean by that is the gifts that came in for the most part did not come from people with enough and more than enough to give. Most of the money came in from people who gave on the level to have to endure the sacrifice from the gift for a while.

People who get Christianity and realize what God gave for us will give more than their ability, like the church at Philippi in Scripture. God's fingerprints were all over this offering, and we had the money for a two-story garage that would seat 200 people furnished with electricity, chairs, and a sound system. Not a building that many here in the states would suffer, but one that they praised the God of heaven for and preached the message of Jesus with to lost people all around their state. That church is still there, doing what it was built to do in that dark place!

Pants

One thing about getting older is that you look back at some things in your life and realize how absolutely wrong you were at the time you believed you were right. Cuba and other mission trips, along with God's grace and mercy and patience, opened my eyes to many things about my teaching that was more tradition than biblical. One such thing was our view of women wearing pants (I'm ashamed to admit I preached this stuff).

Back in the days of my independent Baptist preaching, I was more pharisaical than biblical. I used to teach that a woman should not wear pants because that was what we all preached. We did not go to movies, drink alcohol, smoke anything, or chew. The issues of biblical modesty and holiness in lifestyle were not left to individuals to work out in their own walk. Bless God, we told you what was right, and you had better believe it or you were wrong.

I am so thankful my wife put up with me, and I am sorry for the times I taught such things from the pulpit. I believe that modesty and holiness are biblical and important, and I believe every believer should walk with Jesus in such a way as to please him in our daily lives. I know when I do something that does not please him, and I am sure you do also. Christian people should be free to think for themselves, and as preachers, it is important to be sure what we call God's Word is in fact God's Word.

My wife is a very Godly and modest lady, far past what I deserve. She did not wear pants because I did not want her to. It was not her conviction, it was mine, and she lovingly did as I asked her to do. I was taken to school by God on my last trip to Cuba. I saw people who had never heard of the Bible and of Jesus put their faith in him and begin a walk with him. I noticed how many things I had made major in my preaching was not even relevant to people's lives.

I also began to realize that I liked cigars and was not sinning against God every time I smoked one. So now I was left with a very strange dilemma. How do I explain to my wife and four boys that it is okay to do something I have said for the longest time was a sin? I do not believe in hiding anything or being one thing at home and something else in public. I hate that type of Christianity. So I was trying to find a way to tell my family I smoked cigars and mainly that I was wrong in some of my views as a preacher.

Shortly after I was back from Cuba, my wife and boys were going out to run errands, and I decided to cut the grass. Well, they left, and I thought, *This is a perfect time to smoke a cigar as I am cutting the grass on my riding lawn mower*. I got myself and the lawn mower ready. I got a cigar and my earbuds and was cutting grass with my praise music blasting in my ears and my Cuban cigar in my mouth. I was in hog heaven. My back was turned away from the driveway, and I did not notice that our family van pulled back in and up to where I was in the yard. I turned the mower around to make another sweep across the lawn, and there was my wife and four boys staring at my cigar with shock on their faces.

My wife got out of the van and came up to me asking, "What on earth are you doing with a cigar?"

I looked at her and sheepishly said, "Go buy yourself some pants!"

We had family devotions that night. We read the Bible and sang and prayed together before bed. I confessed to my family that I had been spiritually proud and judgmental in some ways and that I was wrong. I told them that some of the things that I had taught were not true. I asked them to forgive me and also asked God to forgive me.

I also have tried to allow God to teach me how to pastor people and preach his Word biblically. I hope I am getting it. I have tried to live and train my family that what is important in a Christian's life is a daily walk with Christ in his word and in prayer. Each of us should surrender our lives to him and live in such a way as to please him! If we can do that, everything else will take care of itself!

Does God Work for Castro?

I n six weeks, we were on our way back to Cuba. Normally, I would not want to take anyone with me on a trip like this one, mainly because it was potentially dangerous to do the things in Cuba that we were doing. Charles was someone who would be willing to risk his life for a chance to share Christ on this scale, so I felt comfortable with him coming. I also knew God strongly directed me to bring him along. One other businessman came with us who had given money toward the church and was a friend of Charles.

Cuba is a land of strong contrasts. The Cuban people back then could not go to stores or buy and sell goods or go to restaurants or hotels. They could not sell or do business because everything in Cuba belonged to the government. They were not able to raise livestock unless they were registered, and then the stock was property of the state. You could not travel freely unless approved by the government. In a way, everything you would consider normal life for us was illegal for Cubans.

The contrasts I mentioned are that everything in Cuba evolved around the black market. Cuban's bought and sold and functioned almost entirely by doing their business on the black market. Add to the fact that everybody in Cuba was expected to tell the government about any illegal activity they knew about. Everybody in Cuba was expected to be an informant to the government on everybody else. Everything was illegal and everybody was doing illegal stuff and expected to tell the government on everyone else who did the same illegal things they did.

It was a hard thing to wrap your head around if you spent any time in Cuba. For example, Amittay's wife made and sold cakes for birthdays and special occasions. She made more money on her cakes than her doctor husband made each month. Everything she needed for her cakes she bought from others on the black market. In turn, whoever ordered and bought a cake from her was doing so illegally (black market). The government would come to a person and say, "We heard that Dr. Amittay's wife was making and selling cakes (they already knew this), and we need you to tell us when you see her doing this or we will come and take your children away."

They would tell on Amittay and Anita, knowing that Amittay and Anita would do the same on them. Everyone was involved in black market dealings as a matter of survival. Everyone would tell the government on each other when asked, knowing that the government already knew. Each person was always in a position of informing or being informed on. It was a very complex system of keeping the entire population poor, afraid, and controlled. Starvation and fear are the grease on the Cuban machine that keeps the Cuban people under control.

It was a very complex and confusing thing for Americans to wrap our heads around. Cubans were always one step away from being arrested and knew that they were being watched. The same Cuban was in turn afraid of the government and watching their own friends and even loved ones as directed. Everybody operated guilty and was under surveillance constantly, including us, except we were not informants.

Amittay would always tell me to be careful what I said because if there were four people together, one was an informant. I did not understand that until many times in Cuba. Amittay was a government informant on us! Also, a Cuban understood this and did not judge or hold it against other Cubans as it was their way of life.

I had no idea how much this second trip to Cuba was going to change our lives. We arrived at the airport and again made it through customs without incident. I had over $20,000 cash in my pocket, plus my own expense money. I had $15,000 for the church building, and the rest was to help the pastors and people with their needs as God led.

The Cuban pastors were forced to suffer under communism and held to poverty because of their open stand as pastors. Many spent time in jail just because they were pastors. We were all thankful to be able to bring with us a little help for their families. One-hundred dollars of US money could feed a family of four, rice and beans for months.

We made it through customs, and again they searched all our bags and took some of my snacks. It was mostly painless, and we went outside where Dr. Amittay was waiting. We went to his house in Chico and began plans for the next week of travel. Our plan was to deliver our money to Ramon for the church first, and afterward, visit as many of the churches as we could.

We started with a service at Pablo's church in Havana and went from there into the island. Again, God moved in the packed service, and people began their walk with Christ, and for some, a closer walk. It was a blessing to be able to speak for Pastor Pablo, Amittay's father. Over the course of his ministry, he was arrested several times and suffered great hardship in prison just for being a pastor. He had spent a total of over eight years in prison for preaching the truth. He was always nervous listening to me preach but wanted me to do so.

I think of the verse about "So the last shall be first, and the first last" (Matt. 20:16a, KJV). Not many people will ever in this life know the name of Pablo, pastor in Cuba. But the big named million-dollar preacher and their jets will take a backseat to the Pablo's all over the world who suffer and stay faithful to Jesus. They will be first when it counts. I am so blessed to know him and call him friend.

We began the drive to the other end of the island, stopping first at Camaguey and then on to Bayamo to Ramon's. Our trip toward Ramon's was nine and a half hours of driving, so we passed the time, watching the Cuban countryside and the people. It was exciting to be able to see God give Ramon a way to build a church in a country where churches were illegal.

I remembered listening to Ramon and his people talking, and they were asking God in prayer for a building where their church could meet openly as a church. Most churches that were not licensed by the government (illegal churches) met in buildings that had been abandoned or in barns or secret locations. The government licensed some churches (monitored) and allowed them to meet in the old churches that were built before the revolution. Ramon and his people were praying and asking God to open a door that would allow them to build a new building for their church. Impossible by all conceivable means.

A lady in Ramon's church had his last name. She acted like Ramon was her family, and together they asked the communist representative in their area if he could build a garage. Ramon was known as a pastor, and their church was helping a lot of people. The leader recognized the work they were doing and the good that it did for the people. I do not know if the leader knew that Ramon and the lady were not family, but if he did, he did not let on that he knew.

When asked if they could build the garage, the leader gave them permission to build it large enough to seat 200 people. He also told them to dig the footers deep and wide enough to build the first-floor walls and ceilings with enough strength to add a second floor for classrooms. He told them to build an office and a one-bedroom apartment on the end of it in case they needed a place to stay the night. It was in all rights a miracle from God that the permission was given.

We drove into Bayamo and handed Ramon's church the cash money to build and finish the garage (church). Ramon hired government companies to do the labor and bought all the materials on the government market with permission from the government representative. Everything was done legally and above board, and God provided a way for the church in Bayamo to build their own church building in a great location.

I cannot put into words what it felt like sitting around Ramon's living room with Rusty, Charles, Amittay, and Ramon's workers and joining hands and thanking God for what he had done. It was a very sacred time, and God's presence was as real in that circle as anyone else's in the room. It was a God thing. It makes me think of the song "God Will Make a Way." God made a way. An awesome answer to prayer!

As we left the next day, we set our sights on the small fishing town of Niquero where Rafael, Tami, Elon, and Isaac and their church met in a barn. It was a four to five-hour drive along the coast. The Sierra Maestra Mountains were between the city and Niquero. As beautiful as the coast was, we saw on the map what looked like a road through the Sierra Maestra Mountains. It was not clear if it was a road, but it was on the map.

The Sierra Maestra Mountains is a special place in Cuba. It is dense jungle mountains cut off from the main stream of Cuba. It is where Castro and his men hid and lived during the revolution. The mountains had a strong and strange fixation on Castro, and Castro felt the same about the mountains. Castro was revered as a god to many in the mountains of the Sierra Maestra range. The people there lived in primitive huts and mud floors scattered all over the mountainside. No one was allowed into that part of Cuba as tourists, and the people there were not used to cars or anything other than military vehicles.

We rented a minivan and there were five of us with a backseat unused. We decided to try to travel the road and go over the Sierra Maestra Mountains and save time rather than drive around them. The road started out as a dirt road like the ones where you have two dirt tire tracks and grass in between. It was passable for the longest time, but soon we came to where it became more like a four-wheel drive course, but again, it was doable.

We came to a place about an hour in where the road emptied out into a rock bed creek with no road on the other side. We could not tell if it ended or turned right or left using the riverbed as the road. It had just a little water flowing and a lot of the bed was dry river rocks.

We walked up and down a bit and finally decided to turn right down the riverbed to see if the road dumped out on the other side down the way. We drove down the riverbed for a pretty good way having to get out and push a few times with water above our ankles, but still doable. We were just about to turn back as the riverbed was beginning to be more than our rental van could bear when we saw a two-tire track path out the other side. It was an easy little hill out of the riverbed for an old army jeep, but it was a little more of a challenge getting up it in the van.

With the right speed and determination, we popped (literally) right out on the trail/road. As we drove from there, we came into the mountains and the road became more maneuverable. It was even paved in a few of the bigger villages, but mostly it was a dirt road used by military. We were in the middle of some of the most awesome jungle mountain views that I had ever seen. We were quite the sight to the people as many of them had never seen a minivan, much less with one Cuban and four white men. We were the first white men some of the younger people had ever seen. It was like we were a traveling zoo on wheels, and the people were watching us. I felt like a main course on a head hunter's buffet the way some of the people were looking at us.

We were coming up the side of this one mountain with Rusty driving, and I was sitting in the front seat beside him. The mountainside at this area was nothing but little thatch roof huts scattered all around the jungle. I looked over at Rusty, and he was crying. I asked him what he was crying about, and he said to me, "Most everyone of these people have never heard the Gospel and will never hear the Gospel!"

He was right. Most of the people in that mountain range had never even heard of God, much less heard about Jesus. I have never been in a location where so many of the people did not know about God, Jesus, or the Bible. I have been in small villages in the Amazon river where the village had never heard but never a mountain range that took three hours to drive through that did not know about God! Rusty was exactly right. Most of these people had never heard about the Gospel. I looked at Rusty and said, "Then stop and let's tell them."

We drove just a small distance ahead of that spot and noticed a lady with two young boys eleven to twelve-ish in age. Rusty pulled the van over, and he and Amittay got out and started talking with them. The lady was the teacher, and the two boys were her students, and they were just getting out of school.

The teacher and one of the boys walked on, but one of the boys stopped and was talking with Amittay. Rusty asked the boy, whose name is Yorki, if he knew of any churches around the area. Yorki said he had never heard of anything like a church. Rusty told him that a church is where people meet to worship God.

I got out of the car and was listening by this time. Yorki asked Amittay who God was and said he had never heard of him. Rusty told Yorki that God was the creator of all the heavens and the earth and everything and everyone in them. I will never forget Yorki's reply. Yorki said, "If this God fellow is that strong, he must work for Castro!" He had no concept of God other than what he had imagined, if he ever had.

I had a baseball in my pocket and gave it to Yorki, and he knew what it was. No TVs, no radio, but he knew what a baseball was and how to throw it. He started walking toward his hut and we followed, and his mother came out of a path in the jungle and asked what was going on. She was a little shocked seeing her son talking to three white men from a minivan parked on the roadside.

Yorki told his mother we had stopped to talk to him, and she invited us to their house/hut. We all walked down the trail in the thick jungle just a few yards to an opening to one of the most breathtaking views I have ever seen. Their hut was a thatched roof and mud floor hut on the side of the mountain with a view down a thousand-foot drop into the valley with both walls of the mountain covered in thick jungle. You could literally walk thirty feet past their hut and drop to the bottom. It was amazing!

The mom had asked us into their home about the time Yorki's dad walked up. We introduced ourselves and told them we wanted to tell them a story about the God who loved them. Yorki and his mom had never heard about God, but the dad had been in the military and had pledged himself to the government and therefore was an atheist. But he mentioned he had never really given God much thought.

The mom asked us if we would have coffee with them, and we accepted. Yorki went outside to the fire pit and scooped up a handful of coffee beans they had grown and roasted. He brought them into the main room of the hut where a stump with a round hole in the middle about eight inches deep and eight inches wide, rounded out, sat. Yorki poured the roasted beans into the hole and started grinding them by hand.

The hut was one room, maybe twelve by twelve feet, with a curtain covered doorway for the parent's bedroom measuring six by six. On the same side as the parent's room, but other end of the wall, was another curtain doorway to Yorki's room, measuring six by six as well. The main room and bedrooms were under the same thatched roof. Against the opposite wall from the rooms was an open door-way leading out to the cooking area that was open-walled with a lean-to type roof with a handmade clay oven and fire pit. The mom was busy making a fire while Yorki was grinding the beans but still within listening distance to Rusty's discussion about God with the husband.

Rusty was telling the dad that God was creator of the universe and everything in it. The dad said he was not interested in God because it was not good for them to think about such things. Rusty and Amittay shared with them the importance of knowing God, but it was not registering in their minds. Rusty asked the dad about the house, and the man told him that he had made it by hand. When he married Yorki's mom, he built this home just for his family.

Rusty said that he thought the hut had blown together during a storm by accident. The man said that Rusty must be stupid to think that the hut could just fall into place during a storm. He told Rusty he spent weeks cutting the wood and tying it together and making it the right size and shape. Rusty said that he knew that the man had worked hard making the house for his wife and Yorki. Rusty said that he must really love his wife and Yorki, and he said that was why he made them the house. By this time, the coffee was ready, and we sat down on their three chairs and the floor.

Rusty looked at all three of them and said, "How is it that you said I was stupid for thinking that your house just fell together, but you think the heavens and the earth and everything just fell together?"

They looked a little stunned and said they had never thought about it. Rusty then said that just as the dad built their house out of love, God did the same thing building all creation, because he loved them. Rusty told them God had sent us to them so they could know God and his Son. Rusty and Amittay took the next hour or so and shared the story of Genesis to Jesus and then told them about Jesus. We each shared how we accepted Jesus, so they understood how to do the same.

The time came in the conversation for Rusty to ask the three of them to ask Jesus into their hearts. When he did, you could feel the spiritual battle in the room as real as any fight I have ever witnessed. While Rusty was asking them to accept Jesus, the dad was not ready and the mom wanted to wait and Yorki was not sure.

God moved Charles and I at the exact same time to start praying. I turned around on the mud floor and started praying, and Charles stepped outside and started praying. A little chicken kept running under me and pecking me while I was praying (little demon chicken). Charles and I both started begging God to send his Holy Spirit and give these people salvation.

I have a hard time putting what happened next into words. While Rusty and Amittay were reasoning with them for their souls, God had Charles and I both on our knees, begging for his Spirit to fall on them. As sure as if someone walked into the hut, a wind blew in past Charles and myself and blew on all five as they were talking. Charles felt it, I felt it, and not just the wind—God's presence stepped into that mud hut on the side of that mountain in the middle of a mountain range that we were not supposed to even visit.

The dad and the mom started crying, and all three hung their heads. The father took Rusty's hand and accepted Jesus as his Lord and Savior. The mother followed in tears, and finally, Yorki bowed his head and asked Jesus in his life!

To this day, my heart shudders, thinking of how God stepped into that hut and touched the hearts of three Cubans, two of which did not even believe he existed two hours before. The business guy with us remembered that he was in a hurry when he packed for the trip and had put a very nice Spanish Bible in his bags by mistake. He did not know Spanish, he just had the Bible. He ran to the van and brought them a copy of God's Word.

We stood on the mountainside, holding hands, and prayed and committed this Cuban family to Jesus. We hugged and left them with a promise, if possible, to be back some time to check on them.

We walked up the trail, piled into our minivan, and started driving toward Niquero. Not a word was spoken because of what we had just witnessed. God had just put his Spirit in a family in a completely dark area of the world. He had also set it up for them to get a copy of his Word, Old and New Testament.

As we were driving, I was now in the backseat by Charles. I looked over at him, and he was crying just as hard as Rusty had been. I asked, "Why are you crying now?"

I will not forget, and neither will Charles, as he said, "Who is going to disciple them? I would be willing to give everything I own to get a church started here to disciple these people!" The next few chapters will prove just how true God took Charles at his words!

Rusty told Charles that it would be impossible to get a Cuban pastor up into the Sierra Maestra to live. It would be only God, because no Cuban would do it. We spent the next week traveling and preaching and drove back into Havana with just enough time to get to the airport. We stopped by Pastor Pablo's to pray with him and say goodbye. When we walked in, he was meeting with a young preacher and his wife.

After the meeting, Pablo came out to pray and said he was sorry for us having to wait. The couple was a man and his wife who had just finished training. Pablo said, "The funny thing is they said God told them to go to the Sierra Maestra Mountains to work as pastors."

Rusty, Amittay, Charles, and I just looked toward heaven and thanked God for his working in Cuba. I am so thankful to be able to share this with you. That day on the mountain, God did something I always knew he could, I always knew he did, and I always knew he wanted to do. He works where he guides. God answers prayer!

Twelve Hours in Cuba

Soon we were headed back to Cuba to dedicate the new garage for God's glory. We had also collected as much money as we could to give relief to the other churches. It was going to be a twelve-day run through Cuba with a two-day stay in Bayamo for the dedication of the now completed church/garage. Again, Charles and I were going through customs and immigration with little hassle. Charles' wife and my wife, along with other ladies, wanted to do something special for the pastors' wives in Cuba. They bought and packed a large suitcase with all different kinds of ladies' lingerie and make-up, products that they would not be able to get in Cuba.

So as was the Cuban norm at customs, they laid out my suitcases and went through each one. It just so happened that the agent doing my bags was a Cuban woman. I had a bag full of medicines and bandages and antibiotics for Amittay. When she opened the bag with the first aid supplies, she was caught back at first, thinking drugs, but was understanding when she realized it was all antibiotics, fever relievers, and basic needed first aid supplies. A simple cut or wound could turn bad if infection set in and they could not get antibiotics or even pain relievers.

Cuba has some of the best doctors in the world, but their socialized medicine fails to supply medicine. I have watched Amittay give seriously ill babies Tylenol because he had nothing else. The agent was seemingly thankful for the people who would be receiving the aid and let it pass through her inspection. When she opened the next bag (which my wife had packed), it was full of what looked like the new line of Victoria Secret unmentionables. It was packed full of every type of panties and such, and the lady was taken back.

She stared at me and at the bag and started going through it. She called a few of the other women agents, and they started picking out various items and looking at them and laughing. The place was crowded, and people were staring and laughing, and there I stood, surrounded by three customs lady agents who were holding up lingerie and giggling. They took their sweet time and played the crowd as I stood there beet red with embarrassment.

Finally, after every person in the airport had a good laugh, they handed me back the open bags and shuffled pile of unmentionables and let me pass. I do not know how to fold most of that stuff. It was a funny time for everybody but me.

We met Amittay and Rusty who had arrived before us outside and headed back toward Amittay's house. Amittay and his wife, Anita, lived in a modest home above the clinic that Dr. Amittay practiced medicine in. He had two kids, Kelly and Ariel. Kelly was fifteen and pretty, and Ariel was seventeen and autistic.

Anita made and sold cakes for special events on the black market. She made more money than her doctor husband. Amittay was an internal medicine specialist and a geneticist. He was one of the only doctors to be recognized by the government and awarded in his fields and was regarded with high esteem by his peers. He was paid $25 a month and received government rations for food, the same as everyone else. There were often months where he would not be paid because of government shortages in resources.

I remember sitting in their home one day as a government official came to visit. He told Amittay that they were going to arrest him and Anita if she made and sold any more cakes. Jail in Cuba was long and cruel. They let them know that they were being watched (who in Cuba was not constantly being watched?) and would suffer if she kept up her capitalist activity. I was a little worried by the threat, but Amittay said it was constant in Cuba.

It was not thirty minutes after the visit that another government official came to the door and ordered a very expensive birthday cake for Castro's nephew's birthday celebration. He told me that he came to Anita because everybody knew she made the best cakes in Cuba. Amittay said that the two officials probably knew each other.

It was a hard thing to figure out this mental game that is constant in Cuba. The Cuban government tries to keep the people in fear and starvation and under their control.

That evening, we had bought Amittay a box of cigars for himself because he could not afford them on his own. He invited us to have one with him, and we sat around his living room enjoying a Cuban cigar and talking. Amittay asked Charles what he thought was the difference was between Cuba and America.

Charles, a strong patriot and passionate about our American free-doms, responded by just being honest about freedoms that most of us in the US take for granted. As Charles continued talking about our freedoms here in the USA, we noticed Amittay and Anita get quiet and obviously worried. Someone had come up his steps outside his house and was in the shadows, listening. When Amittay walked outside to confront them, they ran when they heard him coming.

Amittay came back and sat down and asked if we could feel the oppression. The truth was that yes, we could feel the oppression of communism. Charles said to me later that his passion for freedom had threatened Amittay and Anita's safety because of freely speak-ing. It was a sobering experience that neither he or I will ever forget.

We rented a van that was what we would call, well, used. It had a diesel engine and the exhaust had been knocked off. A hole was in the floor in the middle just large enough and in the right spot, filling the back of the van with exhaust. The windows were the only working air-conditioning, and off we went headed 900-plus miles to Niquero. I had bought Rusty, Amittay, and Charles a Montecristo Ambassador cigar as was our custom when starting our road trips. They were plugged, and we all threw ours out because they were too hard to smoke.

Charles was sitting toward the back of the van and decided he was going to finish his cigar no matter what. We were driving the main highway through Cuba in a loud exhaust-filled van. Amittay looked back in the mirror and saw Charles' face. He said that Charles was looking a little pale. Charles was sitting in a place where the exhaust was stronger, and his cigar was very hard to draw, so he was having to suck harder on it than normal. He could not hear much, so he was just sitting there, riding along, puffing harder than normal on his cigar. The funny thing about cigars is that you really don't feel the sickness that sometimes a new smoker gets until you are already over the edge.

As we drove, Amittay would look back at Charles and say, "He is getting worse." Charles was sitting still and did not notice the pale, then gray, then green tint that his face was turning. We stopped on the side of the road to use the bushes (sugarcane fields on both sides and empty). Charles said he was a little dizzy, but we piled back in and continued. Just a little while after getting back on the road, Charles said to Rusty, "Hey, man, I need a restroom pretty badly."

We were just coming into a little hole in the wall truck stop in a place called Taguasco. We pulled into the parking lot, and Charles got out and went around back to the one toilet on the property. In Cuba, public toilets often have people who attend them. You give them a small tip, and they give your paper and attend the toilet after you are through with it. This bathroom had no door and was no bigger than a broom closet. No sink and no toilet seat and no running water.

There was an old lady sitting just outside where a door for privacy should be (but was not). She handed Charles paper as he entered, obviously in a hurry and in great distress. Charles did not throw up, but he did empty everything inside his body out in a very short time. When he had finished his reason for needing the restroom, he gathered himself and stepped out of the open door to the lady who had shared his experience with him.

He handed her a US $5 bill. It would be normal to tip a Cuban quarter in this situation. Five dollars there could be a month's pay for that lady. Five bucks there would feed her family for over a month. Charles handed her the bill and said, "Don't worry, ma'am, you are going to earn every penny of it!" It was after that experience, whenever we passed that little truck stop in Taguasco, one of us would mention that Charles still has body parts left in there.

We take so much for granted in America that other people do not have. For one thing, privacy and dignity. What I mean is that common private vented bathrooms are expected even in our poorest settings. That is not so in other areas of the world, like in many Cuban homes. In Niquero, Rafael and Tami had a thatch roof three-sided outhouse in their backyard. It was short to the ground, so you had to squat down and back into it to use it. There was no such thing as privacy with the front of it open. The neighbors would be waving at you while you were doing your business.

One time, when Rusty had to use it, he backed into it, and when he came out, he had a tarantula on his shoulder. After that experience, he helped them turn a small room, just off their kitchen, into a full bath with a shower, sink, and toilet. It was very small but functioning and kept very clean.

Tami and Rafael figured out a way to even have hot water. They took a heater coil from a car and put it in a tin coffee can with small holes in the bottom. They hooked it under the shower spout and connected a 110-watt plug to it. When you turned on the shower, the water would fill the can up over the coil. You then plugged it into the wall socket and it would heat up the water in the can. The holes were small enough so as the water dripped out of the holes breaking the connection, you would not get shocked by the electric current coming straight from the coil in the can. If you didn't touch the can, you would not get shocked.

This bathroom was just three or four feet from the center of the kitchen and had a beach towel as a door. You could see the feet and legs of whoever was sitting on the toilet while you were sitting at the table. You could reach in through the towel from the table if the person inside needed something.

We got to Niquero after twelve hours of driving and my stomach was in bad shape. I am very private with my restroom habits and require privacy to do them. We gathered in the kitchen to get caught up, and I had to go to the bathroom badly. I was not able to do anything about the fact that seven people were four to five feet on the other side of the towel talking while I was sitting on the toilet about to change the constitution of the entire house with my upset stomach. I had just sat down and, with much fear and embarrassment, was about to do what I was in there to do when an arm came past the towel with a cup of coffee. It was Tami, and she said, "Here, Brother Frank, have a cup of coffee."

I told her to set it on the table. I would be right out, because her reaching in had just stopped me from being able to do what it was I was in there to do. The family was so thankful for their bathroom and it was just common in Cuba in many homes that the dignities and privacies we enjoy are not part of their world and they still go on.

Another funny story happened when a friend of Rusty's was in Rafael's home and needed to take a shower. He was a very modest man and was speaking in the service that night and needed to shower. Tami and three ladies from the church were making dinner in the kitchen, and this guy got into the shower on the other side of the towel. He was taller than Rafael and Tami and Elon and Isaac. So as he got into the shower and plugged in the heater and lathered up, he made the mistake of standing up straight under the can. His foot was on the metal drain cover and his head touched the coffee can and grounded him to 110 watts. He took a pretty good shocking and fell onto the ground in a fetal position.

The ladies heard him fall and looked in, and there he was, butt naked and lathered up, laying on the floor, dazed. Without a second thought, the four ladies grabbed his arms and dragged him into the kitchen floor and all began washing off the soap and toweling him dry, just like a baby. They dried him off and started dressing him while he gathered his faculties. Again, to them, it was just another thing, but to the friend of Rusty, it was shocking! To me, it is just plain funny!

Niquero is a place that has so many different memories and special eye-opening things that God did. It is truly a special place to me. We were having a service in the barn/church there, and the place was filled with people. As normal, people were gathered outside around the windows, looking in, and every corner, nook, and cranny was filled to standing room only.

Charles and I were outside, standing by one of the windows looking in with Tami, the pastor's wife. She was telling us stories of the families crowded together inside the service. In the aisle straight in front of our window, in the center of the row, was a younger mother with three boys. Two were toddlers and one was a newborn, just a few months old.

The boys looked healthy, but the mom was very skinny, and her joints looked swollen. You could tell that she had been and probably could be very pretty, but in her present state, she looked starved and close to collapse from malnutrition and stress. In Niquero, many of the people looked malnourished and in poor health because so many of them were.

Charles asked Tami about the lady, and she told us that the woman and her husband were not at all interested in church or faith at first. Tami had been witnessing to her for some time with no effect. Her story goes as follows.

Her husband lost his job and what little income they had was gone. She was pregnant and had two children, and they could not afford to pay their bills or buy food any longer. The husband abandoned the family and left town, leaving her very pregnant and without any support. They were forced to leave their house and were homeless.

As what happens in Niquero, a family who knew their circumstances gave them a place where they could stay. It was a storage shed that was built on the back of their house but never finished. It had three walls with a front door opening with no door frame or door. It also did not have a roof. Basically, it was a six by eight open room off the back of their house with no protection from the elements. When it rained, they all huddled together in the corner and got wet. When it was cold or hot, well, you can imagine.

The lady was thankful for a place to be able to stay. During this time, the lady and Tami became close, and this lady ended up accepting Christ as her savior. She had her baby, a boy, and was doing her best to take care of them and scratch out a living. Tami said that since that lady had accepted Christ, she was a changed person. She read her Bible and prayed every day and went out of her way to help the elderly and with anything the church was doing. What little food she could earn, she shared with others in need. Tami said that the lady was tireless in her work and with her family and with helping others. Her faith was strong, and she was always praying and serving.

After the service, Charles asked Rafael if he could give $100 to him for the lady for food. A hundred dollars in Niquero would feed that family better than they had eaten for over a year. Rice and beans twice a day. Rafael told us that the lady was trustworthy and could handle the money well, and she would use it wisely, feeding her family.

So Charles and Rafael went to the lady, and Rafael introduced Charles to her. Charles told the lady that God spoke to him to give her $100 for food and that she was to use it for her and her boys to be able to eat (it would allow her to get her health back).

The lady looked at Charles and said she was so thankful for his willingness to help. She then told Charles that she could not possibly take it.

Charles asked her why, and she said, "Because God has given me so much already, I cannot possibly ask him for more!"

I was standing there watching, and Charles and I both saw in her face that she was entirely sincere. She and her three small boys slept in an enclosed but open shed with no roof. She had no steady income other than what she managed to earn while also taking care of two toddlers and a baby. Her husband abandoned her, and she sincerely was so thankful to God for all he had given her, she could not possibly ask for more.

I realize that living in an affluent culture like ours, our thinking cannot register this type of poverty. For someone who lives the hardship that this dear lady was walking in daily, it was humbling to say the least. Rafael was able to explain to her that the money was not charity or pity; it was God providing their food needs for a long time to come. She accepted the money, and we were so thankful to be able to watch God do what he does for his children.

The entire trip was God doing something every time we turned around, people being saved and God moving in the churches and throughout the countryside of Cuba. We were able to meet with groups of pastors and visit churches and small groups of people who were faithful in their service to Christ. In that dark land of oppression and godlessness, the Lord had his faithful still serving him. We also met with crowds of people who wanted to hear the message that had been taken from them many years ago when Castro took over.

When we got back to Havana, Amittay drove us to the airport. A police officer on a motorcycle pulled us over. Cubans can own a car if it was made before the takeover in 1960. Amittay's Ford was a '53 so he could own it and drive it. It was, however, illegal for a Cuban to be driving with Americans in their car. Cuban's used their cars as taxis all the time and so on, but it was still illegal.

We had just spent fifteen days driving all over Cuba through checkpoints and roadblocks without any incident. We were within sight of the airport, and we got pulled over. Let me remind you that in Cuba, there is no real justice system. You can go to court and even hire a lawyer, but the government is the final say. Many Cubans are put in jail for years, and some never return and they are with no recourse or rights.

Amittay got out of the car and went back to speak with the officer. He was back there for too long for comfort. He came back to the window and got all our papers to show the officer. Again, he was back talking and taking too long. Rusty mentioned that this could be a bad thing for Amittay. He could end up in jail for forty years or worse over this situation.

Amittay brought back our papers and was obviously worried. He told us that the situation was bad. He walked back to the police officer, and when I looked back at them, it looked like the officer was about to arrest Amittay.

Rusty and I both knew we could end up in jail or dead by coming to Cuba and preaching openly. Charles knew enough to put two and two together and understood risk was involved in traveling to Cuba. The thing I was not willing to risk was for Amittay to rot in jail, leaving Anita and his family homeless and destitute and us being left to go free.

In my thinking, all four of us were in this thing together, and if one of us went down, we all went down together or we all walked away together. But either way, we all went through whatever happened together. I was in the front seat, and Charles and Rusty were in the backseat. I was looking through the rearview mirror and could tell bad things were beginning to happen. I said out loud, not just no, but hell no! I was not sure what I was going to do, but I was going to do something.

I opened the door and got out, walking straight up to the officer's face. I found out later that Rusty and Charles both freaked out and Rusty started laughing and Charles just said, "Oh no, here it goes!"

I knew he had just seen our American passports, but I had to do something. So I got into his face, close and personal, and started shouting at him Russian syllables, staring in his eyes like I was going to bite his face off. I knew he had his hand on his gun and that he could shoot me and us all, for that matter. I looked at Amittay and grabbed and hugged him and pushed him away and started poking the officer in the chest with my finger still shouting Russian syllables at the top of my lungs. I was inwardly hoping he did not speak Russian. I was trying my best to look very upset and important.

The officer asked Amittay something in Spanish (which I also do not speak), and Amittay answered, and the officer looked at me again and I poked him in the chest again and started screaming Russian again. The officer stepped back away from my poking finger and shook his head and waved us on. We both got into Amittay's car and drove away with the officer standing there staring at us as we left. I am not sure what the officer got from what just happened, but I am thankful that the event ended with no one dead or in jail and all of us together.

When we got to the airport and checked our bags, we found out our plane was going to be delayed. We did not realize the delay was going to be twelve hours. I know now God was in the delay, but then it was just a frustration to a very long and exhausting road trip.

We decided to go to the restaurant and order lunch. The concept of a restaurant was a new experience to the Cuban airport, and we were obviously Americans and stood out. We sat down to order our food, and our choices were either a Cuban sandwich or baked chicken with rice and beans and plantains for sides.

We ordered our food, and the waiter was writing down our order. Charles ordered the chicken, and Rusty and I ordered the sandwich. The waiter told Charles that he wanted the sandwich and not the chicken. Charles said to him, "No, I want the chicken." The waiter left and came back and said that the cook said it would take too long to thaw out the chicken and that he should order the sand-wich. Charles had a long and frustrating day, and he wanted the chicken! It was getting kind of funny, because behind us was a table with three Cuban athletes eating chicken.

Charles looked at the waiter and said, "Look, I have the time, I want the chicken," and pointed at the three men behind us with chicken. "I want the chicken just like they have," Charles says.

The waiter pointed to his name tag and said to Charles, "I am the waiter, I decide what you want to eat!" and walked away.

We enjoyed our Cuban sandwiches and joked about how different the mindset between free enterprise and communism is and how far from each other they are in understanding. We ended up being there twelve hours, so that evening, we all had chicken.

What ended up being a twelve-hour delay was really a twelve-hour time for God to speak to Charles and to me. I have already shared my experience with the sugarcane field where I asked God to do a work in and through me. I was also told to start another church but still not wanting to hear that. Charles is the one who should relate his part of this story, but I can share what was going on in his head.

Charles had already decided God wanted him to help me finance the new church I was supposed to start. We had even started survey-ing together places where the needs were the greatest. Also, on this trip, God had again taken both of us to school about the power the Gospel has on and in people's lives. God was dealing heavily with all three of us, and we were stuck in an airport in Cuba.

God was dealing with Charles that he was supposed to help start the church. God was dealing with me that I was supposed to start the church. Neither Charles nor I knew that God was dealing so strongly with each of us. He was doing it separately from each other.

Rusty was just pumped up from seeing so many people saved and a new work built and God doing so many things after eight years of his praying. Rusty has the spiritual gift of seeing what God is doing in someone and bringing it out into the open and helping them process it. During the twelve hours we were there, Rusty spent time with Charles and with me, and we all spoke together about it and knew that God was calling Charles and I to start a church. The Well Church, as we are now named, can easily go back to "Twelve Hours in

Cuba" and how God spoke to Charles and I separately but about the same thing. I am now thankful God did! I am also thankful for my two brothers, Rusty and Charles, for their heart to do what God says!

Rehoboth
"The Well"

R usty had asked Charles to think about something. "What if God has not shown Frank where to start a church because he is waiting on someone else to start it and then call Frank to pastor it?" God clearly was calling Charles into a leadership role in the church he was starting. It was not long after we got back from Cuba that Charles knew he was supposed to help me start a church and one where we already lived.

Soon, Charles and five other families who felt strongly they wanted to help us start a church decided to meet. They were all members of the church where I was serving as assistant pastor. They met and felt that it was God's will for them to do it. They then met with the pastor of the church to inform him that they believed God was calling them to start another church and call me as their pastor. That meeting did not go well as the pastor did not believe God was calling them, and he believed it was more of a church split than a new church.

Charles and the men then called and asked me to meet with them. In our type churches, people leave for the least little thing, and when a group gets together and leaves, it almost always is called a split. I am sure our group seemed the same and may have been for some.

I agreed to meet with them, and we all met at Charles' house to talk about the possibility of forming a church. At the meeting, I shared what God had been doing in my heart and that I had felt him speak to me about starting a new work. I also listened to each of the families tell of their reasons for wanting to help us do it. Charles finished by explaining his part God had called him to, and we prayed together. I told the group I would take a week to pray and fast about the situation and then get back with them with an answer.

My thoughts were mixed about this new start. I was aware that my pastor friend was not at all behind this church starting. One, because it was not his idea, and two, because I had been working in his church, and he was afraid I would be trying to steal his people. I get where he was coming from, and to be honest, that was the main reason I was reluctant to do it. Not stealing his people, but the fact the families were all from his church and he was not in support of the start.

I also was not sure what these people thought the church we were going to start would be like. Charles and I made it very clear that we were not starting another traditional Baptist church in an area where too many already existed. Charles and I expressed to them that the church we started was going to follow the scripture as authority and that we were going to do what God says, no matter what. We were not going to be run by committees or men.

We promised God we would spend our money on people outside the walls of our church and not on ourselves. We also made a promise that has tested our resolve many times. We promised that, as a church, we would never say no to anything God brought to us to do. He would just have to show us a way to do it. We have kept that promise so far!

The facts were The Well looked more like a church split than a church start. The area we were in was saturated with Baptist churches. I still was not wanting to obey God in starting a new church. I knew God was pressing me to do it. I also hate church politics and fighting. I did not like the appearance of our start, but I knew God was doing something in me.

I finally just decided to not try to figure the circumstances out and just seek God's will in the matter. I spent the week in prayer and in fasting and waited on God to give me clear direction. After a time, I met with Charles, and he told me that the group was going to start a church with or without me, and I was good with that. I knew God had called Charles and us together, and besides, God had already given me direction to accept the call.

I officially accepted the church's call at the expense of my pastor friend's friendship. So a few weeks later, we started The Rehoboth Baptist Church! It is now The Well, and after sixteen plus years, it has been a wild but fun ride. Charles and I pastor this church together with three other men, and I am grateful for his call in this church's life!

I have since gone to the pastor of the other church to make things right between us, and both times, he would not talk. I offered my hand to him both times, and he would not take it. It's funny because I still consider him a dear friend, and when I look at it from his perspective, I can't really blame him. I know one day we will work it out on this side of eternity or the other. Time has proven that some of the families who helped start the church were just moving on, and some were called. I am thankful to be part of The Well.

Elon's Seminary

We made it clear to our church family that we were not like a traditional Baptist church, and it was not long after we started meeting in Charles' living room that God tested our resolve. Life is funny sometimes, and this is not a story of one of the funny times. Sometimes life is completely overwhelming.

We often say that God will not put on you more than you can handle. That is simply not true. There are times in life when God allows things to happen that are totally more than a person is capable of handling. In those times, he promises to walk with us through them and help us endure them if (and only if) we draw close to him and allow him to do so.

I received a call from Rusty in Charlotte, North Carolina. He told me that Elon, Rafael and Tami's eleven-year-old son, had been killed in a terrible accident. The kids were playing ball after church in the churchyard, and one of the kids kicked the ball into the street. It was a ball I had given to him and Isaac.

Elon ran out into the street to save the ball from being hit by a truck. There was a communist leader's son driving down the street, drunk, at a very high speed with his lights out. Elon ran right in front of him, and the man hit him and dragged him under the truck for sixty feet or so. Elon was dead instantly and his body was badly mangled. It was a horrible death with terrible circumstances with the condition of his remains.

Rusty said he was leaving for Cuba the next day, and I told him I would grab a flight and meet him in Havana. I packed my bags and flew out the next morning. We met in Havana and grabbed a rental and started the 900-mile drive to the other end of the island. When we got to Rafael's house, Rafael and Tami came out to meet us with hugs and tears.

Isaac (Elon's little brother) was very close to his brother and was very bitter about his brother's death. Rusty and I sat around the table and listened while Rafael and Tami told us the story of what had happened. Elon was trying to save his ball and could not judge the distance because of the darkness along with the truck running with no lights and its high rate of speed. Tami saw him get hit and ran over to him. He was stuck under the truck and was dragged for a long distance.

The driver was too drunk to walk, and Elon was broken up and twisted with a large part of his head missing. Tami held him in her lap and cried and federal police came and whisked the communist's son away before the other police arrived to make a report. The official report did not mention the son or the father's truck. It was swept under the rug because of the father's connections. Elon was dead, and no one was to blame.

The next day, a service was being held at the church. Because of the no embalming, they buried Elon before we got there. We spent the early hours with the family, and around service time, we made our way to the horse barn/church for services. When we got to the location, I was surprised to see much of the village was there. The building, yard, front and back, and the street and side yards were full. It was the largest crowd in Niquero that we had ever seen. It seemed that the entire village was there or everyone who could be was there.

The people of Niquero loved Tami and Rafael because of the clinic and all the help they gave to anyone in need. They were some of the poorest in Niquero and yet gave the most. Isaac and Elon were loved by all as well. I was shocked by the crowd, and after the customary time of standing around visiting, we went inside to start the service. Rusty had informed me the night before that I was going to be the speaker and he the translator.

They sang a few songs, and then it came time for the message. Rafael and Tami were not in their normal places as pastor and first lady. They were on the first row, right in front of me, sitting together, and Tami was crying. I started to approach the pulpit to open my Bible and start preaching when Rusty leaned out of the mic and asked if I understood that this service was Elon's funeral. I had no idea! I thought that since Elon was already buried; they had already had the funeral. No, they had to bury Elon because of the no embalming and climate there. They had waited for us to get there to have the funeral, and this was the service.

That explained the large crowd and the lack of police with that big of a crowd. The Cuban government hates big crowds. Given the circumstances of Elon's death and the communist son's involvement and the government cover up, there were considerably less officials in attendance.

I did not know nor was I mentally prepared to be preaching Elon's funeral. I was very close to Isaac and to Elon. They playfully nicknamed me "Tio Sapo" (Uncle Toad), and my heart was broken at his death and the family, church, and Isaac's loss. Rusty loved this family like his own, and Rafael and Tami were now crying like little babies in front of me. They ended up slipping out of their chairs, sitting on the barn floor, holding each other crying as I spoke.

The crowds were pushed in as close as possible, trying to hear. I could hear nothing but crying from Rafael and Tami in the stillness. I was not prepared for this nor had I prepared a funeral message. I was also overcome with grief from watching Rafael and Tami's pain. The entire crowd was grieving. I stepped back and told Rusty I did not know it was Elon's funeral, and Rusty said, "Well, it is, and you are up."

I took a short moment to gather my thoughts and could not get any. I must say, in forty years of preaching, I had never until then, nor since then, been on the pulpit that close to speaking and be speechless. This was one of the most difficult things that man's fall in the garden brings with it—the death of a child! I stepped up to the microphone and said to the family how hurt I was and how sorry I was for their loss. I spoke to the family and told them that every single person in attendance was there to tell them how much they cared, and they were heartbroken too.

Then I just told the people and the family the truth. I told them I did not know why God had allowed this to happen. I did not know why a young man like Elon would die so soon and in such a horrible way. I do not know why good people had to endure such pain. Then I said this, "I will tell you what I do know!" I just started telling them what I personally knew about God from the years of our relationship. I told them that I know God is not mean or cruel. I know that God loves Tami and Rafael and Isaac and Elon! I told them that he understood every bit of our sorrow and the scope of our suffering.

I told them that God could be trusted even when we did not feel like trusting him. I also told them that Tami was not the only one watching the night Elon tried to save his ball. Tami was watching when Elon was struck by that truck, and so was God. I said that Elon was met by Jesus the second that truck hit him and welcomed him home with him forever. Jesus was kneeling with Tami as she held Elon's mangled body. Jesus was standing beside Isaac who was mad and bitter over losing his best friend and brother. I told the people that just like God was watching the death of Elon, he was watching now the pain of Elon's death on each heart with us that day.

As I was speaking, men started standing up and raising their hands in the air and they were leaving them held up as I continued speaking. Seven or eight men stood there with raised hands as I kept on speaking. I finally said to the crowd that just like Tami and Rafael and Isaac watched their son/brother die, God had one day watched his own son die a terrible, drawn out, and painful death. The difference was Jesus's death was intentional, not by accident.

God the father and Jesus had planned his death out very carefully. It was decided that every sin mankind committed would be placed on Jesus, God's Son. Jesus would then stand before God who sat on his throne of judgement. God would put Jesus on a cross and punish every person's sin debt in full by punishing Jesus in each of our places.

Then I said to Rafael and Tami and Isaac, "You now understand the price God paid so we could be saved. You have just experienced as close as humanly possible what God suffered to forgive our sin and offer each individual salvation."

I asked the people who wanted to ask Jesus for salvation to do so and led the people in a prayer. Many people came to Christ during that funeral service that day, and my stomach hurts now as I relive it with you.

That evening, we sat at the table with Rafael and Tami and listened to them talk. They shared their memories, and we cried and loved on each other. After some time, I asked Rafael why those men stood up and held their hands up in the air during the last part of my message. I had never seen anyone do that in Cuba.

Rafael shared with us that just a few months before Elon was killed, he had come forward in a church service and surrendered to preach the Gospel. Word had spread around the village that little Elon felt God had called him to be a preacher. Rafael said that the men who stood up and held their hands up were telling God that they would preach in Elon's place. It was like a bolt of lightning hit my heart when Rafael said that.

The fact was that Cuba was full of cities, villages, small farming areas where there had never been a church that anyone alive could remember. In all our travels throughout the island, one thing that was urgent and that the island was screaming out for was for preachers to teach the people the Bible. When Rafael said that about the men, I instantly thought about the Sierra Maestra Mountains and the whole of Cuba.

I also felt God speaking to us at the table. Here is the test I was telling you about that was coming for our new baby church. I said to all of us at the table that God was speaking to us to build a seminary for training preachers. I said we should name it Elon's Seminary. The seminary would be for God's glory and to spread the gospel of Jesus in honor of Elon's death. We would take what God began in Elon's service and ask God to give us 100 preachers to train in ten years. They could preach in Elon's place.

This was not a feel-good ploy to try and give meaning to Elon's harsh and tragic death. It was what everyone of us witnessed God start in Elon's service. Rafael was trained by a seminary and could teach seminary classes. That evening, in all the pain and tears and heartache that one can imagine, God birthed a vision.

We joined hands and committed to God that Rafael and Tami would start Elon's Seminary for God's glory. We asked God to give us 100 preachers to go all over Cuba in ten years from that night. I committed for our church to raise the $20,000 needed to buy the land and build the first multipurpose building for the seminary. Rusty too saw the vision and committed his church as well to raise the money and together see it done!

We all joined hands and gave it to God in prayer, in faith, believing. We asked God to take the great pain and loss and build his church in Cuba and for 100 men in ten years to go through the seminary.

As we were traveling back to Havana, Rusty, Amittay, and I tried for hours to find our little family in the Sierra Maestra Mountains. It was heartbreaking. We looked all over and had to leave without finding and encouraging them.

When I got home from Cuba, I shared with our baby church what God had called our church with Rusty's church to do. We were to raise $20,000 and build Elon's Seminary. I shared with them every detail of how it had happened and how each of us at the table understood the same vision from God and that our calling was sure.

When I mentioned it to our families in our church, some of them were not seeing it. They said that God would not call us to build a seminary in Cuba before we built a comfortable building for us to meet in first. Then several said that they were not going to do it. Charles and I had made it very clear that our church was going to be different. One of the families asked for a biblical example of God wanting us to build a building in Cuba for someone else before our own needs.

I mentioned the cross! I reminded the people that as a church, we were going to do what God said and that he had clearly spoken that we were to build the seminary. One of the members said that if we built a seminary for Cuba before we built ourselves a place, they were leaving. Others spoke out with them that they would leave as well.

I reminded the church that we were one of many in our area among which any one of them could attend. We have heard the Gospel so much that people around our parts sleep during most Bible messages. Cuba had whole communities where people did not know about God, much less Jesus. The Gospel getting to the areas of

Cuba where no church exists was much more important than our comfort!

I added that anyone who truly felt that God was concerned about our comfort above lost people getting the Gospel would probably fit better in one of the more traditional churches all around us more than ours. I told them we loved them and that they were free to decide and choose. If they stayed, we were obeying God and building the seminary. If they left, those of us who stayed were going to obey God and build a seminary.

That service, nine of our twelve families walked out of the church as members. Our offerings went from $1,500-plus a week to $150 a week, maybe, if we were lucky. Rusty's church did not lose members. His people understood the Great Commission and believed it. However, his church went through a trial that caused him to take a few steps back. I called him after we realized we had lost so many people, and he told me he had lost people and offerings as well.

Charles and I had already talked about God knowing beforehand that these people were going to leave. We decided to just trust God and continue ahead as planned. Rusty said he realized Satan was trying to stop the seminary and the preachers from being trained. So he had decided to do the same thing as our church. God knew these things were going to happen, so it was decided to trust God for the seminary and now for both of our churches to make it.

At the end of our conversation, Rusty said something that I know to be true and believe, and it has stuck with me and helped during tough hours and lean days. Rusty said, "You know, both of our churches can go away and not be missed in this country. But the churches in Cuba have to make it for the Gospel's sake." He continued, "I am going to keep pushing forward for the seminary, and if both churches fail and we don't make it, when I get to heaven, I am going to tell God I swung for the fence!"

Amen! We both, then and many times since, have swung for the fence! Just a note, the seminary has trained over 100 men over ten years! Thank you, Lord!

I Never Dreamed He had a Son

On our next trip to Cuba, we had a member of Rusty's church with us named Frank. His grandfather was a very great man in Cuba and known by all. Frank came with us so he could reconnect with his roots, you might say. He was a Christian but was struggling in his walk, but he was a brother and a good man. We were going back to visit the churches and to give to the seminary the money we had raised.

We visited our connections in Havana and then started out for the churches throughout the island. We eventually wound up in Bayamo and had a few days where we met with a group of pastors for fellowship and training. Rusty, Amittay, and I answered questions and addressed some issues that we noticed were going on in the churches from bad training or, in most cases, no training. It was fun sitting with these men, listening to their stories about the churches God called them to.

One of the pastors was called to an area back in the mountains that required him to ride his bike back and forth fourteen miles (one way) for the services or as he needed to meet with his people. He was in his forties and was very thankful for his bike God had provided. His bike was one we would not own, but he used it daily to serve his church.

One of the pastors needed his glasses fixed and gave them to me so I could have them fixed here in the states and bring them back next trip. I told him that I was not sure I could hook up with him again, but I would try. This guy was pastoring a church and couldn't afford to get his glasses fixed. It was humbling sitting with these pastors and "training" them when they were suffering just for being a pastor in a communist country. They were looking to us for help, which we did our best to give, when we served in prosperity and comfort compared to all of them. To be honest, I was so thankful to God to just be part of that fellowship of pastors. They were/are the heroes of my faith.

We again saw God move in many ways across Cuba. We were, as usual, constantly moving and getting few hours of sleep each night. Many people were being saved in every place we ministered. We decided to try to locate our family in the Sierra Maestra Mountains again. We had not been able to find them on our previous trip and urgently prayed for God to guide us to them.

After a few hours of looking, we found the trail and walked to the house. Yorkie was there with his friend and his grandmother. He recognized us at once, and we went inside to catch up. Yorki's mom and dad were on their weekly trip fourteen miles one way down the mountain to a little town for supplies. They walked that trip every week or two for trading at the market and to get what supplies they needed. There was only one road up and down from the town, so it would not be hard to find them.

It was about to rain, so Rusty took the car down the mountain with Amittay to the town to find them and give them a ride back. Frank and I stayed at the house so there would be room in the car for Yorki's parents with their stuff. Looking back on it, I am sure Rusty was setting Frank up for what he knew would happen next.

As Rusty and Amittay pulled away, Yorki's grandmother asked us to have coffee with her, and we thankfully accepted. Same routine, she started the fire and Yorki got the roasted beans and started grinding them. As we sat there, Yorki told us about what had happened since the time they were saved and we saw them last. The Bible that we left them had become the nightly entertainment for their family and others.

Each night after work was finished, the dad would bring out the Bible and read it to his family. There was no radio or TV and few books. Word got out that they had a Bible, so other families would come and sit outside and listen as the dad read from scripture. They had several families coming on a regular nightly basis, listening to the word of God being read out loud. It was amazing.

As we sat there, sipping coffee, Yorki's grandmother asked if I would share with her the same thing that Rusty had shared with her daughter and son-in-law and Yorki. She wanted to hear the thing that had changed them so much. She said that Yorki's mom was the one who had changed the most. Yorki's mom was not old, maybe thirty (hard to tell), but she had been through a hard life and was known throughout the mountainside as very angry and 'junkyard dog" mean. No one crossed her, but she was well-liked, also feared by many.

Yorki's stepdad had (cautiously) married her after her first husband died, and he took Yorki as his own son. When the family prayed and accepted Christ, the entire area noticed the change, especially in Yorki's mom. She had become sweet, and her bitterness was gone. She was a natural leader, and the people were drawn to her leadership. When she gave up her anger and bitterness to Christ, the Sierra Maestra region noticed. The entire area changed because of the change in Yorki's mom. The grandmother wanted to hear for herself the message that had helped her daughter so much.

Yorki had a friend with him who also wanted to hear. The rain was just starting, and another man selling bananas stepped inside the hut to get out of the rain and wanted to hear as well. The funny thing was that Frank spoke great Cuban but was not living for Christ as he should be. He was not comfortable translating the

Gospel, because he felt uncomfortable doing so with issues in his life. He was not where he should be. Frank was a brother and war vet and a good man, and truthfully, we all have issues.

He wanted to wait for Rusty to come back, but I was able to convince him to do it. I began telling the story of Jesus from the beginning in Genesis. They had been reading the Bible every night for over a year, and the grandmother could grasp the things I was saying to her a little better because of the Word they were hearing. I came to the place where I shared with her the Gospel. God's Son became a human being and was born from a virgin and lived for thirty-three years so he could die in her place, paying the punishment for her sins.

We told her that because Jesus died being punished for her sins that her sins were gone. They had been punished in full before God, and she could now be 100 percent forgiven and free from death and hell. I told her that Jesus walked out of the grave on the third day, proving she could be forgiven and accepted by God into his family. I explained that Jesus died because of her sins, he being dead had never sinned.

The Bible says that it is sin that brings death, and our sin brought Jesus's death, and now Jesus was dead, and our sins are punished and gone, and he had no sin of his own. So Jesus had to come back alive or the Bible was not God's Word and Jesus was not God and God's Son.

The grandmother had tears in her eyes, and Frank was sweating bullets. Grandma asked how she could get Jesus to forgive her sins. Yorki spoke up and said, "My friend wants to be forgiven too." And the man standing out of the rain also wanted forgiveness.

I told them—or I should say Frank told them, translating my words—that all they had to do was ask Jesus to forgive their sins and to come into their hearts. Frank and I shared that Jesus was listening, and each one of them could bow their head in prayer and ask God to please forgive all their sin. The grandmother, Yorki's friend, and the banana man all prayed and gave their hearts to Jesus. In the same hut where almost two years earlier Yorki's family was saved, three more people asked Jesus into their hearts.

Shortly after the prayer, Rusty and Amittay came back with Yorki's mom and dad. The grandmother told them that now she had what had changed Yorki's mom so much and she understood. We had more coffee and spent some time sharing with the family about the Gospel and answering questions they had from the Bible reading. It is hard to say in words what we were experiencing.

Here on the side of a mountain, in a place where no church was ever known to exist, we were sharing Christ with now six people who had prayed and accepted Jesus into their hearts. Without any help, they started reading the Bible at night and had neighbors coming and joining them to hear. Now they brought friends and family to us, asking for them to get saved. We were witnessing God save and start a little church in the Sierra Maestra, and the people did not even realize it was happening.

Yorki's mom was so thankful her mother was now a Christian and that the others were also. What a time of fellowship we had! I told Frank that it was no accident that God used him in the process and that God wanted a closer walk between the two of them. Frank was seeing God's hand on him in a big way. I am so thankful God uses any of us in his work!

As we were leaving, I asked Yorki if he could get word out across the mountain that we wanted to bring a group of cotton people who talked up here to speak to them. He said that he would do it. He and his mom said they could get everybody to come hear cotton people speak.

413

Our teens at church had a very good puppet ministry, and we had a place where we needed to start a church, and cotton people would do the trick. We promised Yorki and everyone in the hut that as soon as possible, we would return with a group of cotton people who wanted to speak with everyone on that side of the mountain range. We agreed to give them a couple of weeks' notice, and we prayed and went to leave.

On our way out, the little old grandmother asked if she could say something, and Rusty told her of course. She wanted to say she was not a communist and this is why. As a teenager living in these same mountains, she used to sit outside at night and look at the stars. She said she knew that the stars could not be there unless someone made them and put each of them in their own place. She said she would cry because she knew someone greater than herself had made them and she did not know how to know whoever it was.

She continued that she spent many nights talking to whomever made the stars. I will never forget what she said. She prayed, "Dear maker of these stars, will you please let me know you?" She then looked at each of us and stood up a little bolder and said, "I am fifty-six years old, and today, he answered my prayer!" Then she started crying and added, "I know God now, and I never dreamed he had a Son!" She knew his Son now also.

We left the mountains, heading for Niquero, realizing God was starting his own church and he was calling all of us to help them get it started.

Cotton People

Four years and many prayers after that day Yorki and his family came to Christ, a door was opening for us to visit the mountainside where they lived and give the Gospel to that area. We told Yorki's family we would come back and bring a group of cotton people who would share the truth of Jesus to every person in their area who wanted to hear it. What a wonderful opportunity to have, bringing Jesus to a place where more people listening had never heard the name of Jesus than folk who had.

Our church had a teen group who worked very hard at performing puppet shows. I had long thought that Cuba was a prime place for puppets. They did not have the technology and media that America has and so would be drawn to the performance of puppets and would listen intently to their message. Our goal was to bring puppets to the cities and villages in a Gospel platform. We prayed about it and asked for God to open a door if it was his will for it to happen, and he did.

Ramon, one of the Cuban pastors in Bayamo, Cuba, wanted his church to do more evangelistic work out in the areas of his church's influence. I knew that if his teens learned how to do puppets, it would open the door for public meetings that would not draw too much attention from the government. It was not legal in Cuba to hold public gatherings. Puppets kind of took the threat away and would be overlooked because Ramon's church was doing so many positive things with the clinic and aid that Rusty's group had been supplying to the town. Puppets are not a threat, and people are drawn to them.

Our church decided to help our teen group raise the money to buy all the supplies for a puppet team and travel to Bayamo, Cuba, to train Ramon's teen group how to use them and have their own puppet ministry. We all agreed and committed it to prayer, and in a little less than a year, we were flying back to Cuba. Our puppet team consisted of my wife, Sharon, and our boys—Donald, Joshua, John, and Levi—and another teen, Maegan.

They had raised the money for their travel and purchased the puppets and equipment needed to supply Ramon's teens with their own puppet ministry. Some of the stuff we planned to buy in Cuba because it was smarter to do so. In all, they ended up with eight puppets with props, curtain, stage, sound system, and lights and generators.

God was so good to supply enough money for the travel to and from Cuba, expenses to travel while on the island, and money to perform. He also provided much needed monies for assistance to the churches and seminary and the men training. It was $18,000 in aid to the works. It was amazing!

After clearing customs in the airport in Havana, I was approached by a plain-clothed government official who asked me to follow him. I left Sharon and our teens in the lobby of main airport and was escorted outside and into a limousine with two other men in dark suits and sunglasses sitting down on both sides of me. I was taken to a building close by (I could not see outside of the limo to know where we were going). I was then walked into a white room with a stainless steel table and one chair with lights shining toward the chair. I was told to be seated in the chair and to face the blinding lights.

There were four armed Cuban police in different corners of the room. The man in the suit began asking me questions in what turned out to be five hours of questions. Three different suited men came in, each taking up where the last left off, asking the same questions repeatedly. I was asked if I worked for the US government, what I was trying to find out in Cuba, and for whom in the US I was working for, if I had any people in Cuba who were helping me, etc. They went through my briefcase and searched me and asked about the money and who it was for and what it was for.

I told them that I was a pastor traveling to Cuba to visit friends, that our group was visiting churches (did not mention where) and doing puppet shows for them. The money that I had was for our group's travel expenses and that $18,000 of it was help for the churches and people who needed it. I told them the truth about everything but only information they asked for. I was careful not to mention names or areas.

After about five hours, the main suited guy sat down across from me and told me that it was not possible for us to do those things that I was saying we were going to do, especially what I said with the puppets and with the money being given out to people. He explained that this is Cuba and it was not legal to do such things.

I remember telling him that it would be okay. I said that we had no political agenda and that we expected nothing in return for the monies we were giving to the people. I explained that I was visiting as a pastor and would not be preaching unless I was asked and that then I would not stand behind the pulpit when I spoke but that I would stand beside it. I knew that not standing behind the pulpit mattered to them, but I was not sure why.

The man left the room after I said that, and I was alone with the four police. One of them whispered to me not to worry, it was okay, and that when I got back to the states to please tell Sharon Stone he said hello and gave me his name. I promised him I would tell her next time I had lunch with her, and he smiled. A few minutes later, the suited man came back in and handed me my suitcase back and I looked and nothing was missing, including every bit of the money. They walked me out to the limo and drove me back to the airport and to the team who had been left there to wait the five hours. We walked out and met Amittay and went to his house.

We spent two days buying the equipment we needed to go along with what we had and renting a full-sized bus to hold our two puppet teams and all our gear. We knew a driver who worked for the bus people we rented from and paid a bribe so he would be our driver. When we picked up the bus, the driver was not the man we bribed the company to get, so we knew we had an informant for our driver.

We set out for Bayamo from Havana with our team, Amittay and his family, and a few of the teens from their church. It was exciting for them, because a Cuban is not allowed to travel outside of their area without government permission, so most of the people with us had never been on a trip like this before. The bus was a full-sized tour bus and very nice bus for Cuba.

We pulled into Bayamo some 600 miles later and hooked up with Ramon. We started that night with our puppet team meeting and training the teens from Ramon's church. Our team had the entire program they used recorded by Cubans in Charlotte, North Carolina, and put on individual tapes for each one to keep. So after seven months of listening to the skits and songs along with the long hours of practice, they knew them well and got the mouth motion down. None of them spoke Spanish, but they knew the songs and skits.

It was fun to watch our teens pouring themselves into Ramon's teens and training them as puppeteers. They spent the next two days working on the basics, and then we did a show at Ramon's church the second night. It was better than we had imagined, along with the response. The building was packed, and we had the street outside standing room only. The third day was spent doing puppet shows in the open-air all around Ramon's area. Again, we had more people attend and listen than we thought would happen.

Each time we filled the area with kids, teens, adults, and even the men attended. The last show we did had to be done two times because so many people came, we could not do the show for them all. That evening, our puppet team had a meeting with Ramon's guys and gave them everything they needed to have their own puppet ministry. It was an awesome thing to witness because much of the equipment given to this teen group came from hard work and sacrifice and of a lot of their own money and time. It was a powerful service, and the teams finished by asking God in prayer to use them during the next week as we traveled and performed all over Cuba. We spent the next five days in cities, villages, small communities, and in jungle tribal villages a few times.

Our method was simple and effective. We would pull into a town or village and set up our stage and have the locals run and tell everyone we were going to have cotton people do a show. This type of thing had never happened before, so the people flocked to it. Also, every place we drove into, the government turned the electricity to the entire city or village out. Every time this happened, we knew our driver was doing it.

We carried generators and lights, so it did not stop us, and it even helped because when the electricity went out, people could not do their work and would come watch our show. God used the informant and the government shutting off the power to help us reach out to more people. We could clearly feel God working and helping and speaking to these needy people.

The program was very Gospel-oriented, and we had men from our seminary working everywhere we did shows. It was a five-day long trip of sharing Christ to people who did not know it in a way that was not creating a threat to the powers that be. My words lack the ability to capture the power of what God was doing openly in that dark land!

The Sierra Maestra Mountains was a whole new level. This place was sacred to the communists as Castro used those mountains to hide in as he brought his revolution to Cuba. The last day was dedicated to Yorki and his family and those who had come to Christ in that thatch hut on the side of the mountain. Through Charles and Rusty's tears and several years of hard work, now it was time. The plan was to head toward a city at the foot of the mountains, and then at the last minute, tell the driver we changed plans and have him drive into the mountains where Yorki's village meets and have the cotton people do their thing.

Yorki and his family were spreading the word and knew we were coming. Without being from Cuba, it would be hard for you to understand how dangerous and scary it was for Amittay and Ramon and their wives to go into the Sierra Maestra Mountains and openly preach the Gospel. It could cost them their lives in jail or worse. We had created enough stir the four days already where we were all feeling pressure.

Ramon and Naomi, Amittay and Anita, Sharon and I met together in a broom closet the night before we were to go and talked it out. The broom closet would not be bugged. I suggested that they stay in the hotel we were at and we would go and do the program and come back to get them. I was legitimately afraid for their safety (and ours).

Amittay and Ramon and both their wives said that they had served God in Cuba their entire adult lives and were waiting to see this type of thing happen where the Gospel would be preached openly in Cuba. They were not going to miss the finishing meeting of this trip, no matter what happened to them. If you had been with us in that room that night, you would understand the fear, excitement, and thankfulness for God doing this with and through us in those days.

The Gospel of Jesus is often laughed at and discounted as false in more and more of our nation. But sitting in a broom closet so as not to be overheard and planning on giving this same Gospel to people who had never heard it in a country who outlawed it with communism speaks to its power and truth.

The plan was for Rusty to come in from the other side of the mountain the same time we were to start the meeting. We loaded up the bus and started out for a city close to the real destination. When we got to the intersection of the Sierra Maestra or the other city, we told the driver we changed our plans and for him to turn left. It was obvious that he was shaken by the change, but he did, and we drove straight to the middle of the village where Yorki and his family lived.

When we stopped the bus and unloaded the equipment, the driver left the bus and disappeared. Yorki's mom was there, and she had a meeting set up with the communist leader for her area. Nothing happened without this lady's say so. We met together and explained that our team had come all the way from the United States to do a show of cotton people sharing an important message about God.

The communist leader there was very old and was like a grand-mother for the people. She was well-loved and respected. She shared with us that her area had seen such a change in Yorki's mom after her meeting Christ and that the Bible readings at their hut were good for the people. She welcomed the puppet show and sent word for all to come.

We had a couple of hours before the beginning of the show, because many of the people were walking from miles around, and they needed time to get there. It was a hot day, and located just below the place we were at was a waterfall and small swimming hole. So after we set up, our group joined Yorki's family to swim before the show.

We were talking about those who had been saved and how they needed to be baptized as we were swimming. A friend of Yorki's family also wanted to accept Christ. We explained what that was, and she prayed and accepted Christ. She then asked if she could be baptized when we did it. We said yes, and then it dawned on me we had all eight people who had been saved there with the new convert and our team and two pastors from Cuba as well as others. We called everyone together and we all prayed, and Amittay and Ramon baptized the first nine converts of the church that started four years earlier but formed that day.

We got set up, and the time came, and the people gathered. Everybody from that area was there, and Rusty pulled in as we started the show. You could hear a pin drop as the people listened to the Gospel shared by cotton people. At the end of the program, Rusty took his Bible and joined the puppets and explained what had happened to Yorki's family and what the puppets were telling them, and he gave a clear explanation of how everyone there could be a follower of Jesus. As he was speaking, a jeep pulled up full of military guards with the bus driver. They were armed and stood behind the crowd as Rusty kept speaking.

The people paid them no attention, and the lady who was the communist leader of that area backed them off from the meeting. When Rusty finished, the communist leader stood up and invited everyone to a meal. They killed two goats and started cooking.

Rusty and I sat with the leader, and she told us that her area needed what Rusty and the cotton people were talking about. She gave us permission to start a church in the same place we had just swam and baptized people. One of the men from the seminary who was with us mentioned he could meet with the people to start a work.

Some of the men said they would build a meeting place if they could get the wood.

Our teen group heard them talking and asked how much they needed for the wood, and they all gave their own money and paid for the wood. The communist leader invited the military to stay and eat and told them she had agreed for the show to happen, and their threat was gone with her words. We saw our teens preach Christ to many who never heard, nine converts were baptized, and a new church for them was formed, and a pastor we were training was in place to help. God saw Rusty and Charles's tears years before and built his church there.

We finished the trip with Ramon's puppet team equipped to keep it going, and the church in Havana encouraged. That was the beginning of what now is three churches in that area as the first church has since started two more. The people are now doing the work on their own, and God is touching people all over that land. I am amazed at having been able to witness firsthand God's working in that place.

I will forever be grateful to Charles, Rusty, Amittay, Ramon, and their wives for their willingness to risk it all to see God do what only he could do for that great people and country.

Ninety Miles

I often remember hearing Amittay and his wife Anita say the words "ninety miles" whenever we passed the sea wall on the bay in Havana. It was in reference to the fact that the USA was ninety miles away by sea. Ninety miles to freedom.

Cubans often will hit the water and try to make the ninety-mile journey to the Florida Keys. The claim is that one in ten make it. I am not sure how they come by that claim, but that is the number. The ones who do not make it drown or are eaten by sharks. Also, the US has a policy known as "wet foot, dry foot." That means that if a Cuban fleeing to the US for asylum reaches dry land on US soil, they will be given asylum. If they are in the water, they will be sent back to Cuba and given over to the communist government.

I am not sure how God-fearing freedom-loving people can, with a clear conscience, give people seeking freedom back to a communist government where they will face punishment for seeking freedom, but there we have it. It seems that people in communist countries risk their lives to get to America and freedom while some in this country are trying to embrace socialism and even communism.

Amittay was drawing more and more attention from the government with our religious activity, and the puppet tour was the straw that seemingly broke the camel's back. After that trip, the government came out with a nationwide statement claiming responsibility for our puppet team's tour as a cultural education program. They also wrote and changed several laws restricting travel and open-air shows and that type stuff. We made a big enough impression to get laws changed, but unfortunately, that translated into more problems for Amittay with the government.

It became clear enough that Amittay was in danger of being arrested or killed. Rusty and Amittay began to plan ways to get he and his family out of Cuba. Amittay had connections in the government and in the Cuban Mafia where he would be notified if something was going to happen. He would have an hour's notice if they decided to come after him.

Rusty tried to get visas for his family to visit Mexico, and we could get him from there, but nothing was working out, and Amittay was being watched very closely. Secretly, Amittay had a plan that no one knew about. He had a sixteen-foot boat made and hidden with a small outboard motor and enough provisions for three or four days at sea. The deal was that if he got word that the government was coming to take him, he and his family would drop everything and hit the water for the dangerous ninety-mile trip to the states. They had a man who would drive them there, and he would keep the boat after they were in the states.

There was a secret code phrase that Rusty and Amittay had set up that would let us know things were happening while whoever was listening to the phone call would not think it anything other than what it meant.

One day, I received a call from Rusty saying Amittay and his family were missing, and no one had talked with them for a few hours. Rusty made a few phone calls and found out that the order to arrest Amittay had been given and that he took his family and whatever they could carry had fled for their lives. We assumed they had hit the water and were headed for the Florida Keys. We spent a day trying to get any information on them with nothing but silence.

Rusty and I jumped on a flight to Miami and met at the airport where we rented a small plane and pilot to fly over the keys and the international waters looking for them. Several businessmen who knew about the situation funded the trip, and off we went. We had been given a description of the boat and had found out that they had several more people with them as well as the captain.

We flew around what we understood was the location where the currents would land them, trying to spot them. We landed at a small airport in the Keys to refuel and took off again toward all the places where they would have landed. On the last island, we circled and saw a boat that had washed up on the shore. The boat was turned upside down and was in bad shape, but it fit the description of Amittay's boat. We flew around the area looking for footprints in the sand or bodies floating in the water but found nothing. The boat was washed up on shore, obviously messed up and no longer usable. We finally had to return to Miami and try to gather some type of news.

Once back in Miami, Rusty made a few calls, and we found out that the US Coast Guard had found them just a short distance from reaching the shore of the island where we saw their boat. They were picked up (in water) and were on the Coast Guard Ship waiting to be returned to Cuba. At that time, as fate would have it, the man who had the authority to clear Amittay into US custody was a member of my church in the Atlanta area. I will not give his name, but he and his office were the ones who decided who was sent back or who could come to the US, and he had the final say.

I called his cell phone and he answered, and I explained that the Coast Guard had Amittay and his family and were planning on giving them back to the Cuban government. I informed him that Amittay was fleeing for his own and his family's safety and needed to be protected. As a member of our church, he had heard many of the things Amittay had done for the churches in Cuba.

I explained how much danger Amittay and his family would be facing if turned back over to the communists. I can never forget what the man said to me. "I will not get involved and risk drawing political attention to my career."

I explained how urgent it was that he help them and reminded him of Queen Esther in the Bible. I asked him to consider that God may have put him in that position "for such a time as this" and that he had the authority and should use it to help this pastor!

My friend again refused to get involved. He did nothing to help Amittay's family reach safety and freedom. What a great opportunity ignored by a friend I once respected.

Rusty and I spent the next few days trying to get congressmen or senators or anyone with pull to help intervene, but everyone was too afraid to touch it because of the political risks involved. We found out that after being told on the Coast Guard ship that his family would be taken care of, he and his family were taken to Cuba and given to the Cuban government officials. The person on the Coast Guard ship lied to them.

The Cuban government put Amittay, Anita, Ariel (seventeen-year-old autistic son) and Kelly (fifteen) in separate cells in prison and tortured them for four days.

We called everybody we could and begged and pleaded, but no one would go to bat for us to help them. Finally, the then British Ambassador to Cuba listened to Rusty and was able to pull some strings and got Amittay's family released from prison. I have more respect for Paul and his wife, Linda (British Ambassador), and for his country, because when he was made aware of the circumstances, he acted without concern for his own political position and did the right thing, possibly saving Amittay's family from death or extended prison and torture. I am proud of that man and his wife for being a bigger person than any one of our congressmen and senators we contacted, not to mention the man who was already in place but too selfish to make a right decision.

Thank you, Paul and Linda, for your leadership!

Amittay lost his house and everything he owned when he and his family hit the ocean. He was no longer allowed to practice as a Cuban doctor and could not work anywhere else. He was forced to move into a house with his father in Havana. This was the house where the church in Havana was built on the second floor.

The government also came and put a chain and padlock on the upstairs church door with posted signs warning that they were not to be opened. Once a week, he was called by someone in the government saying they were going to kill him. He was watched and under constant fear.

It was during that time that Amittay said he began to see the Cuban people in a different light. God began to renew his love for his own people and renew his burden for how lost so many of his people where. He began to pray and ask God again to use him to help reach his people on a stronger level for Jesus.

As God continued to renew Amittay's heart for the Cuban people, Amittay cut the chains and locks off the church doors and started services again, giving his safety over to God. He continued getting death threats weekly from the government, and Rusty continued working to try to get him and his family out of Cuba. The church has been open ever since, and God is using it to see people come to Christ.

Finally, after two years, Rusty was able to negotiate with a Cuban official ($3,000) for Amittay and his family to be given six-month visas to travel to a church in Mexico to teach music there. The church was a work that Rusty's church in Charlotte helped start, and the pastor there was in on the plan for Rusty to get them safely out of Cuba and to the states. Basically, Rusty bribed the guy in Cuba for the visas, and the church in Mexico had a lawyer bring their family to Laredo, Mexico, where they would meet up with Rusty and I.

The plan was that we would walk across the border with them (on dry land) and ask for asylum. Amittay secured the visas and flew with his family to Mexico. They then started their twenty-four-hour drive to Laredo, Mexico, where we would be waiting.

On the day I was leaving Atlanta by van to get them, Rusty was called out of country to an emergency in Guatemala (Jose's work). So a pastor friend of ours, Karl, from Flipside Church in California, flew in and met me in Laredo, Texas, and we both went over the border to scout out the meeting with Amittay the day before. I thank God for Karl and his heart and passion for missions and Christ. We found out that Laredo, Mexico, was a wild and crazy place and dangerous for Americans to travel to.

The next day, Karl and I went across the border to the location set up for us to meet Amittay and his family. We waited several hours past the time for the meeting, and Karl had to leave and catch his plane back to California. About an hour later, Amittay and his family pulled in, and it was a scary happy time.

We had a mile or so to walk to the border, and they said their goodbyes to the lawyer, and we began our walk to the United States of America. When we got to the bridge over the river between the two countries, we began across with no problem from the Mexican side. In the middle of the bridge was a line with United States of America written on state side and Mexico written on our side. We got to the line, and I watched in thankfulness to years of answered prayer as all four of Amittay's family stepped over the line onto American land on dry ground.

FRANK PENLEY

I crossed the line after them and approached the US border agent at the end of the bridge ahead of them and told him that I was an American pastor and had a Cuban family with me that was fleeing Cuba for their lives and seeking asylum in the US.

I will never forget the reaction of the agent. He walked around the counter he was standing in front of and saluted them. He said, "Welcome to the United States of America!" And he gave them his word that they were now safe! It was an unbelievable experience to watch as Amittay (not expecting that kind of welcome) was treated with respect and kindness. God was giving them what they needed at that moment through that US border agent. I still see it now in my memory.

We walked into the customs building where they were assigned a person to help them begin the process of entrance to our country. It took twenty-six hours for them to be cleared from customs. I was able to check on them and bring them food. It was about 10:00 a.m. when they walked out of customs into America.

I took them to my hotel room so they could shower and freshen up. Afterward, we loaded the van and started toward Atlanta. I forgot to tell them that just outside of Laredo, Texas, was a checkpoint that was impossible to get around. They were just settling down for the trip, and as I drove over a little ridge, there it was—this huge military type checkpoint with guards, dogs, weapons—and we were driving up to the entrance.

I should remind you that Amittay and his family were told by the US Coast Guard that they were fine and would be taken care of and then turned over to the Cuban guards and tortured for four days. Kelly, Amittay's fifteen-year-old daughter, saw the checkpoint and was immediately sick. We rolled the window down, and she threw up just before we got to the first guard post who was supposed to search our van.

I stopped the van and got out and told the guard I was a pastor and that they were Cubans who had gotten close before, only to be turned back over to Cuba by the American Coast Guard and horribly mistreated. I then shared that I forgot to warn them about this stop, and little Kelly was freaking out, thinking she would be sent back to Cuba. It was my fault for not preparing them for this stop, but it was clearly traumatic to them, especially Kelly.

The guard asked for the asylum papers for all four of them, which I showed her, and she walked up to Kelly's window and told her not to worry, she was protected by the US now, and she cleared our van from the process and escorted us through and out the other side with no search. We drove away, and it began to sink in to them that Amittay and his family were now safe.

It was fun taking them to truck stops and restaurants and hotels. They did not know how to do simple things like buying snacks or ordering from a menu, but it did not take them long to learn. I took them to a Golden Corral buffet to eat one night, and Anita burst into tears when she saw the buffet. She had never seen that much food cooked and ready to eat at one time and in one place before, and it was hard for her to process it.

The first night in a hotel, they were afraid to use too many towels. It was a shock to them to see the wealth and abundance that this country takes for granted. Ariel (autistic son) would go into the snack area at every stop and load up his pockets with all they could hold. I did not have the heart to stop him. I told him not to worry, he would be able to eat again next meal time, and he would just pat his pockets and smile and say, "Yes, I know I will."

The next Sunday, Amittay and his family had their first church service in the United States at our church. As we started the service, Amittay and his family shared a testimony with us that I must share with you. It was when they were out at sea in the middle of the night, fleeing Cuba. They had eight or nine adults in a sixteen-foot boat, sixty miles or so out to sea with thirty more to go. The motor stopped working and a storm blew in and waves started hitting the boat. The rudder broke off and sank, and they were without power or ability to steer and had no lights.

As the storm grew worse, the waves began to come over the sides, filling the boat. Ariel (autistic son) began to ask his mother if they were going to be eaten alive by sharks. Anita told him that God was going to take care of them. About thirty minutes later, a huge wave came over the side from the darkness, filling the boat almost to the top.

Ariel screamed to his mom, "God better hurry up if he is going to help!"

The captain of the boat told everyone if another wave like that one hit them, the boat would sink. It was dark and raining and high waves with lightning striking all around them. Kelly started singing a Cuban song about how God would put his hands under you and keep you in the storm. As she was singing, another wave like the last big one hit them and filled the boat to where the sides were all the way underwater.

Amittay shared that the people were screaming and Kelly was still singing and the boat was seemingly lost. What happened next was hard to explain by any other means than the hand of God. Amittay and Anita and everyone else in the boat felt like a hand went under the boat, lifting it above the waterline. Everyone started bailing out the water.

Kelly kept singing, and they all could tell that God was putting his hand under them and keeping them through the storm. Kelly stood up in our service and sang that song for us in her language, remembering that night. Our church was able to get a slight glimpse of God's hand under his children in a dark and terrible storm.

During the message, Ariel got up out of his seat and walked over to the American flag and hugged it. Our church was given a reminder of just how much we have in the freedom we enjoy. So many of our men and women have sacrificed for us to have it.

Today, Amittay is working with Pastor Rusty Price at Camino Church in Charlotte, North Carolina, and he, his wife, Ariel, and Kelly are now all US citizens. They are serving in their church, and Amittay is working in a medical clinic that Camino runs for their community. I am so thankful God kept his hand under them and on them and brought them safely to this country.

I thank Rusty and Amittay for allowing me and our church to walk with them during these events, and mainly, I thank God for over 100 men preaching in over 100 churches throughout Cuba, and especially for the three churches in the Sierra Maestra Mountains.

Guatemala

When starting our church, God impressed us to never refuse his leading, no matter how big it seemed. We promised as a church body that we would operate by faith and would obey God's leading in anything if he would show us the way to do it. That not only proved true in Cuba, but in several other countries and here at home as well. It is in our DNA "to do what God says" and to trust him to provide no matter how big the call. We have done our best to do just that, and these next few chapters are testimony to God's call and provision and his answered prayer.

Jesus asked the question when he was here, "When the Son of Man returns, will he find faith?" Notice he did not ask, "Will he find churches?"

I sometimes think that so many people do not trust in him because so many of his followers do not trust in him either! After all, one cannot run a business by faith!

Rusty met and led two men from Guatemala to faith in Christ. Both of these men eventually joined his church and became leaders. Before long, God began to burden both men for their home village. They eventually gave up their successful business and sold their homes to return to their little town and share the Gospel and plant churches. I knew both of these men and have great respect for them. I was touched by their willingness to leave a $250,000 house in Charlotte, North Carolina for a mud-floored house the size of their living room back in the states.

I was invited to visit them in Guatemala with Rusty, and I gladly took the trip. I was impressed with the sacrifice and tenacity with which the men labored as they tried to share Christ with their people. Both men were starting churches in their different locations, which did not have a Gospel-centered church. Rusty was very close to these two men and shared their burden for that part of Guatemala. Rusty also had open doors in other parts of Guatemala that he was praying over and researching on this trip.

One day, we were invited to speak to the children in a local school house in Jose's village. The school was three small classrooms and one open gym type square block building used for meetings and such. They had two small bathrooms, and the teachers were poorly paid and without much-needed teaching tools or classroom supplies.

I could not help but notice how dedicated and driven the teachers were at their job. The children were all attentive and very cheerful, all despite the school being three times too small for the number of students it was trying to help. They were in great want for much needed space and supplies, but the children were so thankful to be given a chance to have an education. It was also very clear to us that the parents wanted their children to have better, and this little pitiful school was the villages main chance.

That night, Rusty and Jose and I were talking, and Jose was sharing his frustrations with the work. The women and children were coming, but the men were not willing to come, much less commit to the church. The area was mainly farming and it was also under strong control of the local drug cartel that controls much of that part of the country of Guatemala.

While we were talking about all of this, I could not help but think of all the dads that had stopped work to come see the kids' program at the school that day. Jose said that the government had been planning on building a new building that would give the school enough room and bathrooms for all the children, plus some. They were waiting on the money to do so, and it had been several years of talk.

Jose said the amount needed was $5,000. Cement and blocks and labor are almost free, and that amount would build the new school building. That night, we felt the Lord speak to us that we could build that building through Jose's church, and doing so would touch the men of the village hearts and show them the *love* God had for their families. I also knew in my heart God wanted our church to supply the need for them to build it.

I spoke to Rusty and Jose about it the next morning, and we all agreed it would be best when Jose promised the money, we followed through fast enough as to give the right message. Our church was all in when they heard that we were invited to help reach that part of Guatemala. We joined Rusty and Jose's church in this call and agreed to give the money.

Jose approached the government with the idea that his church would provide the money needed for them to build the school if they would supply it with what was needed for the children's supplies. It would be their building. We would just build it for the children in the village to have a decent school. They agreed, and God helped us raise the money in just a few short months. In less than a year, the building was built.

When it was finished, we decided to throw a big party in the village to celebrate the building of the school and to dedicate it. We had Jose buy a full-grown massive bull and barbeque that bad boy and invite the entire village and surrounding houses to come to the dedication. Then after everyone had eaten, we assembled, and Jose dedicated the new school to the people of the village and prayed over the children and the teachers. It was a very great day.

The government officials came, and everybody who was anybody came. The newspapers and TV news came, and the mayor acknowledged Jose and his church as the one who provided the building as a gift to the village and its children. Unfortunately, the leader of the drug cartel was in attendance as well.

It was not long after this that the church began to grow. The men started bringing their families, and many of the men made decisions to accept Christ into their hearts. God used Rusty's church to help Jose acquire property to build their church a place of their own to worship. God opened that area up for the Gospel and blessed the sacrifice and surrender with the people coming to faith. Finally, Jose and his team began to see answers to years of prayer for these dear people.

It is hard to write the next part of this story, but as history has proven true with his church, God has used what I am about to share for his glory and for his church to grow.

Soon after the new church property was bought and new school building was finished, Jose was contacted by the drug cartel that he was to start giving a percentage of his support to them or else. Also, some of the men who were working for the cartel (more like slaves to them) had come to Christ and would no longer work for them. The cartel told Jose that they needed an answer, and Jose told them he would not give God's money to them. He had an understanding of who he was dealing with and what their threats could mean. He also knew that God had called him to give his all for the cause of Christ and these people he now was serving.

A few weeks later, one of Jose's church members, in a second church Jose was starting up in the mountains, called Jose to come to his house late one night for an emergency. As it turned out, the man was a plant from the cartel, pretending to be a Christian, and the call was a trap. In a remote part of the road leading to the new church, Jose and one of his workers were ambushed. They killed the worker who was with Jose instantly, and they executed Jose with their style of execution so everyone would get the message.

The police and the ambulance would not come to the scene until the next day because of fear of the cartel. Jose's wife was called by an unknown person and told about it as it was happening. When she got to the place where Jose was, she sat with both bodies until the next day to keep the wild animals and dogs away from the bodies. The cartel then put a hit contract out on Jose's wife and children and on Vicente and his pregnant wife. The contract was sent out all over Guatemala for anyone who wanted the reward. Jose's children were three, five, and eight, and Vicente's wife was pregnant.

Rusty called me and a pastor friend from California named Karl. We all grabbed as much money as our churches had and met in Guatemala the next day. Jose's village and church is a five-plus hour drive from Guatemala City. We all met at the airport early as possible the next morning and were trying to get local contacts to help.

When at the airport, one man who was very influential in the military called Rusty and told us to abandon Jose's family and Vicente and his wife and leave the country. He also told us to throw our phones away. He said to never contact him again.

We went and checked into our hotel and met in a cigar bar close by and began to plan our next steps. Some of the men in the church grabbed Jose's and Vicente's family and were bringing them to us the next day, but they were safe for now. They came so fast that they left their important papers behind showing that three of the children were US citizens. It was decided that Rusty would go to the US Embassy and try to get them to harbor the families and get them to safety back in the states. Karl and I would drive up to the village and get the needed papers so as to be able to get them out of the country.

In the cigar bar, I spoke with the bartender and let him know that we needed to meet someone who could sell us a few guns. I let him know the guns were for protection, and we had cash. A few minutes later, he came over and asked me if I had considered buying bodyguards instead of guns as they were less expensive. We called a missionary friend who had worked in the country for twenty years or so, and he already knew the situation. He gave us the name of a man who could do the job and was trustworthy and willing.

We contacted him, explained the situation and who they were protecting these people from, and he came the next morning with four other men and loaded for bear. These guys were ready, willing, and appeared very able to protect Jose and Vicente's family if attacked. They had serious weapons and looked ready for a small war.

The next day, when the families arrived, we put them in a small hotel inside a compound surrounded by walls and a gate with armed security. It was decided that we move them every morning to a new location and keep them behind locked doors guarded by two men at each door and one hidden, watching the entrance. Karl and I drove up to get the papers that evening and were back the next day.

Rusty went to the embassy to ask for help and was told that we needed to get out of the country as soon as possible and leave our friends; we could not help them. They informed him that if he brought them to the embassy, they would not let them in and would turn us all away. They referenced the power and money and political connections the cartel had all the way to DC.

We were left with no other option but to get them out of the country ourselves. We had the bodyguards for another day and needed to move quickly anyway. Our church, Karl's church, and Rusty's church had $15,000 between us for everything. Rusty had mission works all over central and south America and the Caribbean. Vicente's wife had family in the mountains. It was the cartel's area, but all who knew her family and town said she was safer there than anywhere else.

So Rusty started setting up locations to send Jose's family, and Vicente would go somewhere and come back for his wife as soon as he could do so safely. That night, Karl and I drove Vicente's wife five hours up into the mountains to where her family were waiting on her to take her to safety. We got to the place where we met her transport late in the night and dropped her off with them.

It looked like a small town in the middle of the mountains that could be in a spaghetti western with Clint Eastwood smoking a cigar. One guy was leaning against a light post as we stopped to let Vicente's wife out. They just walked away into the shadows. It seemed that we were alone in that place, but I could feel the eyes and tell family was all around and protecting their own.

On the way back to the hotel, we came to where the mountain road turns onto the main highway leading us the three hours back. We were stopped and surrounded by multiple police. It was very late—or very early, depending on your view—but the highway and road were empty. We had five cars and men with loaded weapons pointing at us, asking to check our papers. It was very obvious who they were working for, and at that moment, Karl and I knew that they had our lives in their hands.

They kept us there for twenty-plus minutes, surrounded and at gunpoint. Karl and I knew that it was up to God on what they decided to do. Finally, the leader gave us back our papers and suggested we be careful for the rest of our stay in Guatemala. We got back to Guatemala City the next morning, and by that night, we had everyone safely out of the country and hidden.

That evening, we sat in our hotel room and thanked the Lord that he had answered prayer and protected everyone and that everyone was safe.

There are three churches there in Jose's and Vicente's locations. Some of the men in the village found out who killed Jose, and they killed them. The cartel then killed some of those men, and as I understand it, there has been a truce of sorts, and another family is now serving in that church with another one ready to go if needed. God has blessed that church with growth and it has been birthed from the blood of Jesus and the blood of Jose and his helper.

God has used that situation to teach me that money given must be done with care and knowledge of the individual field. I am not saying that our offerings led to Jose's death, but I am saying that since Jose's death, I think long, hard, and spend time in prayer to know how God wants us to help and how to give in such a way that God's work is blessed and not hindered.

Throughout history, God has built his church with the blood of the men and women who lay their life down in service to Christ. I hurt for Jose and the pain his death caused his family, Rusty, and many others. I stand and salute his memory and the work his life accomplished. See you again, my friend!

Haiti

We had Steve Horne visit our church and speak. He shared with us that he and Bobby Price had been offered a large plot of land in Haiti. It was next to a town called Perches. They had a vision of starting an orphanage. There are many orphans in Haiti, and Bobby and Steve had raised the money and built an orphanage that could hold up to seventy-five kids.

When they opened the orphanage, 150 kids needed a place and easily more could be gathered. When Steve shared with our church the need for more orphans to be taken care of, we knew that God, a God of orphans, wanted us to do something about the need. We as a church began asking God how to help and how to pay for the help.

I went with Steve and Bobby to Haiti, and we visited the town of Perches. Having never been to Haiti, I was not quite ready mentally for what I was about to experience. We flew into the Dominican Republic and planned to walk across the border into a small town and drive to Perches where the orphanage is located. We entered customs on the Dominican side of the bridge and were preparing to show our passports to walk across.

The Dominican agent just looked at us and said, "If you are crazy enough to go in, there you can go." Also, the only line were people trying to get out of Haiti and into the Dominican Republic. No one was in line to get into Haiti but our team. We walked outside of the port of entry and approached the bridge to enter Haiti.

As we walked over the bridge, it was like we were leaving a plush jungle country and entering a war-torn one. Literally, it was like a battlefield after months of fighting, just without the war. The place was like a scorched desert with trash everywhere. The Haitian people were gathered at the border, burning any and everything they could in protest of something. Just over the bridge was a tank and a group of NATO Peacekeepers guarding the bridge exit. They looked at us like we were crazy walking across the bridge toward and through the crowd of protesters.

We met up with our ride and did the three-hour trip into the backcountry to Perches. We set up our gear in the almost complete orphanage building and began the three-hour walk into town. Perches was a town of several thousand people and was very poor. We walked to the market that was filled with people, but very little was worth buying. We then headed back toward the orphanage through the town. I noticed from time to time people were left lying out in front of their houses, dying, and some were already dead. In this town, they collect the dead in the mornings, and people lay out their dead and dying throughout the day.

The orphanage was filling up fast with the kids as word spread of our arrival. We stopped by a house, and in the backyard was a young boy—probably twelve to fourteen, we thought—with a rope around his neck and tied to a tree. He was just like a dog sitting there, lifeless. We cut the rope and brought him with us to the orphanage. Kids were walking around the countryside who lived outside on their own—no name, no home, no identity. They were like stray dogs running in packs.

A simple infection here was deadly, and these kids had lost their parent(s) or were cast out because of lack of food. I had not seen this type of poverty and suffering since Albania! There was also no value placed on human life here and little care for the sick or dying.

The kid with the rope around his neck is called LiLi. He was the slave of a powerful woman in the town who had tied him to a tree in her backyard and had fed him scraps. She beat him with sticks and treated him like an animal. That night, as we were eating, I gave my plate to LiLi sitting beside me. The generator broke, and we lost our lights and were eating in darkness. I was patting LiLi on the back, and it seemed that his back was eaten up with bug bites or sores of some kind.

I got the first aid kit and a flashlight and was about to treat his sores when I pulled up his shirt. I realized his sores were not bug bites or sores, they were scars from being beaten so often. He was forty-five pounds and knee-high to a grasshopper, and his back from neck to waist was covered in scar tissue as if he had been beaten with a bullwhip. I thought, "How in the world can there be slaves and children tied to trees and beaten in our day?" I also thought about how God saw every day of LiLi's life and heard his prayers for help.

The woman who claimed she owned him actually came to the orphanage and demanded $1,500 payment for LiLi. She did not get any money or LiLi.

Fast forward to a year or so later where we were now in the small fishing village of Aquin. The orphanage in Perches had been stolen from Bobby and Steve by the church that they were helping. We took what children we could and those who needed the most help and were looking for a place to rent to house them. Aquin was far enough away from Perches where the kids would be safe. Our church had raised $16,000 to help Steve buy a house for the orphans as Bobby and their church had left Haiti and were no longer willing to help after the loss of the building and property being stolen.

Haiti is corrupt, and justice is no competitor with money or influence. I told Steve our church would support the new orphanage if we could find a place where the kids would be safe. We spent the night in a small hotel in Aquin, praying and asking God for a safe place for our kids. God answered our prayers, and the next day, God gave us a house and we had an orphanage in Aquin, Haiti, for thirty-plus kids.

Our plan was to build a second story on the house and start a bakery. The kids would run the bakery and sell the products for the support of the orphanage. Each kid would get a percentage of his part to put into a savings account so that when he or she got old enough to be on their own, they had enough money to get on their feet and start a small business on their own. We raised the money, and after three years, we had the bakery built.

God answered the prayers of our group and the kids. They started a church on the property of the orphanage, and people from the area came and worshipped with them. They did the worship, and even the preaching, and they started and continued the church from their own heart without anyone telling or asking them to.

I remember sitting in the back of the thatch roof hut with eighty other people having church with them and crying from the spirit that was in that little work of grace.

We had a man in Aquin who was paid to look out after the property and the kids. They were in a school, getting a good education, and were eating two meals a day. They were safe and clean with a good bed, and any needs they had were met. God gave us six or seven good years, and we were so thankful to be a part of the work. Steve had raised monthly support for it, and people gave and the work was going forward.

Our church built the bakery, and our vision of turning a fish into a fishing pole was almost complete. We had a man named Farrell, who felt God call him to leave his job two years before retirement with benefits, to move to Haiti and make the oversight of the orphanage a little more hands on.

One day, I got a call that an earthquake had hit Haiti and half a million people were dead. Steve was not able to get a hold of anyone at the orphanage, and no flights were going in or out of Haiti. Steve, Farrell, and I gathered all the money we could from our church and his project and flew to the Dominican Republic. Once there, we rented a taxi to the border. We rented a 4x4 truck and driver and filled the truck up with food and water and first aid supplies and headed into Haiti.

It was about two hours from the border to the fault line in Port-au-Prince. I was sitting in the back of the truck we had rented to keep our supplies from being stolen. About five miles from the airport at Port-au-Prince, the sky was filled with buzzards flying toward the earthquake zone. It was the third day after the earthquake, but we could smell the death from five miles out.

We drove past the airport in Port-au-Prince, and the fault line of the earthquake was a straight line with little damage on our side and total devastation on the other side. It was like an atomic bomb had gone off. The streets were no longer passable, and it seemed like all the buildings were collapsed into them with trails through the rubble.

We spent several hours trying to find the family of one of our work-ers. We did find them, and all but one had lived. There were bodies scattered all around, partially sticking out of rubble and lying dead in the street. It looked like everybody was dead. At one point, we had parked the truck and were walking through the wreckage, try-ing to find someone. I remember cutting my leg on a piece of rebar sticking from one of the collapsed buildings I was crawling over.

I stood up, surrounded by total devastation and death, and thought about the verse in the Bible that mentions the Lord sending in the death angel into the enemy camp that threatened Judah during Hezekiah's day. That night, the Lord sent an angel into the enemy camp and killed 150,000 of them. The Bible in the KJV says that the next morning, they woke up, and everyone was dead.

Until that moment, I never understood that wording, but standing there surrounded by over a quarter a million dead and everything destroyed, I understood exactly what that wording was saying. I almost felt guilty for being alive, and in that setting, my life seemed unimportant and insignificant in that level of death. I cannot put it into words the experience.

We took the rest of the day traveling the road (what was left of it) to the orphanage. It was seemingly impossible to continue at times, but finally we made it. Our kids were all okay and safe. The building was damaged but repairable. Our deep water well was the only real damage, and we had to dig another one. We left the supplies and headed back for Port-au-Prince to help the families we knew there.

We got back the sixth day after the earthquake. The US had landed at the airport along with aid groups from all over the world. The smell was worse, and people were still lying dead all around. I have never seen a quarter of a million dead before and a city with half the size of Atlanta, Georgia, and as many living there completely devastated and the confusion that followed. I will never forget it.

Shortly after that, we hired a lawyer to get our kids' papers so we could move the older ones to Nicaragua to teach them Spanish. Our goal was that they could then move to the Dominican Republic for employment in some of the new Haitian cities that were starting up as a result from the quake.

The Haitian who ran our orphanage took care of the lawyer and the paperwork, and we trusted him. In the meantime, Farrell decided to go to Dominican Republic and set up housing and the language school through Bobby Price who was now working there and running the school. The lawyer and our guy and another Haitian in the church where Steve went in Charlotte had the paperwork the lawyer drafted and given to them for proofing. We could not read the French Creole document, and they said it checked out.

What I along with Steve and Farrell did not know was that the four of them were together in drafting a document that turned the deed title and operation of the orphanage over to them. So basically, Steve and I signed over the property to them legally without knowing it.

They kicked the kids out onto the street and took over the property. Farrell was in the Dominican Republic waiting on our kids to get there, and they were not coming. Our church had $64,000 in the property, and Steve and his group had great loss as well. Farrell had sacrificed his retirement to be there, and God allowed the work to be stolen out from under us and the kids put back on the streets.

It was a hard pill to swallow, and I took a while before I was able to give it to God and trust Christ with it.

It is crazy when Christians steal and lie to you in the work. Putting orphans back on the streets was hard for me to suffer, but we could not do anything about it but tell Jesus on them. I have heard they now have other church groups helping them get money for the ministry there. I have given them all to Jesus, and he will work it out. I am amazed when brothers in ministry cheat, steal, and other things. We must keep our eyes on Jesus, not men.

Also, when we gave the $64,000 over eight years to that work, we gave that money to God for his glory. I do not like what happened, and I will do things differently dealing with those types of things in the future, but ultimately, we gave what we gave to God to help those orphan kids. Many were saved. They had eight years of education and safety. They were old enough to survive when they were put out in the street. God will take care of both the orphan and the men as only he can do. I am thankful for being given the chance to try and help such needy children!

Nicaragua

Farrell knew God had led him to walk away from eighteen years at his job two years before retirement with full benefits. The work he had surrendered to was stolen out from under our control, and our kids were back on the streets in Haiti. He was now in Nicaragua with no understanding of why God would allow that to happen nor understanding of what to do next. He was sure God had called him to do it, and yet now he was in a different country than he was planning on going to with his work nonexistent.

One thing about life, it does not always make sense. Farrell was in a town called Matagalpa, Nicaragua, with no ministry, having just walked out on his retirement because he thought God told him to. As he was trying to figure this out, he met a boy living on the street, begging for food. The boy had a bad cleft palate and was filthy.

Farrell bought the boy some food and took him home and had him get a bath and some new clothes. The boy, named Harvey, told Farrell that he lived with his grandmother who had eleven living in their house. Farrell told the boy he would help him if he was willing to go back home and live and get off the streets.

Harvey told Farrell that if he saw his house, he would not ask him to go back there. Farrell took him up on the offer and took Harvey back home to his grandmother. Farrell was not prepared for what he was about to witness.

In that part of Nicaragua, there is a giant landfill garbage dump that takes the garbage from that side of the country. It is huge. There are what has turned into three cities of people who have set up plastic and stick huts for their homes. They live off the garbage that is dumped there three times a week. There are 60,000 people (easily) in these three areas, and they are the poorest of the poor.

Harvey's grandma lived in a hut made of plastic and sticks and mud floors. The house was smaller than our average living room. When Harvey showed the house to Farrell, he was instantly touched by the living conditions. Not only was Harvey's family living in horrible circumstances, thousands of people were in this place living in these same conditions. It was heartbreaking and unbearable.

On top of all of this, the mission groups and churches in that area did nothing for these people. Why is it that the poorest people are ignored by the churches? Farrell had barely enough support to take care of himself and was not even sure now how long he would be in that area. What could one man with no money to speak of do for Harvey and 60,000 others who, for all practical purposes, were too poor for anyone to help them? Prayer is what Farrell could and did do.

God did a work in Farrell that began a new thing in that area of Nicaragua. Farrell began a work helping street kids from the trash dump cities go back to school. For a kid to go to public school there, they must be on their age's grade level, keep their grades up, and be able to provide their own uniforms and supplies.

Farrell, from his own support that was limited, hired three teachers and set up a classroom to start teaching the street kids. When they reached their grade level in their understanding, they qualified for public school, which was decent. He would then buy their clothes and supplies and get them registered into their local schools. He started with Harvey.

Soon, he had thirty-seven kids, which grew into 157, and now he has over 400. Our church joined him, and Steve heads up the ministry in the states. It is called The Hope Project. God took Farrell to Nicaragua to reach a people who were ignored by the churches and missions groups in Matagalpa. The poorest of the people are often ignored by Christian ministries, but no one is ignored by God, only by his people sometimes. God always sees and cares!

The Hope Project now has over 400 children being taught and fed a hot meal each day. Often, this meal is the only meal the child gets, and many of the kids get five good meals a week, which is more than they were getting.

Farrell has had numerous brick homes with running clean water and a tin roof built for some of the families. His ministry is constantly raising money and building these homes. He has started several training programs for the parents to learn skills, like sewing, to give the mothers a trade. Most of the time, the moms are single with no education or skill. He has medical teams visit the kids and other groups who provide clothes, shoes, beds, etc.

Harvey has had his cleft palate repaired and is finishing his education, now living at home with his grandmother in their brick house. While the kids would eat their lunch each day, the aged began gathering outside the school so they could eat any food that would be left over after the kids were fed. In that culture, when a person gets too old to bring food into the home, they are left to scrounge food for themselves.

When there was enough food left over, they started feeding the aged. Soon the ones gathering outside showed another great need. Prayer was offered, and now he is feeding the aged. God has brought help from God's people, and Farrell and his team are now building a community center. God took a bad thing and turned it into a good thing. Farrell is now doing in Matagalpa what Haitian people stopped him from doing in Haiti. Our church has visited and taken teams down and will again. It is unbelievable what God is doing.

Farrell's sacrifice has begun a work that is transforming a poverty cursed area, and even churches from the town are beginning to follow Farrell's leadership and reach out to the poor. You know Jesus is involved in any work that sees the Gospel being given to the poor. Farrell is still living on a tight budget for himself, but through Farrell's willingness to allow God to show him a people who needed his Son, Jesus, and Farrell's prayers and obedience and trust, God is doing a thing that is truly only a thing God would do! I am so thankful God cares for the poor and the helpless. I pray we will allow God to open our eyes and see the ones he loves and wants to help!

Two Deaths and One Question

God speaks to us in different and sometimes unexpected ways. We have a family that lives a few houses down from ours. They have six kids that my wife brings to church with her. We love the kids, but I do not know their mom and dad that well.

The father of the dad and mom, granddad of the kids, moved in with the family due to health problems. Lonnie was in the last stages of cancer and was finishing his life living here with this family. The mom and my wife are friends, and they asked if I could come and talk with Lonnie about his death and answer any questions that he had. I had the flu and was not able to visit for two weeks. By the time I could go visit, Lonnie had progressed to not being able to communicate and was taken to a local hospice to be looked after until the end.

I went to visit Lonnie and his wife and daughter in his room at hospice and to pray with them. I walked in the room and introduced myself and talked with them about Lonnie's death. They informed me that for most of Lonnie's life, he had served the Lord and even preached as a lay preacher sometimes. It seemed that his questions about his cancer and death were more from his dying and his medication and its effect on his thinking than doubt.

In any case, Lonnie was a believer, but for some reason, not my place to question, he had left church. Well, the nurse came in to do some things, and I left the room for a few minutes with intentions to return and pray with them.

Out in the hall, I looked in a room a few doors down, and it had thirty plus people in it. One of the ladies came out of the room and hugged me. I realized she was a mother who owned and ran the restaurant where I often ate lunch. Her girls were the waitresses, and I knew most of them. Her sister was in the room, dying, and all the family was there to be with her. Sons, daughters, grandkids— the room was packed.

The lady dying was in her last moments, and I went into the room, and we all had prayer, asking God to do what man's words cannot in these times. I told the sister of the lady dying that our church would help them if they needed. I left the room and went back to Lonnie's room and prayed with the wife and daughter for God's grace during Lonnie's passing.

As I was leaving, I went by the other room where everyone was upset and crying. The dear woman had just passed, and everyone was heartbroken. I went in the room and prayed for them and hugged the sister, gave her my number, telling her that our church would pray for them and help if they needed anything.

This brings me to the reason for this chapter. The next day, within the same hour, I got a call from both families. They asked me the same question almost exactly. They both told me that the death was unexpected and their family was not prepared for the cost. They both wanted a church ceremony but did not have a church home or a pastor. Both the deceased were to be cremated because of financial reasons.

Then here was the thing God spoke to me about. Both people were nervous asking me if they could use our church for the funeral and if I would do the services. They apologized for not having a lot of money and wanted to know what our church would charge and what I charged for doing a funeral. One family even asked if they could make payments!

In the space of one hour, two families came to me with the exact same question, showing the exact same fear. They do not know each other and have no idea of the other's circumstance. After I hung up with them, God began dealing with me about what they were saying and what he wanted me to see. I spent some time thinking about what God was using these hurting people to teach me.

I wrote down what I knew about their situation and here is what I came up with. Both families were believers. Both families were out of church and were bothered by that fact or at least acting guilty about it. Both were painfully heartbroken. Both had the responsibility to decide for the family. Both families were not able financially to pay for everything that was needed. Both persons sounded desperate and reluctant to ask me for help.

The truth that the facts were the same for both families let me know God was speaking. I prayed and asked God to let me see what he was showing through this situation, and here is what I saw. It is not my place to question why they left church. They would not come to me for help if they did not have to do so. They were desperately needing Jesus to help them and their families. Their understanding of how to get Jesus's help was to come to the church and ask.

Here is what God showed me that broke my heart and opened my eyes at the same time. Both families were wanting to get help from Jesus but were afraid to come to the church because of guilt and money. It broke down to this. "We need Jesus to help us. How much will it cost?" They did not feel worthy, were nervous around Christians they did not know, were afraid of how much Jesus's help would cost!

Jesus is the place anyone can come to and at any time to find grace and mercy to help in their time of need. The safest place to run for anyone, anytime, is to Jesus. The church is Jesus's servants. Why would the lost or broken be afraid to run to us for help? They are afraid of what the church will charge them. They are afraid to come to Jesus because of us (the church).

Our churches are broken, and we will each have to give account to God for how we treat the ones God calls us to serve. I am asking God to show us how to show people, every person, how much God loves them.

Our church is serving both families with our property. We are giving them keys to the building and providing a speaker for their service. We are cleaning the building and fellowship hall for them after they leave and plan on giving them anything else they need at no cost. The only money that will be passed is if we give them a love offering.

Jesus is a safe place to run to in times of need, and our church and myself as a pastor are asking God to open our eyes and change our thinking. I pray we are not making the grace and mercy of God something we can market or control. God, help your church to open our eyes to the lost and broken! Help us show them not to be afraid to come to us when needed!

The Well

The purpose in writing this book is not so much to tell about my life. Yes, in the early part of the book I wanted to share some of the funny and not so funny stories, because I feel they are funny and may give some entertainment (hopefully). But in the progression of the book, my hope is that the reader will be able to see God and his work through prayer.

God answers prayer and he does amazing things, some of which I have recorded with my best memory for you to enjoy. Join me in praising God for his work and his answers to prayer, and I praise him for not giving up on broken people. Also, pray and allow God to show you his heart for you and your life.

The Well Church has seen God do much more than this book tells, and God is still working today. The great things recorded in this book are in no way intentionally exaggerated or imagined. I have tried to be factual and true. The past eighteen years of this church's life have not been without pain or sorrow. Our church has seen God bring in huge amounts of money for missions and his ministry, but we as a church have seen many lean times and struggles over money too. I can say God has always supplied, but often, when great victory was the case overseas, we were next to closing our doors. God would step in at the last minute and meet the needs, almost always as an answer to prayers of his people. My family lost our home to foreclosure and we have not been able to receive a full salary as our budget does not allow at this time. I am convinced that God was in this and that he is the God of what we do not have as much as the God of what we do have. It has not been easy these years, and the spiritual battles that come along with this type of work are often harsh and long. But God has showed himself to us in ways that are impossible to deny his existence. Also, it is an honor and a privilege to serve the Lord and the cause of Christ.

Many people have not understood our giving and our walk. Our goals and purpose do not meet with the traditions of many churches, and I hope it never does. Our mission is the Great Commission, and our vision is loving people to Jesus. We strive "to do what God says," and still we promise to never say no to a project or call God brings to our table.

We pray two things. First, that when Jesus returns, he will find faith lived out through our church. Secondly, that you and any other person we can tell about Jesus will come to a place of understanding that you/they can start a relationship with the Jesus and God of the Bible and that your/their heart will come to the full knowledge of Jesus and be fulfilled with life's purpose. Turn over your life to Jesus by telling him your sins and problems and ask his forgiveness and his help. Watch and see what God does in your story and through your prayers.

About the Author

Frank Penley served as pastor for over thirty-five years. He travels and speaks for groups and churches in the US and in several countries for missions work. Frank spent his early adult life as an atheist and became a follower of Christ at twenty years of age.

Frank believes strongly that many people have given up on church and faith; so many hurting people who do not see a way or answer for their pain and suffering. He knows God is the answer and Jesus is the way to true peace and forgiveness and happiness. He intends on spending his days telling the forgotten and the broken that Jesus is real and God loves them and has a way for them to get help in any area of their life.

Jesus is the answer and life is best lived in a real relationship with Christ. Frank did not believe that God could or would save him, but Jesus did. If God would save him, he will save anybody who will ask him. That's who Frank is and what he does.

CPSIA information can be obtained
at www.ICGtesting.com
Printed in the USA
BVHW081023230919
559147BV00001B/40/P